DARK SECRETS OF CHILD

Media power, and public s

Fred Powell and Marga   ...un

First published in Great Britain in 2015 by

Policy Press
University of Bristol
1-9 Old Park Hill
Bristol
BS2 8BB
UK
t: +44 (0)117 954 5940
pp-info@bristol.ac.uk
www.policypress.co.uk

North America office:
Policy Press
c/o The University of Chicago Press
1427 East 60th Street
Chicago, IL 60637, USA
t: +1 773 702 7700
f: +1 773-702-9756
sales@press.uchicago.edu
www.press.uchicago.edu

British Library Cataloguing in Publication Data
A catalogue record for this book is available from the British Library

Library of Congress Cataloging-in-Publication Data
A catalog record for this book has been requested

ISBN 978 1 4473 1785 2 paperback
ISBN 978 1 4473 1784 5 hardback

Cover design by Andrew Corbett
Front cover image: Getty
Printed and bound in Great Britain by CMP, Poole
Policy Press uses environmentally responsible print partners

If you want to keep a secret, you must also hide it from yourself.

George Orwell, *1984*

Contents

Acknowledgements

The authors wish to acknowledge the financial support offered by the Irish Research Council that made this study possible. We would also like to thank the Institute of Social Science in the 21st Century at University College Cork for their support and encouragement. Finally, we would like to acknowledge the valuable contribution made by Rebecca Jeffers in producing this manuscript.

Introduction

> The mythology of child abuse must surely begin with the story of Medea. Her grisly legend, as conveyed by Euripides and by Seneca, is instructive of the shock and outrage expressed, both publicly and privately, in response to the spectrum of damage that has been inflicted upon children, by adults, from antiquity up until the present day. It is instructive further in relation to the intelligibility of such abhorrent acts as emanating not so much from devils and stereotypical perverts as from members of that same outraged public – real people.
>
> Medea, a sorceress, having aided Jason in his quest to obtain the Golden Fleece, became his consort and, subsequently, mother of their two sons. Jason later abandoned her and she, in a ferocious state of negative passion, burned down their palace, murdered the King of Corinth and the princess, her rival, and then fled to Athens with her own children whom she ritualistically slaughtered en route. This catalogue of carnage and destruction was not, tragically enough, directed specifically at its subjects but rather at Jason for his betrayal. A nemesis with its victim at one remove; the immediate sufferers being secondary to the noumenon of the act, but suffering supremely, nevertheless. This resonates with the diffuse, and often unintended, consequences wrought through the exercise of modern forms of social control. (Chris Jenks, 2005: 92)

This classic fable tells us that child abuse is as old as civilisation itself. It also tells us that driven by emotion human beings are capable of transgressing the most deeply embedded cultural codes in society. Medea's pursuit of revenge drove her to kill her innocent children. Her wanton violence amidst the pathos of this tragic tale is so shocking that it confronts us with deeply unsettling questions about humanity. It also highlights the uses and abuses of adult power over children. In doing so, the Medea fable touches on deeply embedded cultural taboos. Finally, the Medea narrative leaves us searching for explanations. How could any parent wreak such violence on an innocent child? Why does child abuse happen? What can be done to stop it? Is it possible to understand child abuse sociologically? Jenks' (2005) narration of this classical fable about Medea starts the process of contextualising these questions. He doesn't find any simple answers. There are none! But he does make a historical link between antiquity and the contemporary world; a world in which we are witnessing the re-emergence of public interest in child abuse. Jenks (2005: 94) concludes that child abuse cannot 'simply be explained' because it belongs to the anthropological realm of encoded meanings by which 'a society attempts to render meaningful and coherent the relationship between existing cosmologies and emergent behavioural anomalies'. Lalor (1998: 4) found the first written evidence of child sexual abuse in Ireland in the 6th century, written into the penitentials (confessional manuals used by the clergy). These works contained an exhaustive list of proscribed behaviours and appropriate sanctions. The penitentials were later adopted in England and subsequently Western Europe as the moral code of the medieval world.

In contemporary reality the mass media has made child abuse a major focus of public interest. The mass media, composed of newspapers, journals, books, radio, films, television and the internet, plays a defining role in constructing our cultural and social reality. It embraces news and information as well as culture, entertainment and advertising. Furthermore, the mass media takes many cultural forms from elitist to populist and is culturally essential to the process of meaning-making in all its social complexity. In this book we analyse the relationship between the mass media and childhood in contemporary society through the prism of child abuse enacted in families, institutions and the community.

'Knowing childhood', media representation and cultural contradictions

The study of childhood is poised to succeed the study of class, the study of gender and the study of race as the most recent arrival in a series of demands to know. While historically representation of women and children as occupying the same social space dates from antiquity, the liberation of women in modernity has not been accompanied by any change in the marginalised status of children (Cohen, 2007: 2). Childhood has proven to be an even more complex area of study than women, gender and ethnicity. Why? Ada Cohen (2007: 3) suggests the explanation that 'unlike biological sex, the very definition of childhood is unstable, its reality shifting no less than its cultural parameters; in other words, there is no stable pre-existing definition of childhood on which to anchor its evolution'. Within the binary oppositions used to socially and culturally differentiate children from adults, we represent this division as 'natural' in media imagery. We know a child when we see one, or do we? Childhood can, after all, be subdivided into temporal frameworks – infancy, childhood, youth, adolescence, young adults and so forth, underlining its cultural and representational complexity (James et al, 1998). Much of our thinking about child welfare and protection is framed within the discourse of parental care (and its failures). The mother is culturally represented as being in the central position of responsibility within this discourse of care, which is linked to the domestic sphere and family life. Care and loss are the twin poles of this socially and culturally constructed world of the ideal family. Children are portrayed within this family ideal as innocent and vulnerable in the adult world of social responsibility (Higonnet, 1998).

In modern society childhood has become simultaneously popularised, commercialised and sexualised by the mass media and market values (Higonnet, 1998 and 2002). One of the key challenges in conceptualising childhood is the issue of what Anne Higonnet calls 'Knowing Childhood'. The romanticisation of childhood in popular media representations stands in marked contrast to social reality – many children live in poverty. This is the paradoxical relationship between the commercial image and the social reality of childhood. Child abuse has created a crisis for the ideal of childhood, which has come to a head in recent times in the media. Middle-class conceptions of childhood in the Anglo-Saxon world repress the social reality of plural childhoods. They are profoundly challenged by the evidence of child abuse reports. Civil society is confronted with the task of 'Knowing Childhood' through a diversity of media images that challenge the 'simplification and popularisation of the image of the child' as 'innocent' (Higonnet, 1998 and 2002). The commercialisation and sexualisation of childhood in media advertising stands in sharp contrast to the idealisation of childhood innocence and the rhetoric of condemnation in the media's reportage of child abuse. Modern capitalist society is confronted by child abuse with its cultural contradictions in relation to childhood. Fundamental moral and social questions emerge regarding adult–child relations and media representations of childhood that raises profound cultural and policy issues.

'The abuse of childhood': popular culture and social myths

Chris Jenks (2005: 91) has interrogated 'the seemingly unprecedented increase in child abuse in Western societies', which he views as a modern myth. He offers an explanation of his myth thesis:

What I suggest then, is that the phenomenon of child abuse has emerged as a malign and exponential growth towards the conclusion of the twentieth century not because of any significant alteration in the pattern of our behaviour towards children but because of the changing patterns of personal, political and moral control in social life more generally which have, in turn, affected our vision of childhood. (Jenks, 2005: 92)

Jenks (2005: 93) further asserts:

Progressive society provides us with few reasons for indignation, the child abuser, we might suggest, is the last domestic variety. All 'decent' and 'right-thinking' people know that adults regard childhood as a state of dependency that we relate to through strategies of care. Physical, sexual and psychological abuse have no part in either the moral or the material contexts of adult–child relationships. The invocation of the normative assumptions inherent in the notions of 'decency' and 'right-mindedness' is a deliberate device to open up their ideological connotations ...

The French social theorist, Jacques Donzelot, in his book *The Policing of Families* (1980), presents the child's welfare and protection as a social metaphor in terms of family adaption to the normative standards of postmodern life. What Donzelot (1980) calls the 'tutelary complex' is manifest in the governance of everyday family life under the careful gaze of professional social workers, psychologists, paediatricians and psychiatrists, who, he argues, form a social police force – enforcing societal norms. In order to uphold the 'tutelary complex', public attitudes towards child abuse have both the characteristics of social myth-making in its media representation and social reality as documented events in everyday life. As Jenks (2005: 103) puts it, 'child abuse is real, but it is equally a device for constituting reality'.

By arguing child abuse is a myth Jenks (2005: 103) is not suggesting that it isn't real. Rather he is arguing that it belongs to the fluid realm of meaning-making in our cultural imaginary, where childhood is culturally and socially constructed. He unpacks this myth thesis by locating the abused child in what he calls the 'new liminality [threshold phase] of the postmodern child' (Jenks, 2005: 103). Jenks (2005: 111) asserts:

... late modern society has readopted the child. The child in
the setting of what are now conceptualised as postmodern
cultural configurations, has become the site or the relocation
of discourses concerning stability, integration and the social
bond. The child is now envisioned as a form of 'nostalgia',
a longing for times past, not as futurity.

In risk society, according to Ulrich Beck (1992: 118), the foundations
of the family are constantly threatened by upheavals (eg, divorce): '[t]he
child becomes the *final alternative to loneliness* that can be built up against
the vanishing possibilities of love'. Jenks (2005: 114) concludes '[w]hat
is being so jealously preserved through the new, "nostalgic", vision of
the child is the metanarrative of society itself', adding: 'to abuse the
child today is to strike at the remaining, embodied vestige of the social
bond and the consequent collective reaction is, understandably, both
resounding and vituperative'. This is the context of media portrayals
of child abuse as grotesque and alarming in its imagery of paedophile
priests and Satanists, as well as 'incompetent' social workers (eg, Orkney
Report (Clyde, 1992)). Society's public anger, articulated through the
voice of the media, espouses deeper moral concerns about the absence
of affection in an increasingly individualised and atomised society.
Children have become the last remaining guarantors of meaning and
love in this barren postmodern landscape. But who are they? Are they
not citizens with rights? What are these rights? What is childhood after
modernity? Is it simply a cultural and social construction? We will
explore these fundamental questions. Our focus in this introductory
chapter is on locating contemporary childhood through the prism of
child abuse. In adopting this approach to understanding childhood we
are conscious of Priscilla Alderson's (2013: 7) observation 'if children
are mentioned in the mass media or policy debates they are usually
portrayed negatively as villains or victims, or as needy dependents,
and their wide ranging views and activities are seldom reported in
the way adults appear in the media'. She is, of course, correct. The
mass media is skewed towards the adult world, but its debates also have
the potential to transform public consciousness about the issues of
the day, including the treatment of children. Equally, the mass media
can sensationalise, trivialise and distort information. It can also create
moral panics and witch hunts (Furedi, 2013). We hope our study will
reflect these contradictions and complexities and thereby bring greater
understanding and purpose to the discussion of child abuse.

Civility and childhood

In order to understand the child's social reality this book explores the wider context and experience of the child citizen, the cultural life of the child, childhood's hidden history and various experiences of being 'othered'. Essential to the child's life world is her/his position as a citizen in a rapidly changing society that affords children a right to care and protection but denies them the right to participation in the polis. At the core of adult–child power relations is civility, which governs human behaviour and speech in daily life in terms of good conduct between citizens. People lack civility when they act disrespectfully and aggressively towards each other (Brandsen et al, 2010). A rupture has occurred in modern democratic society, where 'the traditionalist premodern emphasis on social hierarchy, order and family privacy has been replaced by institutional changes interwoven with changes both in the general culture of society (civility) and of its political culture (civicness)' (Brandsen et al, 2010: 44). Child abuse is a fundamental challenge to civility and civicness in modern democratic culture, because it challenges the social myth that we live in a 'civilised' society, where people (including children) are treated with dignity and respect.

Childhood: real or imagined?

The facts of child abuse are undeniable, as we shall demonstrate in this book by examining the supporting and the opposing schools of thought on the matter.

In explaining childhood Priscilla Alderson (2013: 20) has pointed to the importance of 'recognising that real existence (ontology) is separate from thought and imagining (epistemology)'. This raises a key issue in the theorisation of childhood between foundationalist and antifoundationalist accounts of the body. Foundationalists view the body as:

> ... a real, material entity which is not reducible to the many different frameworks of meaning to be found cross-culturally ... At their most basic, foundationalists assume that there is something out there, so to speak, which functions independently (if not fully so) of the social context in which it is found. The body is an entity which is experienced and lived... (James et al, 1998: 148-9)

Alderson (2008) locates her own theoretical position within the discourse of critical realism, which she advocates as an approach to childhood studies.

On the other hand, James et al (1998: 148–149) argue that 'antifoundationalists are unwilling to make this distinction between the body and the representations that are made of it'. In its most extreme form the antifoundationalist perspective denies the existence of the body. Therefore, there are two distinctive approaches to the explanation of childhood. One (foundationalist) views the embodied child as an empirical reality. The other (antifoundationalist) denies the material body (which is bracketed out) and instead focuses on public discourses about childhood (James et al, 1998: 147).

Our research problem seeks to address childhood in the context of media representations of child abuse reports. It is, therefore, broadly located in the sphere of discourse analysis. However, we take the view that the child's body is a real material entity. The child abuse reports we seek to analyse are about the *real* lives of *real* children. They also belong to the realm of material reality. On the other hand, media representation of these texts is, in our view, not simply shaped by the empirical facts or medico–legal narratives. Media reports of child abuse reports are representative of wider sociocultural encoded meanings and exist essentially in the realm of discourse. The selective focus of media discourse in child abuse cases is on the symbolic construction of the child. James et al (1998: 152) assert:

> This relatively denaturalized or antifoundationalist childhood body ... has taken on a highly significant symbolic form in late modernity in relation to child abuse, which is cited here as an extended example. There is, it would seem, a revival of the focus on bodily purity, with the child's body seen as a temple of the sacred. Children's bodies are to be preserved at all costs, any violation signifying a transgressive act of almost unimaginable dimensions.

In relation to the analysis of media reports of child abuse reports, we are addressing a three-dimensional Zizekian reality: the *real* real, the *imagined* real and the *symbolic* real. Yet, we cannot escape from the fact that child abuse is part of modern social life. It cannot be sociologically conceptualised away as the product of a moral crusade, public witch hunts, societal mistrust or greater risk awareness, as some recent commentators have sought to do (Kampmark, 2012; Furedi, 2013). Binoy Kampmark (2012: 6) asserts:

... child-centric demagogues are dictating the broad agenda of how adult–child relations are formed and developed ... The very legalization of child protection and the proliferation of legal regulations threatens to undermine not merely the welfare of the child, but those of adults. Laws designed to protect children risk subverting their safety. They also enclose society in a net of suspicion.

His concern about the negative consequences of 'sacrelizing' childhood raises questions about the epistemological basis of child abuse enquires. This sociological critique is taken up by Frank Furedi in his book *Moral Crusades in the Age of Mistrust*, published in 2013, which focuses on the topical Jimmy Savile scandal where a dead celebrity has become the focus of a major media scandal in the UK.

Professor Furedi (2013) views child abuse as an exemplar of a loss of trust in community and institutions. He argues that 'the media and campaigning organisations are often attracted to the idea that behind every headline there lies a hidden agenda, and that the focus is not on the story but on the story behind the story' (Furedi, 2013: 10). He concludes that 'instead of investing so much energy in dredging up the misdeeds of previous decades, society would do better to learn how to give meaning to its own experience' (Furedi, 2013: 10). If we were to accept Furedi's conclusion we would ignore human rights violations committed against children in the past, which constitute vital historical evidence regarding the abuse of adult power in society and the role of survivors and media campaigns in exposing child abuse. Furedi (2013: 16) counters this argument by asserting 'memory is far from being a reliable instrument for capturing the truth. All too often reading history backwards encourages anachronism, an act of reinterpretation that says more about what actually happened in the past'. We hope the evidence that we have assembled in this book and in a previous study (Powell et al, 2012a) will conclusively disprove Furedi's 'false memory syndrome' case. Furthermore, some inquiries, such as the Irish *Report of the Commission to Inquire into Child Abuse* (CICA, 2009), also known as the Ryan Report, were purportedly informed by the principles of truth and reconciliation. However, we acknowledge that Furedi raises important questions about why it took over 20 years for some witnesses to report these events (Furedi, 2013: 30). The Ryan Report (CICA, 2009: 4: 6.43) provides an answer: 'witnesses reported that the power of the abuser, the culture of secrecy and isolation and the fear of physical punishment inhibited them in disclosing abuse'.

Childhood and vulnerability

The challenge of writing a book about the dark side of childhood has been very considerable. It has at times seemed like a strange and unpredictable journey through the dark side of a planet that likes to hide its secrets. Truth is illusive. Myths are prevalent. Scandal is endemic in media reports. Cultural anxiety is all pervasive. Yet, one senses being on a journey to the core of power relations and truth-telling in modern civilisation. Along this stony road, littered by child abuse reports, is an unfolding narrative of the abuse of adult power over children, especially vulnerable children from socially deprived backgrounds. This chilling social reality makes the authors' task emotionally and intellectually very challenging. Both of us are parents. We know about the world of children's experience at first hand, yet we are not part of the child's psychic world. Our cultural landscape is different from theirs, because of children's exclusion from it.

The shocking events of war in various global theatres during the summer of 2014 remind us of the fragility of our civilisation. Child victims of these terrible wars stand out as signifiers of the sheer barbarity of these horrifying events in places such as Gaza. They also remind us that children are so often the innocent victims of apparently uncontrollable adult violence. The abuse of adult power over vulnerable children is part of our social reality.

The social construction of child abuse: 'What is child abuse?'

At the outset it is important to pose the question: 'What is child abuse?' The answer is complex because child abuse is socially constructed in public discourse. In traditional society (in so far as a conception of child abuse existed), it was associated with child abandonment, infanticide, child prostitution, child labour (including 'white slavery') and cruelty. There was a clear linkage with poverty. The 'rediscovery' of child abuse in modern society has classified it into four categories: physical abuse, sexual abuse, neglect, and emotional abuse. The Ryan Report (CICA, 2009: 3: 1.09) defines each of these categories:

Physical abuse:
The wilful, reckless or negligent infliction of physical injury on, or failure to prevent such injury to, the child.

Sexual abuse:
The use of the child by a person for sexual arousal or sexual gratification of that person or another person.

Neglect:
Failure to care for the child which results, or could reasonably be expected to result, in serious impairment of the physical or mental health or development of the child or serious adverse effects on his or her behaviour or welfare.

Emotional abuse:
Any other act or omission towards the child which results, or could reasonably be expected to result, in serious impairment of the physical or mental health or development of the child or serious adverse effects on his or her behaviour or welfare.

Latterly, sexual abuse has been foregrounded, particularly in relation to celebrity culture. This public construction in the media has coincided with the emergence of 'historic abuse' in institutions where children were placed, usually arising from structural poverty, as seen in the Ryan Report (CICA, 2009). There have also been allegations of historic child abuse against members of the clergy in the community, which has been covered up, as shown in the Ferns Report (Murphy et al, 2005) and the Dublin Report (DJELR, 2009).

The core task of the book is (1) to report on child abuse inquiry reports in keeping with the conditions of our research grant from the Irish Research Council (these conditions being to write a 'report on reports in Ireland', based upon media representation that contextualises their public reception) and (2) to locate child abuse within its wider political, cultural and historic context. In approaching the research task, we have endeavoured to place the local in its global context. This book will be (we hope) of interest to a wide international audience because child abuse is universal and the media globalised. Since the publication of Marshall McLuhan's *The Guttenberg Galaxy* (1962) and *Understanding Media* (1964) and *The Medium is the Message* (1967), we have become aware that we live in a 'global village' in which our collective consciousness is shaped by the modern mass media. Sociologists refer to 'reflexivity'; a permanent interaction between change and consciousness. Yet all villages, from the dawn of civilisation to the age of globalisation, contain dark secrets, often cloaked in encoded messages. Child abuse is one of the darkest of dark cultural secrets. It invites civilisation to look at itself in the mirror. But as Ciaran McCullagh (2002) in his book *Media Power* points out, when we look at child abuse our perspective is distorted by 'fractured glass'. The reality we perceive presents an image too painful for society to take ownership of in terms of collective culpability, so we displace the blame on to the 'other'. We describe the events as 'scandals'. At the core of media representations of child abuse is the populist process of 'blaming and shaming', which frequently represents perpetrators of abuse as 'monsters' or 'demons'. Social workers are often at the receiving end of society's rejection of collective responsibility and are framed in the media as 'incompetent' or even 'negligent'. This cultural practice of 'scapegoating' is perhaps best encapsulated in the UK Cleveland case (1987) in which the media displaced the blame for parental abuse from parents onto social workers doing the job of protecting children. Other groups have claimed that they are also being scapegoated, such as the Catholic clergy, as seen in their response to the Ryan Report (CICA, 2009) on child abuse in Irish industrial and reformatory schools (Flannery, 2009). The Ryan Report (CICA, 2009: vol 4, 6.20) fundamentally disagrees and states that the Catholic religious orders protected clerical perpetrators of child abuse while handing over lay perpetrators to the police. But perhaps they are making a deeper point about culpability – the historic collusion of Irish civil society in child abuse over the centuries. We hope this book will shine a light on these dark cultural secrets. They cannot simply be consigned to a 'murky past' that we can afford to forget about. History is a living experience in a dialectical relationship with the past.

Children historically have lacked human rights and visibility. Agency over their lives is denied to them: they have been the possessions of their parents and, latterly, through the principle of *parens patriae*, they have become 'welfare subjects' (Pinkney, 2000) of the state in its role as ultimate custodian of the child's right to care and protection. The dependency of the child's status in this legal and cultural framework is challenged by child abuse reports, which point to adult failures to discharge their responsibilities towards children, who are culturally framed by the media as 'innocent and vulnerable'. Increasingly, questions are being asked about the child citizen (Keane, 2008). Should children, along with other historically disempowered groups (eg, women, ethnic minorities, people with disabilities, and so on) not be empowered? Why do children lack a public voice? Does this denial of a basic human right facilitate child abuse? These are difficult questions that threaten the normativity upon which our cultural world is constructed. Article 12 of the UN Convention on the Rights of the Child (1989) proclaims children do have a right to public expression of their views in relation to their welfare – 'the child's voice'. Its implementation promises to transform children's human rights (Young Bruehl, 2012).

This book is primarily an exercise in deconstruction through discourse analysis of child abuse inquiry reports, their public reception and media representation. We seek to step behind the looking glass to analyse the interplay between texts (inquiry reports) and counter-texts (media representation of inquiry reports). Our search behind the looking glass is for explanations grounded in social reality that may be cloaked in cultural defences, and characterised by displacement, denial and dissimulation, and sometimes even by demonisation. It is a media-constructed world of 'monsters', 'perverts', 'incompetents' and assorted undesirable characters who are blame for child abuse. We also explore child culture for evidence of the symbolic construction of child abuse and the social risks posed by the electronic media.

Our journey is towards making sense of past events, while looking forward to a future where children will be recognised as actors in the making of their own biographies. When we step back out through the looking glass, we have learnt that narrative participation and agency are essential to child citizenship, a core element in combating child abuse. Only the powerless are abused. If there is a fundamental lesson to be learned from child abuse reports, this is it. The social reality behind child abuse reports is the documentation of plural childhoods in which poverty makes children particularly vulnerable to abuse and exploitation. The UN Convention on the Rights of the Child (1989) has enshrined social policy within the 3 Ps (provision, protection and participation). The 3 Ps offer answers to child abuse, but their implementation depends upon cultural change, an active state and a civil society that is willing to embrace social justice and human rights.

Discourses of child abuse: media, professional and human rights

The conceptual language of child abuse takes a number of distinct discursive forms. First, there is the simple descriptive language of moral condemnation contained in traditional words like 'cruelty', 'neglect', 'ill treatment', 'indecency', 'incest' and, latterly, 'torture', 'grooming', and 'exploitation', that have framed popular media conceptualisations of child abuse. This is the language adopted by the media in reporting child abuse cases. It reflects back to the public its own moral outrage and condemnation, which some commentators argue can form moral panics (Fitzgibbon, 2012). Second, during the 1960s the professionalisation of child protection led to the emergence of a new medico–legal language (physical abuse, neglect, emotional abuse and sexual abuse), which has become the dominant official discourse (Kempe and Kempe, 1978). This discourse is articulated in official guidelines, procedural manuals, professional training and student texts. The third discursive form is the language of universal human rights, which has challenged traditional thinking about childhood. Human rights discourse emerged out of the atrocities associated with the Second World War and the emergence of totalitarian societies. Article 1 of the Universal Declaration of Human Rights (1948) boldly proclaimed 'all human beings are born free and equal in dignity and rights'. The UN Convention on the Rights of the Child (1989) became the first international treaty to improve basic standards regarding the treatment of children. In addition, the European Convention on Human Rights (ECHR) has established basic standards within the European Union regarding the treatment of citizens, which are enforced by the European Court of Human Rights (ECtHR).

All three discourses inform public responses to child abuse in quite distinct ways in case reportage. The mass media (as already noted) tends to use the populist language of moral outrage and condemnation. For example, in the recent UK trial of Daniel Pelka, a four-year-old abused and killed by his parents, the *Daily Mail* (1 August 2013) declared 'the Polish monster who tortured and killed his four-year-old stepson had been jailed in this country three times … But despite his serial offending he was never put on a plane back to Poland'. The *Daily Express* (4 August 2013) informed its readers 'Daniel Pelka's evil mother revelled in being cruel … she swore, took drugs and was often seen in the company of older men, who degraded her calling her a "slut" and a whore in the street but she seems to enjoy it'. This populist language of media condemnation evokes the Maria Colwell case that prompted the first media crusade against child abuse. Subsequent UK child abuse inquiries such as the Cleveland case (1987), the Orkney case (1992), the Victoria Climbié case (2003) and the Baby P case (2007) have all attracted major media outrage.

The mass media's reportage stands in sharp contrast to the medico–legal language of public inquiries. The Ryan Report (2009), which was examining a historical event in the sense that its investigation of child abuse in Irish industrial and reformatory schools was about institutions that have been closed for many years, chose to adopt a medico–legal approach: physical abuse, neglect, emotional abuse and sexual abuse. While physical abuse was the dominant mode of abuse identified by the survivors in their evidence, sexual abuse featured heavily in media reportage, partly because of the moral paradox of clergy sexually abusing children, which became a media angle.

Finally, the human rights approach to the conceptualisation of child abuse is part of a humanistic discourse that challenges unaccountable adult power. It confronts society with much deeper questions that cannot be easily accommodated in media conceptualisations, albeit the media can lead the debates. For example, the Kilkenny Report (McGuinness, 1993) and the Roscommon Report (Gibbons, 2010) exposed the absence of children's rights in the Irish Constitution, necessitating a referendum in 2012. The media played a key role in leading the debate for constitutional change through its reportage of these inquiries' findings. Probably the most successful media campaign waged by human rights activists on behalf of children has been the outlawing by the ECtHR of corporal punishment (Holohan, 2011: 56-8). However, there are profound issues arising from plural childhoods, in which many children become victims of child abuse because of poverty, which the media does not address.

The media, child abuse and civil society

While it is undoubtedly selective with the news, the mass media has had a powerful influence in augmenting children's rights within civil society, simply by reporting child abuse. Paradoxically, this has come from challenging the secrets of the adult world, yet it is important to acknowledge that this is a debate about children from which they are excluded. Survivors of child abuse become the spokespersons – 'the child's voice' as victims of adult power (CICA, 2009; Deetman, 2011). Their narratives enable us to assemble an account of the child's historic experience in care. Buckingham (2000: 104) cautions that 'in the process, we are inevitably making assumptions about who these other people are – and in this case, about what "childhood" is, or should be'. The invisible audience is the court of public opinion. Inevitably, the presentation of the issues shapes the public response – demanding more effective services for children. But there are also deeper issues involved, notably the use and abuse of adult power over children that tend to be framed in terms of accountability within the public realm. Justice must be done and seen to be done. This is, of course, right and proper. There is, however, a missing link in this nexus, which centres on the role of civil society in framing social and moral discourse of adult–child power relations. The sociocultural context of the debate is often lost in the public discourse of condemnation and denial.

Kampmark (2012: 60) observes 'the cult of the sacred child leads to distortions in the way civil society is ordered'.

However, civil society is not monolithic. There are various strands within civil society: conservative, liberal and radical (Powell, 2013). The conservative strand defends traditional values, organised religion and class interests. It finds its media voice through populist right-wing newspapers, such as *The Sun*, the *Irish Daily Star, The Express* and *The Mail*. These national organs have many local imitators. Liberal civil society on the other hand tends to be more progressive, reflecting the liberal views of the middle class intelligentsia, though newspapers like *The Guardian, The Independent* and *The Irish Times*. These are very much the minority in terms of newspaper sales, but they are highly influential in terms of shaping elite public opinion. On the other hand, the voice of radical civil society tends to be expressed through the fringe media and protest. Television and radio, which have a much larger audience, present news to mass audiences in increasingly tabloid form. However, there are key programmes, such as the British Broadcasting Corporation (BBC) Radio 4 *Today* programme, the Raidió Teilifís Éireann (RTÉ) radio programme *Morning Ireland*, the BBC Two programme *Newsnight*, the RTÉ television programme *Primetime* and Channel 4 News, which offer deeper news analysis and discussion of current affairs aimed at the intelligentsia.

Beyond the mainstream print broadcasting media is the internet with its blogosphere, where citizens debate the issues of the day in the largely unregulated world of cyberspace. Some call this 'cyber democracy', but the internet can be very destructive. Social media sites, such as Facebook and Twitter, have introduced a new dimension to public discourse. Young people are particularly active in social media. We will discuss cyberbullying later in the book (see Chapter 7). This has led moral conservatives to call for more regulation. A growing literature has begun the task of evaluating the impact of the internet on civil society in relation to child abuse (Butler and Drakeford, 2012; Fitzgibbon, 2012). They particularly focus on the impact on social work and probation. Silverman and Wilson (2002) were the first to address this task in the United Kingdom on a larger societal basis. In their study, Silverman and Wilson (2002: 1) focus on the media's public enemy number one – 'the paedophile'.

All of these studies focus on the capacity of the media to manufacture scandal and foment moral panics among the public. As the issue of child abuse has evolved since the Maria Colwell Report in 1974 (Field-Fisher, 1974), public interest in and engagement with child abuse has grown, enveloping the media itself, as in the ongoing Jimmy Savile case. Civil society is no longer only confronted with child abuse within the family or care institutions but also among the cultural elite, notably in the media. This changing sociocultural context frames mass media responses to allegations of child abuse, especially when the accused is a celebrity, into morality theatre. The narrative has moved on and the media must now report on itself. That has proved to be a challenging task for the media.

Aims and structure of the book

The child abuse inquiries of the last few decades have been hugely significant in revealing the tragic circumstances under which some children lived and died. In the book, however, our main focus will not be on what these inquiries reveal about abuse *per se*, but on what they reveal about contemporary Irish society and the changing relations between a number of key institutions, particularly the Catholic Church, the state and the media. Through the 'lens' of the child abuse inquiry we will consider a number of issues, including: the changing status of children in Irish society, the emergence of campaigning groups as a significant political force, the growing power of the media, and the development of childcare policy. We will then explore the wider context (political, cultural, historical) in which adult–child power relations are conducted. These essays address discrete metathemes that, we hope, will enable the reader to contextualise the debate about child abuse and theorise it from a critical social perspective. This will, we believe, offer a uniquely original analysis of child abuse.

Part 1 of the book constitutes 'a report on reports', and will:

- Explore the origins of a number of inquiries. We will trace the events leading up to each inquiry. For example, was there public pressure to carry out investigations? What was the role of campaigning groups and of the media in initiating the inquiries?
- Explore the sociohistorical context, including civil society and the state. Why did child abuse inquiries first begin to take place? What were the conditions that made this possible?
- Critically analyse the inquiry reports.
- Analyse media representation of the inquiries and reports. What was the nature and extent of media coverage? This is a key issue as (arguably) most people do not read child abuse reports, and depend on media interpretations. In addition, the coverage of clerical child abuse represented a shift in power in church–media relations as the media increasingly hold the church to account for its actions.

- Consider the implications of the inquiries for the Catholic Church, the social work profession and the development of childcare policy.

Part 1 of the book is divided into five chapters.

Chapter 1: The construction of child abuse as a social problem

In this chapter we will map the emergence of child abuse as a major social issue in western countries, focusing in particular on developments in Britain, Ireland and the United States. We take as our starting point the late 19th/early 20th century, during which time the foundations of contemporary child protection and welfare systems were laid. The second period of major change runs from the 1960s to the current day, a period in which the main focus of anxiety commenced with physical abuse (the 'battered child syndrome') and finally focused on the sexual abuse of children as the 'paramount evil' to be confronted (Coldrey, 1996: 370). During this period, we also see a shift in emphasis from intra- to extrafamilial abuse, particularly within institutional settings. These developments will be situated in the wider context of changing conceptions of childhood and the family, and the emergence of the media as the 'fourth estate' that brought the issue of abuse to a mass audience and acted as a powerful catalyst for change.

Chapter 2: The public child

The aim of this chapter is to provide a critical perspective on the public debates surrounding the Kilkenny case, an area that has hitherto been largely overlooked in academic research. A central issue is whether the inquiry team, the media and key stakeholders attributed responsibility for 'why action to halt the abuse was not taken earlier' to the individual practitioners involved in the case (doctors, police, social workers) or to the system and structures within which they operated. Comparisons will be made with the UK, where a number of high profile inquiries ascribed responsibility for professional 'failures' to individual practitioners, who were subsequently pilloried in the media (Fitzgibbon, 2012). We also consider the controversy surrounding the sentencing of the abuser. While the focus of public anger in high profile child abuse scandals is often on social workers and child protection, in the Kilkenny case much of the initial outrage was targeted at the judge and the criminal justice system. Finally, we will explore the 'emblematic' features of the case – what appeared to be the wider implications of the Kilkenny case for Irish society at that time? Our research suggests that while recent child abuse scandals in the UK have been seen to represent the breakdown of the traditional family (Fitzgibbon, 2012), in Kilkenny it was the sanctity of the family that was seen to be problematic, as it discouraged disclosure of abuse and outside intervention.

Chapter 3: The Catholic Church, scandal and the media

In this chapter we explore the role of the media in exposing clerical child abuse in Ireland, focusing in particular on how a series of television documentaries paved the way for two major inquiries (Ferns and Dublin), and the media's subsequent coverage of the inquiry reports. We look at how the controversy surrounding the clerical child abuse inquiries embodied key features of an 'institutional scandal': social norms were transgressed leading to moral outrage; the actions of individuals brought the Catholic Church as a whole into disrepute; and allegations of institutional 'cover-ups' proved to be as damaging as the acts they sought to conceal.

Chapter 4: The Ryan Report and the charity myth

This chapter provides an analysis of the Ryan Report, which became and international story.

The publication of the Ryan Report during 2009 was a seminal event in the process of disclosure and truth-telling. Its revelations are thorough and deeply shocking, identifying over 200 institutions. Most of the alleged abusers were members of the clergy. These are stark facts that underpin the powerful testimony of the survivors of these abuse regimes that went on during most of the 20th century. The Ryan Report reveals that over a 35-year period child abuse was endemic in the industrial and reformatory school system in Ireland. Its revelations have been reported around the world, exposing the failure of Ireland's human rights record in relation to children to critical international scrutiny. The crimes against children described in the Ryan Report are on a systemic scale and involve a degree of sadistic cruelty that is difficult to comprehend. Public reaction has been one of shock and horror.

Chapter 5: Child abuse, cultural disbelief and the patriarchal family

In Chapter 5 we analyse four major Irish child abuse inquiries that revolved around family violence. All four were patriarchal families with a domineering and overbearing father who abused his power relations with his children and his submissive spouse. We explore the cultural context of social work intervention with these families and the role of wider state agencies. In particular we examine the influence of traditionalist values that led to a culture of disbelief, constraining social work intervention and children's rights. We also discuss the politicisation of family rights and the consequences for child protection.

Part 2 of this book will (1) seek to analyse the contexts of child abuse (historical, cultural and political) and (2) through the medium of four discreet essays, magnify the global boundaries of the debate about child abuse. It will:

- Explore the changing meaning of childhood in postmodern society.
- Discuss the case for rethinking children's rights through an analysis of public discourse on child citizenship rights, and explore the implications of the UN Convention on the Rights of the Child.
- Analyse the nature of child culture and the impact of adult influence on shaping the child imaginary. We will discuss the symbolic construction of child abuse in children's literature and cinema and the implications of the internet on the sustainability of childhood. We will also look at the internet's potential as a site of child abuse.
- Examine the hidden history of child abuse through an analysis of the historic evolution of child abuse. The 'othering' of vulnerable children will be discussed in the context of plural experiences of childhood, and its implications for locating child abuse within the wider context of social inequality and deprivation will also be considered.
- Evaluate the contemporary reality of child abuse and its linkage to the social marginalisation of migrants and other vulnerable children.

Part 2 of the book includes four substantive chapters and a conclusion that offers steps forward on the road to recognising children's right to be treated as citizens in societies that profess to be democracies (at least for adults).

Chapter 6: Rethinking children's rights

In this chapter we pose two seminal questions regarding child citizenship: 'Can children become full members of civil society?' and 'Do they have the capacity to enjoy its rights of association and property, legal protection and citizens' power to vote for representatives of their choice, in free and fair elections?'. There are two principle schools of thought regarding children's rights: (1) a child liberationist or self-determinationist model; and (2) a child protectionist or nurturance model. It is important to note that the UN Convention on the Rights of the Child (1989) incorporates elements from both models as aspects of human rights thinking in relation to children's rights. However, the two models do represent two notably divergent ways of approaching children's rights, contrasting active and passive citizenship. Child liberationists want to equalise children's rights with adult's rights (active citizenship). On the other hand, child protectionists want to shield children from adult exploitation (passive citizenship). The issues are further complicated by Article 12 of the UN Convention on the Rights of the Child, which asserts the child's right to participation in civil society in accordance with the age and maturity of the child.

Chapter 7: Child culture and risk society

This chapter poses the questions: 'Do adults and children occupy the same cognitive world of shared meanings or do adults culturally construct (and arguably) control the imaginary lives of children?' 'Do fairy tales contain culturally encoded messages?' and 'What is the meaning behind these messages?'. We will seek to explore how media forms culturally construct the child's reality, often paradoxically through the agency of adult fantasy. The media's primary cultural target is children's imaginations. The chapter also explores the advent of the electronic media, which has arguably, given the child imaginative agency. The chapter poses two further questions: 'Is the emergence of child agency on the internet deconstructing childhood?' and 'Is this a positive or negative development?'.

Chapter 8: Angelmakers: the hidden history of child abuse

In this chapter we examine the power dynamics of child abuse through the sociological lens of 'othering'. We set the analysis in its historical context, tracing developments up to the present day. Parental indifference historically emerges as a key issue, reflecting a wider societal indifference to abandoned children. Jonathan Swift in his satirical essay, *A Modest Proposal*, penned during the early 18th century, sought to confront society with its hypocrisy by advocating cannibalism. His use of the pamphlet as an instrument of media power was shocking. Swift intended it to be shocking, but he failed to break the silence. Media silence was the product of cultural collusion. There were 'known-knowns' but they were also unmentionables. Why? The answer lies in the cultural dynamics in which vulnerable groups are 'othered'. It resulted in devastating consequences for socially deprived children. They were allowed to die with societal complicity during the 18th century. The 19th century witnessed their segregation in institutions, where children were brutalised and exploited, that offered no material change in their circumstances. This saga continued until the late 20th century. What is striking about this tragic narrative is its unrelenting bleakness. Genes and poverty underpinned the exclusionary process of 'othering'.

Chapter 9: The cultural politics of child abuse

In this chapter we examine the cultural politics of child abuse. The chapter takes the narrative right up to the present day. We focus on two groups of children: (1) those from asylum-seeking backgrounds housed in direct provision accommodation and (2) the contemporary reality of children in care proceedings. What emerges from our analysis is that the issue of child abuse continues to be a disturbing reality in Irish civil society and the state remains reluctant to take responsibility for many child citizens who are born in Ireland. Their ethnicity clearly is an ongoing factor in abuse and social service failure.

Chapter 10: Conclusion

In the conclusion to this book we will summarise the issues arising from our 'report on reports' of child abuse. We will then take an overview of the wider contextual implications for civil society, the state and human rights. Finally, we will pose the questions: 'How can we combat child abuse?' and 'What steps are required?' We don't pretend there are simple answers but we argue that there are fundamental changes that could significantly contribute to combating child abuse.

Research contribution

The book builds upon research in several disciplines.

Social and historical studies

The book connects with a growing body of literature concerned with social change in Ireland. It will contribute to the analysis of different aspects of social change, including: the modernisation of Ireland from the 1960s (Ferriter, 2004; Garvin 2004); the development of the welfare state; the changing status of children (Burns and Lynch, 2012); the social construction of childhood in Ireland and internationally (Buckingham, 2000; James and James, 2004; Powell et al, 2012b); and the construction of child abuse as a social problem (Ferguson, 1996).

The book will also build upon previous studies on the history of the Catholic Church (Inglis, 1998; Keogh, 1996; Whyte, 1980); and contribute to debates concerning the impact of the child abuse inquiries, and other 'scandals', on the church's position in Ireland (Ferguson, 1995; Kirby, 1995; Donnelly and Inglis, 2010).

Child protection and welfare

The policy implications of certain inquiries – particularly the Kilkenny Incest Investigation – are discussed in the child protection literature (Ferguson, 1993; Ferguson, 1995; Lavan, 1998; Lalor, 2001; McGuinness, 2012). The book builds on this literature while also providing a new perspective by considering the sociocultural context of the inquiries. Consequently, the project should provide a more in-depth understanding of the inquiries and a broader perspective on the development of child protection policy.

Media studies

Although the role of the media in publicising the findings of child abuse inquiries in Ireland has been discussed (Donnelly and Inglis, 2010), there has been no systematic research study of media coverage of the inquiries along the lines proposed in this book. We make an original contribution by conducting a number of in-depth case studies of television and newspaper reporting. The book also contributes to the international literature on the media's representation of child abuse and child abuse inquiries (Franklin and Parton, 1991; Skidmore, 1995; Wilczynski and Sinclair, 1999; Kitzinger, 2000; Ayre, 2001; Kitzinger, 2004; Cheit et al, 2010).

International studies

There is a considerable body of international literature on different aspects of child abuse inquiries, particularly in the UK (Reder et al, 1993; Corby et al, 1998; Corby et al, 2001; Parton, 2004; Kuijvenhoven and Kortleven, 2010). This book is situated within the context of this international research; comparisons will be made between the Irish experience of inquiries and that of other countries.

Cultural focus and social change

Over the last two decades, a series of high profile inquiries and reports have revealed the abuse of children, both in their own homes and in church-run institutions. An analysis of the social and cultural context within which these investigations took place – and the reaction from the media, politicians and the public – reveal much about our changing attitudes to children, particularly in terms of their need for protection and their rights as citizens. The setting up of these inquiries is also indicative of changes in church–state relations and of a gradual decline in deference towards authority figures, including the clergy, politicians and social workers. Indeed in some respects, child abuse inquiries could be seen as barometers of social change, providing us with an insight into what issues are of public concern and how these issues are framed or constructed. Moreover, they raise intriguing questions as to why the investigations were held at that particular point in time. Prior to the 1990s, there were no child abuse inquiries in Ireland since the inception of the state in 1922, even though many children suffered or died at the hands of their parents or other carers (Ferguson, 1995). The high profile revelations concerning *clerical* child abuse in particular would have been unthinkable 50 years ago. What has happened in the intervening decades to make these inquiries possible? This is one of the questions that we hope to address in the book. We will consider child abuse inquiries and reports in their social and cultural context, exploring their origins, reception and impact.

While our primary focus in Part 1 will be on Ireland, the issues raised are of international significance: child abuse inquiries have been a feature of several western countries, with profound consequences for the Catholic Church and for those agencies charged with the protection of children, particularly social services (Kuijvenhoven and Kortleven, 2010; Munro, 2011). Part 2 of the book moves the argument onto a global plain and poses questions about the meaning of child citizenship in postmodern society.

Irish child abuse reports and children's rights

While the Ryan Report (CICA, 2009) has been justifiably awarded totemic significance by the international media, it is only one of the series of reports that highlight the pervasiveness of child abuse in

Ireland. There have in fact been a series of major child abuse reports in Ireland over the past two decades and these are listed here under the names under which they are commonly known, with the author/date of each report in parentheses. They can be subdivided into four categories:

(1) Inquiries dealing with abuse within the family

The Kilkenny Incest Investigation Report (McGuinness, 1993)

The Kelly Fitzgerald Report (Houses of the Oireachtas, 1996)

The McColgan Report (West of Ireland Farmer Case) (Bruton, 1998)

The Monageer Inquiry (Brosnan, 2009)

The Roscommon Child Care Report (Gibbons, 2010)

(2) Inquiries concerning abuse in institutional settings

The Madonna House Inquiry (Department of Health, 1996)

The Ryan Report (or the Report of the Commission to Inquire into Child Abuse (CICA, 2009)

The Report on the Inspection of St Patricks Institution (Reilly, 2012)

The Report of the Inter-Departmental Group on Mother and Baby Homes (DCYA, 2014)

(3) Inquiries into clerical sexual abuse

The Ferns Report (Murphy et al, 2005)

The Dublin Report (DJELR, 2009)

The Cloyne Report (DJELR, 2011)

(4) Inquiries into community care

Report of the Independent Child Death Review Group (Shannon and Gibbons, 2012)

Interim Report: Child Care Law Reporting Project (Coulter, 2013)

The revelations of these reports have underlined serious human rights violations in the Irish Child Care system. While some of these reports provide a historical narrative covering the 20th century, others address the shortcomings of the contemporary child protection system in the 21st century. All of them have received media attention and contributed to changing public consciousness about the importance of children's human rights, the need for social policy to reflect practical problems on the ground and the rights of children to care and protection. These media reports have questioned the arguably arcane principals upon which the 1937 Constitution rests and that idealise the family at the expense of the child.

PART 1
The reports

ONE

The construction of child abuse as a social problem

> To strike at the child is to attack the repository of social sentiment and the very embodiment of 'goodness'. Indeed such an act epitomizes absolute evil. And yet child abuse is a constant feature of the historical process as well as being a preoccupation of the contemporary collective consciousness. (James et al, 1998: 152)

Over the last 50 years, there has been what is often described as an 'explosion' of interest in the issue of child abuse. In western countries an ever expanding range of laws, policies and procedures have been introduced to address this problem, while media coverage of child abuse scandals has at times reached saturation point. Revelations of child sexual abuse by Roman Catholic clergy – and its 'cover-up' by church authorities – have given rise to one of the greatest institutional scandals of modern history. Moreover, the paedophile has emerged as 'the bogeyman of our age' who inspires fear and public loathing, 'often beyond all moderation' (Silverman and Wilson, 2002: 1).

The current preoccupation with child abuse does not, of course, mean that this is a recent phenomenon, or even that it is on the increase (Lalor, 1998). Historians have found that the mistreatment of children (including infanticide, abandonment, severe physical punishment, child prostitution and harsh labour) has existed throughout history. According to deMause (1974: 1), 'the further back in history one goes, the lower the level of child care, and the more likely children are to be killed, abandoned, beaten, terrorized, and sexually abused'. He views the history of childhood in evolutionary terms, as 'a nightmare from which we have only recently begun to awaken'. Other historians have taken a less censorious view of childhoods past, arguing that although living conditions and general standards of care for children were far lower than those of today, and although children often had to undertake hard labour, this was largely a consequence of harsh economic conditions (Corby et al, 2012: 19). Historians are also divided over societal attitudes to the mistreatment of children: while some have argued that there was widespread indifference to the mistreatment of

27

children who were viewed as little more than possessions, others dispute the notion that it is only in recent times that societies have shown any concern about this problem (Pollock, 1983; Corby et al, 2012: 22-3).

What is beyond dispute, however, is that the issue of child abuse has over the last 50 years achieved a significance never seen before. The current level of state intervention in the life of the family, in particular, would have been unimaginable in previous generations, as would the 'explicit frankness' with which issues, such as sexual abuse, are now discussed (Coldrey, 1996: 371). Indeed, until recently child sexual abuse hardly existed as an academic or public policy issue in the West (Lalor, 1998: 49).

In this chapter we will map the emergence of child abuse as a major social issue in western countries, focusing in particular on developments in Britain, Ireland and the United States. We take as our starting point the late 19th/early 20th century, during which time the foundations of contemporary child protection and welfare systems were laid. The second period of major change runs from the 1960s to the current day, a period in which the main focus of anxiety commenced with physical abuse (the 'battered child syndrome') and finally focused on the sexual abuse of children as the 'paramount evil' to be confronted (Coldrey, 1996: 370). During this period we also see a shift in emphasis from intra- to extrafamilial abuse, particularly within institutional settings. These developments will be situated in the wider context of changing conceptions of childhood and the family, and in the emergence of the media as the 'fourth estate' that brought the issue of abuse to a mass audience and acted as a powerful catalyst for change.

'Discovery' of child abuse in the late 19th and early 20th century

The latter half of the 19th century saw a flurry of activity around the issue of child protection. The conception of the child that developed during this period, and which informed subsequent practice and policy, saw children either as vulnerable and in need of protection (the child as victim) or as impulsive, unsocialised and in need of guidance and control (the child as threat) (Foley et al, 2003: 106; Parton 2006: 10). Corby et al (2012) identify four categories of young people who were of particular concern to the state: children of the street (termed as vagabonds, beggars or street traders), young offenders, children at work and children looked after in Poor Law authority institutions. Unease about the welfare and control of young people took on an added significance as the population of England and Wales expanded rapidly in the course of the 19th century (from under 10 million in 1801 to 32 million in 1901) with those aged under 14 never falling below 30% and for much of the period the figure was nearer 40% (Parton, 2006: 11). The proportions living in urban areas similarly increased from just over half in 1851 to three-quarters by 1901. These demographic changes, brought about by the demands of rapid industrialisation, led to new problems and concerns about the upbringing of children and the emergence of new forms of state intervention. The main pattern of responses was for issues to be initially taken up by philanthropic societies of different religious persuasions acting as pressure groups, followed by government intervention and state legislation (Corby et al, 2012: 26).

By the end of the 19th century, a number of philanthropic organisations had been set up in Britain and Ireland to address the needs of poorer children, some of which exist to the current day (eg, Barnardo's). The most influential of these organisations was undoubtedly the National Society for the Prevention of Cruelty to Children (NSPCC). While today state agencies have the primary responsibility for the investigation and management of child abuse, in the years between the 1880s and the Second World War, the NSPCC was uniformly recognised as the primary organisation in the formulation of child protection policy and practice in both the UK and Ireland (Ferguson, 1993: 16). The first Society for the Prevention of Cruelty to Children (SPCC) was founded by Elbridge Gerry and Henry Bergh in New York City in December 1874 (Myers, 2011). Their involvement in the rescue of an eight-year-old girl, Mary Ellen Wilson, from her abusive guardians had persuaded them of the need to organise a society to protect children. Others followed their example and by 1922 some 300 nongovernmental child protection societies were scattered across America. In 1881, Thomas Agnew, a banker from Liverpool, visited the New York SPCC and was so impressed by what he saw that, on his return to Britain, he set up the Liverpool SPCC. In 1884 the London SPCC was established and by 1889 it had opened 32 branches or aid committees across England, Wales and Scotland (Corby et al, 2012: 27). In the same year the name of the organisation was changed to the National Society for the Prevention of Cruelty to Children. In Ireland, a Dublin branch was formed in 1889 and was soon followed by branches in Cork, Belfast and Waterford (Ferguson, 1993).[1]

---

[1]   In 1956, the Irish Society for the Prevention of Cruelty to Children (ISPCC) was founded as a successor to the NSPCC, which had operated in Ireland from 1889 to 1956.

One of the main concerns of the early NSPCC was that there were no statutory means of protecting children before cases of parental cruelty were tried and no means of ensuring continued protection once convicted parents were released (Corby et al, 2012: 27). NSPCC inspectors were appointed to seek out and report instances of abuse and neglect to the police, while shelters were established to provide places of safety for children pending prosecutions. Accounts of child mistreatment and fatalities were publicised in order to influence public opinion and generate resources (Ferguson, 1993). Moreover, relentless parliamentary lobbying led to the introduction of the first legislation specifically outlawing child cruelty and giving public agencies powers to protect children within their home – the Prevention of Cruelty to Children Act 1889. Further Acts followed in 1894, 1904 and 1908, the effects of which were to consolidate and extend the original Act. Corby et al (2012) note that by 1908 the main components of child protection law that exist today were in place. The Children Act 1908 was aptly called 'The Children's Charter'.

Child sexual abuse within the family, previously ignored as a social problem, was also being addressed by the NSPCC, though it was not publicised in the same way as physical abuse and neglect cases. Corby et al (2012: 29) argue that this response 'reflected the general attitude to the issue, which was akin to a conspiracy of silence'. Nonetheless, pressure from the NSPCC and the National Vigilance Association did help to pave the way for the introduction of the Punishment of Incest Act 1908. While the impact of this legislation may have been limited, incest was now officially recognised as a crime and this at least 'created the potential for more effective intervention' (Corby et al, 2012: 29). Concerns about the sexual exploitation of children *outside* the family were more publicly acknowledged and became the subject of public debate and controversy on a number of occasions. Early feminist and 'social purity' campaigners, for example, highlighted how working-class girls were trapped into prostitution (Kitzinger, 2004: 33). In 1885, public opinion was scandalised by the publication of a series of salacious articles in the *Pall Mall Gazette*, describing the sale of young girls for sexual services, under headings such as 'Confessionals of a Brothel-Keeper' (Kitzinger, 2004). The newspaper was subsequently banned by major newsagents and the government came under considerable pressure to raise the age of consent. Following a mass demonstration in Hyde Park in London, and amidst fears of national riots, the Criminal Law Amendment Act was passed, raising the age of consent to 16.

As can be seen, there were considerable shifts in thinking about state intervention into family life between 1870 and 1914, largely in response to growing concerns around the welfare of children. However, there was a definite shift in focus away from this issue between the two world wars (Coldrey, 1996; Parton, 2006). A number of possible reasons have been put forward for this, including the decline of the women's movement following the granting of universal suffrage and changes to the NSPCC, 'to whom the government was happy to leave the responsibility for child cruelty', which became more bureaucratic and less campaigning (Parton, 2006: 16). Moreover, Ferguson (2011: 28) argues that the NSPCC stopped publicising information about child deaths in the manner that it had done in the pre-war period because the 'disclosure of such failures to protect children threatened the authority, optimism and trustworthiness of the child protection system'. By the late 1930s, information about deaths in child protection cases ceased to be made public and had disappeared from view. While there was an upsurge in interest in the welfare of deprived children after the Second World War and a number of significant policy developments (Corby et al 2012: 30-4), it was not until the 1960s that the issue of child abuse again began to enter the public arena as a significant social problem.

The 'rediscovery' of child abuse

The 'rediscovery' of the problem we now call child abuse began in the USA during the 1960s and is particularly associated with the work of Dr Henry Kempe and his colleagues. In a landmark article, published in the prestigious journal of the American Medical Association, they coined the term 'battered child syndrome' to describe a clinical condition in young children (usually under the age of three) who had received serious physical abuse, generally from a parent or foster parent. While this syndrome was a significant cause of childhood disability and death, it was frequently not recognised. Kempe et al (1962) argued that difficulties in diagnosing the condition stemmed in part from parental denials of abuse and from the battered child's own reluctance or inability to disclose details of their injuries. Therefore the use of x-rays to aid diagnosis is stressed: 'to the informed physician, the bones tell a story the child is too young or too frightened to tell' (Kempe et al, 1962: 144). However, Kempe and his colleagues also highlighted the fact that even where there is clear evidence of parental abuse doctors are often unwilling to acknowledge it as such. This was a major stumbling block to the recognition and treatment of the condition:

> In addition to the reluctance of the parents to give information regarding the attacks on their children, there

is another factor that is of great importance and extreme interest as it relates to the difficulty in delving into the problem of parental neglect and abuse. This is the fact that physicians have great difficulty both in believing that parents could have attacked their children and in undertaking the essential questioning of parents on this subject. Many physicians find it hard to believe that such an attack could have occurred and they attempt to obliterate such suspicions from their minds, even in the face of the obvious circumstantial evidence. The reason for this is not clearly understood. One possibility is that the arousal of the physician's antipathy in response to such situations is so great that it is easier for the physician to deny the possibility of such attack than to have to deal with the excessive anger which surges up in him when he realizes the truth of the situation. Furthermore, the physician's training and personality usually makes it quite difficult for him to assume the role of policeman or district attorney and start questioning parents as if he were investigating a crime. The humanitarian-minded physician finds it most difficult to proceed when he is met with protestations of innocence from the aggressive parent, especially when the battered child was brought to him voluntarily. (Kempe et al, 1962: 146)

Kempe's article is in some respects a call to arms for the medical profession: physicians are urged to interrogate parents (rather than accepting their explanations at face value) and to report suspected abuse to the authorities. Crucially, the authors argued that the welfare of children should be prioritised above all other considerations: 'the bias should be in favor of the child's safety; everything should be done to prevent repeated trauma, and the physician should not be satisfied to return the child to an environment where even a moderate risk of repetition exists' (Kempe et al, 1962: 153).

The work of Kempe and his colleagues had a significant impact on the development of child protection policy in the United States (Nelson, 1984). Physical abuse of children came to be seen as a major social issue, attracting national publicity. While local media had always reported 'noteworthy' cases, as when a child was beaten to death, coverage by national media was uncommon prior to the 1960s (Myers, 2011). However, following the publication of 'The Battered-Child Syndrome', national news outlets like *Newsweek*, *Saturday Evening Post*,

Parents magazine, *Time* magazine, *Good Housekeeping*, and *Life* published emotional stories of abuse, often citing Kempe's work. Similarly, there had been little professional research and writing about abuse prior to 1962 but after this point 'a trickle of writing became a torrent that continues to this day' (Nelson, 1984: 129; Myers, 2011: 9).

Growing concerns around the physical abuse of children also led to the introduction of reporting laws (Nelson, 1984). By the end of 1963, thirteen US states had enacted statutory reporting laws whereby professionals who suspected abuse or neglect were legally required to report this to the police or a childcare agency (Parton, 1985: 52). Ten more states were added in 1964, 26 in 1965, and by 1967 every state had passed some form of reporting law. Therefore by the mid-1960s in the USA 'there was a recognition of a new and distinctive problem called 'the battered child syndrome' which, while it begins with a pattern of injuries to the child, is really descriptive of a pattern of conduct on the part of the parents or others who care for children' (Parton, 1985: 52).

A number of reasons have been identified for the re-emergence of this age-old problem at this particular time. Technological developments such as the use of X-rays certainly played a part and were a key component of Kempe's work on the diagnosis of battered child syndrome. However, as Corby et al (2012) point out, broader considerations also need to be taken into account. The climate was right for the greater focus on the care and upbringing of children. The relative affluence of the 1960s, particularly in America, created the conditions for people to pay greater attention to the needs of children and to the quality of parent–child relationships. Moreover, by giving child abuse a medical label – battered child *syndrome* – and seeing it as treatable, new forms of intervention into family life were not seen as threatening the independence of families in general 'because they were aimed only at the families that had the "illness"' (Corby et al, 2012: 34). Nelson (1984) argues that in the United States public and state interest in child abuse was also part of a larger social current which was pushing issues of equity (eg, civil rights, feminism) to the fore during the 1960s.

Rediscovery of abuse in Britain and Ireland

Awareness of the problem of child abuse developed more slowly in Britain and was heavily influenced by developments in the US, particularly Kempe's work on the battered child syndrome (Parton, 1985). The medical profession initially played a key role in establishing this as a significant issue. Of particular note was an influential article on 'battered baby syndrome' by Griffiths and Moynihan, two orthopaedic surgeons, which was published in the *British Medical Journal* in 1963. Like Kempe, they asserted that the condition was being misdiagnosed and that doctors should always consider that babies may have been injured by 'brutal violence' with 'the culprit' almost always the parent (Griffiths and Moynihan, 1963: 1560). The article was well received and paved the way for further debate within the medical profession. The amount of medical literature devoted to this issue developed steadily throughout the 1960s with paediatricians and forensic pathologists leading the way.

By the late 1960s, awareness of the problem outside of the medical profession was still minimal. However, with the establishment of the NSPCC Battered Child Research Unit this began to change. The Unit became crucial in sustaining and disseminating publicity to other professional groups and was, according to Parton (1985: 58), 'the primary influence on the way the problem was taken up by the media and civil servants, so that its definition of the problem, its explanation, management and resolutions became dominant'. As part of its dissemination strategy, members of the NSPCC unit had seventeen articles published in a variety of professional journals between January 1969 and 1973. In addition, two of their reports (1969, 1972) brought the problem to the attention of the media and central government for the first time. Indeed, Parton argues, media reporting of the issue during this time seems to have relied largely on outputs from the NSPCC unit. Moreover, the professional journals, including those of the medical profession, increasingly saw it as the focal agency. Interestingly, it seems that social work generally was relatively slow to respond to the problem compared to other professional groups. A review of the social work journals for the period demonstrates that apart from the articles produced by the NSPCC unit there were no articles on the problem written by social workers (Parton, 1985).

While the NSPCC and sections of the medical professional undoubtedly helped to raise awareness of child abuse during the 1960s and '70s, the problem was still not seen as a major priority and was given a relatively low profile in many professional groups, the media, and central and local government. One writer to the letters column of the *British Medical Journal* noted prophetically that 'what is really needed is a *cause célèbre* with front page treatment in the press' (Parton, 1985: 55). In 1972, the tragic death of Maria Colwell proved to be just such a case, establishing child abuse as a significant social problem and ushering in major changes in policy and practice.

In Ireland, there was little public or professional acknowledgement of the problem of child abuse for much of the 20th century and the state appeared reluctant to legislate on behalf of children: the Children Act 1908 provided the main legal framework for child care for over 80 years. Indeed, according to the Task Force on Child Care Services (1980: 182), 'the most striking feature of the child care scene was the alarming complacency and indifference of both the general public and the various governmental departments and statutory bodies responsible for the welfare of children'. However, from the 1970s onwards, policy makers and professionals began to 'rediscover' child abuse and were particularly influenced by events in Britain and the US, including Kempe's work on the battered child syndrome (Ferguson, 1993). In 1976, the Department of Health established a Committee on Non-Accidental Injury to Children whose work included the production of guidelines on the identification and management of non-accidental injury (Lalor, 2001: 7). The introduction of the Child Care Act 1991 is generally acknowledged as a key moment in the development of the child protection and welfare system in Ireland (Ferguson, 1995; Lavan, 1998) and will be considered in detail in Chapter 2.

Discovery of child sexual abuse

The child abuse that was being 'rediscovered' during the 1960s was primarily physical abuse: professional and public concern over the sexual abuse of children did not begin to emerge as a serious problem until the 1970s (in the USA) and 1980s (in Britain). In some countries, including Ireland, public awareness of child sexual abuse lagged further behind, only emerging in the 1990s when a series of high-profile scandals and inquiries revealed both familial and clerical abuse (see Chapters 2–4). Despite the fact that there was clear evidence that children were being sexually abused in earlier parts of the century, there was widespread avoidance and denial both among the public and professionals themselves. Parton (1991: 85) notes that research studies and case reports on child sexual abuse had been available in Britain during the 1950s, '60s and '70s, but these did not spur the professional community to determine the incidence of child sexual abuse or provide specialised services for those affected. Similarly, Kitzinger (2004: 34) argues that throughout the 1920s and 1930s, women active in organisations such as the Association for Moral and Social Hygiene and the National Vigilance Association fought to have sexual abuse taken seriously, but the legal profession and the media evaded their efforts. Moreover, where sexual abuse was detected, it was often dealt with as something else, usually neglect. Ferguson's (2011: 29) research into the archives of child protection agencies found that where girls and young women did disclose child sexual abuse, including incest, the case was taken as neglect because there was evidence of that and it was easier to get cases of neglect through the courts. Some who disclosed sexual abuse were not only disbelieved but punished. All of this began to change from the 1970s onwards, resulting in significant developments in the field of child protection and heightened media and political interest. The feminist movement played a key role in laying the groundwork for the recognition of child sexual abuse. In particular, women's refuges and rape crisis centres helped to expose the problem of incest. As Kitzinger (2004: 45) points out, years before this issue entered the public/media domain, workers in these feminist-inspired initiatives were having to address the needs of women who were fleeing to protect their sexually abused children.[2] Moreover, feminist writers and activists provided an important sociological perspective to the understanding of sexual abuse within the family. It was argued that such abuse was perpetrated almost exclusively by men and reflected the subordinate position of children and women within a patriarchal society (Parton, 1991: 88). Unlike the 'family dysfunction approach', which attempts to ensure that those implicated in an abusive relationship 'assume their traditional roles as child, mother and father', a feminist approach stresses the prevalence of male power as a central explanation and focus for intervention (Parton, 1991: 88). Consequently, feminists see child sexual abuse as more of a societal than a familial issue (Crosson Tower, 1996: 131). The testimonies of survivors and the formation of survivor support groups were also crucial to raising public awareness of this problem. Adults who had been sexually abused as children wrote books based on their experience or contributed to documentaries and other forms of media reporting on the subject (Kitzinger, 2004).

Writing in the US context, Myers (2011) also argues that groundbreaking research in the late 1960s and 70s helped to launch the issue of child sexual abuse (hitherto largely invisible) onto the national stage. Of particular note was De Francis's (1969: vii) study of 250 sexual abuse cases from Brooklyn, the results of which suggested that the incidence of sexual abuse was 'many times larger than the reported

[2]   The prevalence of childhood abuse was also exposed through consciousness raising groups as women shared their experiences. In the late 1970s and in the 1980s, a number of conferences, including the New York Radical Feminist conference and the National Women's Liberation conference, provided a forum for discussions on child sexual abuse (Kitzinger, 2004).

incidence of physical abuse of children'. Further studies (Finkelhor, 1979; Russell, 1983) also helped to reveal the prevalence of child sexual abuse, particularly by family members, exploding any notion that sexual abuse was either rare or benign. As with the earlier issue of child physical abuse, the US authorities acted quickly to introduce reporting legislation:

> By the end of the 1970s, the United States enjoyed for the first time a nationwide system of government-sponsored child protection. The influential CAPTA [Child Abuse Prevention and Treatment Act] of 1974 included sexual abuse in its definition of maltreatment. By 1976, all states had reporting laws requiring professionals to report sexual abuse. The expanded child protection system, particularly the reporting laws, wrenched sexual abuse from obscurity. (Myers, 2011: 12-13)

During the 1980s and 1990s, a series of scandals and public inquiries into the handling of child sexual abuse cases attracted widespread public, media and political attention. The first major inquiry into sexual abuse in the UK concerned the Cleveland case, in which 121 children from 57 families were taken into care over a five month period in 1987. The children had been examined by paediatricians Marietta Higgs and Geoff Wyatt who diagnosed them as showing signs consistent with abuse. The parents vehemently denied these charges, arguing that the test used by the paediatricians was unreliable and that the children had been misdiagnosed. They were supported by the MP Stuart Bell and significant sections of the media who presented this as a case of over-zealous social workers and doctors snatching children from their loving families. While the allegations were disputed, Cleveland nonetheless represented a further step in bringing the issue of child sexual abuse within the family into the open as Parton (2006: 34-5) points out:

> Cleveland was about sexual abuse and touched a range of sensitivities which were rarely evident in earlier concerns about physical abuse and neglect: it reached the most intimate, hidden and private elements of family life and adult–child relations; it represented a major set of debates around patriarchy and male power and thereby opened up a range of political arguments around gender never evident in the official discourses previously; and for the first time, the issue threatened middle-class and professional households.

No longer could child abuse be seen as only associated
with the marginalised and disreputable sections of society.
It seemed to permeate 'normal' families.

In Ireland, there was a growing awareness and recognition of child
sexual abuse among professionals from the early 1980s (Lalor, 2001:
8-9). Nonetheless, the concept of child sexual abuse did not exist
in the public domain in any meaningful way nor was it seen as a
significant area of practice or policy. In 1993, however, the controversy
surrounding the Kilkenny incest case – in which a man was found
to have physically and sexually abused his daughter – catapulted the
issues of sexual violence and child care policy to the top of the political
agenda. Following the man's trial, the Minister for Health immediately
announced an inquiry that was chaired by Senior Counsel, Catherine
McGuinness. While the Kilkenny case concerned both physical and
sexual abuse, it was the latter – perpetrated over 15 years during which
time the victim became pregnant and gave birth to a son – that gave
this case its notoriety and attracted huge media publicity to the issue
of sexual violence within the family. The unfolding of the Kilkenny
scandal, and the media's coverage, is considered in detail in Chapter 2.

Institutional abuse: 'pindown' and other scandals in the UK

When first identified, the problem of child abuse and neglect was
perceived as occurring within the family context with parents as
the perpetrators (Department of Health, 1996). However, during
the 1990s, new concerns came to the fore regarding the treatment
of children in various institutional settings, including residential
homes, hospitals, mainstream and special schools (residential and day),
playgroups, nurseries and daycare. The shift in official and public
concern from familial to institutional abuse is clearly illustrated by the
types of inquiries undertaken during this period. In the UK between
1991 and 2000, there were at least 12 public inquiries into abuse in
institutional settings, outstripping the number of inquiries of abuse
of children in their own homes (Corby et al, 2012: 45). This is in
stark contrast to the 1970s and 1980s when there were only three
inquiries into institutional abuse (in Lewisham, Belfast and Greenwich)
compared with nearly 50 into abuse by family members.

One of the most significant inquiries into institutional abuse in
Britain concerned a system known as 'pindown', which operated in
children's homes in Staffordshire from 1983 to 1989. 'Pindown' referred
to a range of punitive measures used to control young people, including

isolation in special areas or units; removal of ordinary clothing and the enforced wearing of shorts or nightclothes; persistent loss of all 'privileges'; non-attendance at school; and lack of access to television, radio and reading materials (Staffordshire County Council 1991:120).[3] This system operated for over six years until a complaint by a 15-year-old girl to a solicitor representing her in care proceedings set in motion a series of events that led eventually to the setting up of an inquiry by Staffordshire County Council (Butler and Drakeford, 2003: 205). The media – most notably a Granada Television programme shown in June 1990 – played a key role in these events, transforming 'pindown' 'from a local to a national phenomenon' and drawing in more powerful voices to the growing chorus of concern around events in Staffordshire (Butler and Drakeford, 2003: 207).

Significantly, in their analysis of the Staffordshire inquiry, Butler and Drakeford (2003) found that there was no evidence to suggest that any sustained attempt had been made to *conceal* the practice of 'pindown' within residential homes. Senior managers and external visitors entered these premises on a regular basis and detailed logbooks recorded the measures used. At the time, far from being considered scandalous, 'pindown' appeared to have been an accepted, even approved way of controlling young people. To understand *why* this apparently routine child care practice subsequently became the source of a major scandal, it must be located within the wider context of changing perceptions of children's rights. The scandal was, according to Butler and Drakeford (2003: 215), largely a matter of timing:

> Central to the scandal of pindown is the question of children's emerging status as rights-holders. This was a scandal precipitated by a lawyer and pursued through the courts. It was 'sponsored' by organisations such as NAYPIC [National Association of Young People in Care] and engaged with by groups with an interest in civil liberties. At the centre of the abuses of pindown was the restriction of children's liberty, their isolation, their exclusion from education and normal social intercourse and the degradation and humiliation at being denied even their own clothes. It is their civil rights that were at issue rather

---

[3] The origin of the term 'pindown' was said to be the use by one staff member of the words, 'we must pin down the problem' (Staffordshire County Council 1991:120). The children began to speak of being in 'pindown'.

than the more obvious cruelties or abuses that formed the substance of previous scandals.

In the aftermath of the 'pindown' scandal, the British government commissioned a special review of residential care in England, which was undertaken by Sir William Utting and published as *Children in the Public Care* (Utting, 1991). The report highlighted the low status of residential care which was commonly regarded as an unimportant, residual activity in which the skills required were inherent or intuitive. Consequently, Utting made several recommendations aimed at raising the profile of residential child care work, particularly in relation to better training for staff. Other recommendations concerned the need for improved management through better planning, inspection and monitoring. Significantly, Utting also recommended that children and young people be given a greater say in the decisions that affected their lives. Increased participation for young people, together with closer managerial oversight, were two key themes that were to grow in significance over the coming years (Parton, 2006: 43).

As the 1990s progressed, a series of scandals concerning the sexual abuse of children in care dealt a further blow to the reputation and morale of the residential sector. Inquiries into institutional abuse were held in various parts of Britain, including Shropshire (Brannan et al, 1993), Leicestershire (Kirkwood, 1993), Islington (White and Hart, 1995) and Northumberland (Kilgallon, 1995). Allegations of the widespread abuse of children in residential homes in North Wales led to the establishment of a 'tribunal of inquiry' in 1996 (see Chapter 2). At the same time the government commissioned a national review of safeguards for children living away from home, which was again chaired by Sir William Utting (1997). Further reports, regulations and initiatives followed. However, by the late 1990s confidence in residential services had been seriously undermined (Corby, 2004). Both local authorities and voluntary organisations were accused of having failed to protect those most in need of care, many of whom came from very damaged backgrounds. Indeed, Stanley (1999: 16) argues that concerns about abuse in out-of-home-care settings may even have had 'the effect of making the use of care orders [to remove children] seem as risky a strategy as leaving children in abusive home situations'.

The various scandals and inquiries into institutional abuse in the UK had a major influence on the development of policy (Stanley, 1999). While the growing interest in the welfare of children in care during the 1990s was certainly welcomed, by the end of the decade there were also concerns that the sheer volume and complexity of the ensuing regulations and guidance was becoming a problem in itself (Butler and Drakeford, 2003: 217).[4] In some cases policy reforms were developed within a narrow frame of reference, being unduly influenced by inquiries and media coverage (Stanley, 1999: 38-9). Moreover, the inquiries themselves were criticised by some observers for their over-reliance on hindsight, outdated findings and financial cost, and for undermining staff morale resulting in more defensive practice. According to Corby (2004: 127), the North Wales Tribunal, in particular, embodied all of these problems and indicated the need to find 'a more systematic, independent and public way to review or inquire into all cases of abuse in residential care in a more routinised way'.

Institutional abuse in Ireland

In Ireland, the issue of institutional abuse of children entered the public domain in 1993 when allegations of misconduct were made against members of staff employed at Madonna House, a residential home for children in Dublin, run by the Sisters of Charity. One staff member (a maintenance man) was subsequently convicted and jailed for indecent and sexual assault, perpetrated over a five-year period between 1985 and 1990 (Department of Health, 1996: 93[5]). Parallel to the criminal investigation, the Sisters of Charity and the Department of Health appointed an inquiry team in September 1993 to review the operation of Madonna House, focusing in particular on staff qualifications and competence, and 'the manner in which care duties were discharged by staff members ... in light of the various allegations made' (Department of Health, 1996: 5). The inquiry team was composed of representatives from the Health Boards and the Sisters of Charity, and chaired by Fred Donohoe, former Programme Manager Community Care in the Eastern Health Board. It was not a statutory inquiry and all those who participated did so voluntarily.

In March 1995, a copy of the Report of the Inquiry Team was submitted to the Minister for Health (Department of Health, 1996: viii). However, following advice from the Attorney General's Office, it was decided that certain sections could not be published because of 'the need to protect the identities of certain parties and to avoid interference with ongoing investigations and legal proceedings' (Department of

---

[4]   Similar issues were later raised by Munro (2011) in a review of the child protection system.

[5]   See also *The Irish Times* 1 June 1994 'Madonna House to close down'.

Health, 1996: viii). However, the decision to publish an abridged version of the report (in May 1996) was greeted with scepticism by the press and the Irish Association of Care Workers (IACW). Indeed, in a statement, the IACW asserted that 'more confusion now exists in relation to the issue of abuse in Madonna House than prior to the publication of the report'.[6] Concerns were also expressed that the roles of the Sisters of Charity and the Eastern Health Board had not been sufficiently scrutinised, and that an independent inquiry would have been more appropriate.[7]

By the time the abridged version was published by the Department of Health (as the *Report on the Inquiry into the Operation of Madonna House*) in May 1996, the home had already closed down. Nonetheless, the findings and recommendations had a wider significance and subsequently impacted on the way in which residential facilities for children were run (Lalor, 2001). Like earlier reports in the UK – which are cited extensively – the Madonna House Report highlighted concerns around the recruitment and retention of suitably qualified staff: most staff were found to have had either no qualification or a qualification that was not appropriate to their role; there appeared to be no expectation that these staff undertake the necessary training; and there was a high staff turnover, particularly for more junior posts (Department of Health, 1996: ch 8). In terms of the running of the home, the report was particularly critical of the failure to provide aftercare services for those young people leaving care, who were ill-equipped for the practicalities of everyday living and at risk of becoming homeless (Department of Health, 1996: 88, 90). Comparatively little was said about the abuse that was alleged to have taken place within Madonna House and a number of sections dealing with this issue had clearly been retracted. Nonetheless, the inquiry did consider the factors that might inhibit effective disclosure of abuse, including the isolation and vulnerability of children in residential care, and in some cases their apparent acceptance of physical discipline as 'normal' or 'appropriate' (Department of Health, 1996: 80).

While the focus of the report was on Madonna House, the inquiry team were nonetheless emphatic that the abuses which occurred there had to be viewed in the wider context of a 'dysfunctional social system' (Department of Health, 1996: 96). A number of 'external contextual factors' were identified, including the absence of statutory

---

6   *The Irish Times* 19 June 1996 'Criticism of the abridged report on Madonna House'.

7   *The Irish Times* 10 May 1996 'A lost opportunity for a more in-depth inquiry'.

regulation in relation to residential care services, the strain on services and professionals as they attempt to cope with ever increasing demands and the 'inadequacies of the legal system' in relation to child abuse (p 101). Moreover, the inquiry team concurred with Utting's view that residential care tended to be seen as a Cinderella service and that measures had to be taken to raise the status of the sector as a whole: 'If residential care is to meet the needs of extremely vulnerable children who have been damaged by child abuse and neglect, it needs to be valued, resourced, and integrated fully into the spectrum of community-based family support services' (p29). The need to recognise and assert the rights of children is also highlighted – echoing earlier reports in the UK and the Kilkenny Report (McGuiness, 1993). Given the 'unique vulnerabilities' of children who have been taken into care, the report recommended that a Statement of Children's Rights in Care be developed as a matter of urgency.

The Madonna House Report, while highly critical of certain aspects of the operation and management of the home, also acknowledged its 'many remarkable and impressive features' (Department of Health, 1996: 6) and the positive experiences reported by a number of former residents (pp 85, 89). Crucially, the published report contained none of the damning accusations of concealment and 'cover-up', which characterised later inquiries into institutional and community-based clerical abuse (see Chapter 3). The fact that the only person convicted was a maintenance man (rather than a member of the religious order) no doubt further mitigated the damage to the reputation of the Sisters of Charity. Nonetheless, the Madonna House Report was published at a time when there was a growing awareness of institutional abuse and religious orders were almost inevitably going to be subject to scrutiny, given their primacy in providing residential care for children in Ireland for most of the 20th century. The influential drama–documentary *Dear Daughter* had been broadcast on Raidió Teilifís Éireann (RTÉ) only a few months earlier (February 1996), detailing the physical and emotional abuse endured by children in Goldenbridge – an orphanage run by the Sisters of Mercy – during the 1940s and 1950s. Former residents described savage beatings and being so hungry that they were forced to scavenge for food in the rubbish bins at night. In the ensuing controversy there were calls for an independent inquiry,[8] for reform to the residential care system in order to better protect children[9] and

---

[8]   *The Irish Times* 24 February 1996 'FF wants inquiry on orphanage' and *The Irish Times* 28 February 1996 'Inquiry into abuse allegations urged'.

[9]   See, for example, *The Irish Times* 26 February 1996 'State child care reforms urged'.

for greater openness and transparency when child abuse scandals did occur.[10] A police investigation was also announced into the allegations made in *Dear Daughter*.[11]

The public were further sensitised to the issue of institutional abuse through extensive press coverage during which Goldenbridge was likened to Romanian and Chinese orphanages, where widespread abuse and neglect had been uncovered and reported in television documentaries.[12] While the Sisters of Mercy order was at the centre of this controversy, the Irish state was also criticised for a dereliction of duty to vulnerable children and for its failure to regulate and monitor church-run institutions. It was against this backdrop of heightened awareness of institutional abuse – and of the apparent failure of both church and state to protect children – that the abridged version of the Madonna House Report was finally published in May 1996.

In 1999, RTÉ broadcast a three-part series, *States of Fear*, which documented the systematic abuse of children within the former industrial and reformatory school system. The harrowing revelations led to a public outcry and to the setting up of the landmark Commission to Inquire into Child Abuse in 2000, the findings of which were published in the Ryan Report (CICA, 2009), which we discuss in detail in Chapter 4.

In June 2014, the care of children in church-run institutions again made national and international headlines when it emerged that 796 children, most of them infants, had died at a former 'mother and baby home' in Tuam between 1925 and 1961. A local historian, Catherine Corless, sourced details of the deaths from public records. Even by the standards of the time, the mortality rates at this institution – run by the Sisters of the Bon Secours – appeared disturbingly high. Figures subsequently published by the Department of Children and Youth Affairs in July 2014 show that most of these deaths were attributed to 'debility from birth', premature birth, respiratory diseases and a range of other illnesses (including measles, influenza, whooping cough and gastroenteritis), which raised questions about the living conditions and standards of care within these types of homes. The Catholic Church again came under public scrutiny, though there was also recognition that the state and Irish society must shoulder some of the responsibility for the fate of these children and their mothers. Politicians and media

[10]   See, for example, *The Irish Times* 27 February 1996 'Child abuse cases raise doubts on church role'.

[11]   *The Irish Times* 26 February 1996 'Gardai to investigate child abuse claims'.

[12]   *The Irish Times* 17 February 1996 'Forgotten Babies'.

commentators described the case as a reminder of the 'darker' side of Ireland's history when women who became pregnant outside of marriage were often ostracised by their families and forced in some cases to seek refuge in church-run institutions. Writing in the *Irish Independent*, the historian Diarmaid Ferriter asserted that the mother and baby homes were one of the means by which state and church 'colluded to get rid of an embarrassment to Catholic Ireland'.[13] For families and communities, these homes provided a solution to the stigma and shame of pregnancy outside marriage 'by removing from circulation those who were deemed to have transgressed'. Alternatively, many single mothers moved from rural areas to Dublin city or migrated to Britain to begin a new life (Department of Children and Youth Affairs, 2014).

One of the most controversial aspects of the Tuam case concerned the burial arrangements for these children, which became the subject of sensational media coverage both in Ireland and internationally. According to the *Irish Examiner* and the *Irish Daily Mirror* the bodies had been 'dumped' in mass graves.[14] Press headlines announced that the babies had been interred in a sceptic tank – an image that seemed to symbolise the indignity of their lives and untimely deaths.[15] One of the most lurid headlines, provided by *The Washington Times* (3 June 2014), claimed that the 'Catholic Church' (rather than the nuns themselves) had 'tossed 800 Irish Orphans into [a] septic tank grave'. In *The Irish Sun* and the *Sunday World* the death and burial of these children is compared with the holocaust and Cambodia's 'killing fields'.[16] There was also considerable speculation as to the possible scale of deaths in other homes. The *Sunday World* claimed that Tuam was 'just the tip of

[13] *Irish Independent* 6 June 2014 'Families saw these homes as a solution to their shame and stigma'.

[14] *Irish Examiner* 5 June 2014 'Tuam mother-and-baby home is a scandal of church and state'. *Irish Daily Mirror* 7 June 2014 'Gardai begin probe into 800 babies dumped in mass grave'.

[15] Examples of headlines included: 'Mass grave of 796 babies found in septic tank at Catholic orphanage in Tuam, Galway' (*Belfast Telegraph* 4 June 2014); 'Mass baby grave in Tuam, Galway: Laid to rest in septic tank, shameful fate of 800 little children' (*Belfast Telegraph* 5 June 2014); '800 skeletons of babies found inside septic tank at former irish home for unwed mothers: report' (*New York Daily News*, 3 June 2014). 'Bodies of 800 babies, long dead, found in septic tank at former Irish home for unwed mothers' (*The Washington Post* 3 June 2014).

[16] *Sunday World* 9 June 2014 'Ireland's holocaust: special report on the Tuam killing field'; *The Irish Sun* 6 June, 2014 'Mass grave "is our holocaust"'.

the iceberg' and that there might be as many as 10,000 babies buried in unmarked graves in a network of homes around the country. Writing in the *Guardian*, Emer O'Toole claimed that women were 'incarcerated' in mother and baby homes up until the 1990s when most had in fact ceased to operate decades earlier (DCYA, 2014: 11), and that there were 'outrageous' child mortality rates in each of these institutions.[17]

As Tuam escalated into an international scandal, some voiced concern at the media's sensational reporting of the case, including Catherine Corless herself. In an interview with the *Irish Times* she claimed that her research had been misrepresented in some quarters and that she had 'never said to anyone that 800 bodies were dumped in a septic tank'.[18] The crucial issue at stake here was that (contrary to some media headlines) the bodies of the 796 children had not actually been *found*. While there were a number of theories as to the *possible* location of the burial site, these had not been substantiated. Consequently much of the media-generated outrage around burial arrangements was based on very shaky foundations. The Associated Press and a number of newspapers – including *The Guardian* and *The Washington Post* – subsequently issued corrections and changed the online headings of articles about the Tuam case.

Notwithstanding that Tuam was the original focus of this controversy, related issues of death rates, burial arrangements and general conditions have also been raised with regard to Mother and Baby Homes in other locations (Department of Children and Youth Affairs, 2014). In response to public outcry, the Irish government announced the setting up of a Commission of Inquiry, the scope of which is currently under review. The commission is to be headed by Judge Yvonne Murphy who previously chaired inquiries into clerical abuse in the Archdiocese of Dublin and the Diocese of Cloyne (see Chapter 3).

Institutional abuse internationally

Institutional child abuse has been reported in a number of other western countries, including the United States, Canada, Australia and the Netherlands. In the United States, the proliferation of civil lawsuits, criminal investigations, inquiries and survivors' accounts

---

[17] *The Guardian* 4 June 2014 'Tell us the truth about the children in Galway's mass graves' (the original title of the article published on 4 June was amended on 10 June 2014 and was not available on the online copy of the paper).

[18] *Irish Times* 7 June 2014 'Tuam mother and baby home: the trouble with the septic tank story'.

have brought this issue into the open. The Catholic Church has been subject to particular scrutiny: the recent wave of sexual abuse complaints against clergy can be seen as beginning in Louisiana with the case of Father Gilbert Gauthe, against whom civil and criminal charges were brought in 1984 (Keenan, 2012:17). The case attracted publicity across the country and in the following decades the Catholic Church became embroiled in a series of other scandals concerning the abuse of children in both institutional and community settings. In Canada, examinations of child abuse revealed patterns of extensive abuse in child welfare and educational institutions that were under church or government control (Mian et al, 2001). One of the most publicised institutional abuse cases was at Mount Cashel Orphanage in Newfoundland where boys suffered chronic physical and sexual abuse at the hands of the Christian Brothers. Following disclosures of abuse, the Newfoundland government and the Catholic Church eventually established commissions of inquiry that made a number of recommendations to prevent similar occurrences in the future.

In 1997, the Law Commission of Canada was asked to look at ways of addressing 'the harm caused by physical and sexual abuse of children in institutions operated, funded or sponsored by government', including residential schools for Aboriginal children, schools for the deaf and blind, training schools, long-term mental health care facilities and sanatoria (Law Commission of Canada, 2000: 1). Some of the issues raised by the commission resonate with the findings of the Ryan Report (CICA, 2009), namely that: (1) the majority of children placed in institutions came from the most underprivileged or marginalised groups in society; (2) a significant power imbalance existed between the children and those in charge of these institutions, one that went beyond the obvious power imbalance between a child and an adult in a position of authority; (3) there was little independent monitoring of what went on inside these institutions and the desire to preserve the good name of an institution took precedence over a concern for the welfare of children (Law Commission of Canada, 2000: 1-2). The experience of Aboriginal children in residential schools was an issue of particular concern 'because their presence in residential schools was the result of a policy of assimilation sustained for several decades by the federal government, with the cooperation of many religious organisations'. The report goes on to say:

> Deprived of their native languages, cultural traditions and religion, many Aboriginal children in residential schools were cut off from their heritage and made to feel ashamed

of it. As a result, the residential school system inflicted terrible damage not just on individuals but on families, entire communities and peoples. (Law Commission of Canada, 2000: 2)

Australia has similarly had to confront 'the large-scale maltreatment of children' in the past, including the forced separation of Aboriginal children from their families and placement in institutions as part of the country's assimilation policy (Hatty and Hatty, 2001). A Royal Commission was established in 2013 'to inquire into institutional responses to allegations and incidents of child sexual abuse' in Australia – its work is still ongoing (Royal Commission into Institutional Responses to Child Sexual Abuse, 2013). A major inquiry is also underway into the abuse of children in residential institutions in Northern Ireland between 1922 and 1995 (The Historical Institutional Abuse Inquiry, 2014). Other historical inquiries have focused on particular institutions or religious denominations. At the request of the Catholic Church in the Netherlands, a commission of inquiry was set up in 2010, headed by Wim Deetman, to carry out a study of the abuse of minors in Roman Catholic institutions and parishes during the period from 1945 to 2010. Like inquiries in other countries, the commission found that church authorities were aware of the problem of sexual abuse but in many cases failed to take adequate action to protect children. As we shall see in Chapter 3, it was this failure to act and the deliberate concealment of the problem that were to cause the greatest damage to the reputation of the Catholic Church.

While investigations into the abuse of children in church-run institutions have been carried out mainly in western, industrialised countries, there is little reason to doubt that similar abuses occurred in other countries.

The media's role in constructing child abuse

The media played a key role in the construction of child abuse as a major social problem during the latter part of the 20th century. From a largely unacknowledged issue (prior to the 1960s) reportage of child abuse has now reached saturation point (Kitzinger, 2004: 36). Moreover, the issue has been covered across a range of genre (including news programmes, television drama, films, call-in shows and soap operas) thereby reaching a diverse range of audiences.

While acknowledging the importance of the media in raising awareness, a number of commentators have also noted that the media's interest is very recent and has generally relied on others (eg, activists, professional groups) to lay the groundwork. Rather than being in the vanguard, the media has generally brought up the rear. The groundwork for the recognition of child sexual abuse, for example, lay in early activities by feminists and survivors, and involved international links within the women's movement across the world. According to Kitzinger (2004: 45):

> Without this range of interventions the media might never have discovered the issue. Certainly, to many of those active throughout the 1970s and early 1980s, the media seemed tardy in the extreme in taking this issue on board. Journalists were sceptical of the allegations, or did not take them seriously, or considered them too shocking for a family newspaper.

In relation to the 'rediscovery' of physical abuse in Britain during the 1960s, Parton (1985) argues that the media, far from campaigning in its own right, simply reflected the views and publications of the NSPCC Battered Child Research Unit. Similarly in the US, it was only after the publication of the 'The Battered-Child Syndrome' that the national media began to take an interest in the subject (Myers, 2011). Despite the fact that there had been widespread abuse of children in church-run institutions in Ireland throughout the 1950s and 1960s, this issue was not reported in the media until the 1990s. However, when the media did finally become involved in highlighting the issue of abuse, the impact was enormous. As we mentioned earlier, extensive coverage helped to transform events – such as the use of 'pindown' in residential homes – from local events to national scandals, requiring substantial government intervention. Moreover, the media has been instrumental in calling powerful institutions – notably the Catholic Church – to account for their handling of child abuse allegations (see Chapter 3).

Media representations of sexual abuse not only transformed public knowledge, but also had profound implications for 'private' knowledge. In her research, Kitzinger (2004) found that, up until the mid-1980s, survivors of abuse often struggled to make sense of what had been done to them within the inadequate conventional categories available to them at that time. Because of the culture of silence around incest, abused children and adult survivors had to process their experiences in an almost total cultural vacuum. They often had no words to define what was happening to them, other than the explanation offered by their abusers. However, from the 1980s onwards media representations began to provide victims of abuse with a framework for thinking and talking about their experiences:

> During the late 1980s and early 1990s many adult abuse survivors finally began to find words for what had been done to them. They started to reassess what had happened to them, finally realising that it was not normal or that they did not deserve it. Others found that media coverage forced them to confront memories that they had been trying to ignore. One woman comments that until the media started to discuss incest 'I just had these funny ideas floating around in my head – I had no way of making sense of them.' Another states that, in spite of recurring nightmares, 'It was not part of my waking day at all.' The media helped to change this. Indeed, among those I interviewed during the 1980s it was media coverage, rather than comments from friends or family, which is most often identified as a trigger for confronting childhood abuse and 'grasping' what happened to them … Recognition on TV and radio, in newspapers, magazines and films became a vital part of women's process of making sense of their memories. Women refer to the importance of representation in every form; from agony columns in magazines to press reports, from soap operas to current affairs documentaries or discussion programmes. (Kitzinger, 2004: 41)

One of the key moments in media coverage of child abuse in the UK came in October 1986 with the broadcast of a major British Broadcasting Corporation (BBC) programme, *Childwatch* (Parton, 1991: 91; Kitzinger, 2004: 35). The *Childwatch* programme was accompanied by a remarkable expansion in attention to child abuse, particularly sexual abuse, from other television formats as well as the print media. Reporting of sexual abuse in *The Times* newspaper, for example, increased by 300% between 1985 and 1987 (Kitzinger, 2004). Moreover, sexual abuse within families became the subject of a number of flagship UK documentary series, including *Brass Tacks* (BBC Two, 1987), *Everyman* (BBC One, 1988), *Antenna* (BBC One, 1989) and *Horizon* (BBC Two, 1989). Kitzinger (2004:36) has also noted the importance of fictional genre in highlighting this issue. By the early 1990s, child sexual abuse had begun to appear in British and American drama series and became the subject of 'true crime' features. It also featured in soap operas, most notably *Brookside* (Channel 4), which ran a two-year storyline on a family traumatised by an abusive father.

In Ireland, some of the most shocking and influential media coverage concerned clerical child abuse. The first major clerical child sexual abuse scandal concerned the case of Brendan Smyth, a priest with the Norbertine Order, who in 1994 pleaded guilty to 72 charges of indecent and sexual assault and was sentenced to 12 years in prison (Keenan, 2012). Through a 'brilliant piece of investigative journalism', Chris Moore, a reporter with Ulster Television's *Counterpoint* programme, showed that the clerical authorities had known for years of Smyth's crimes but had dealt with it by moving him on and essentially covering up his actions (Ferguson, 1995: 247). The infamous Smyth case opened the floodgates for further revelations. Of particular note was the broadcast of a number of powerful documentaries detailing the abuse of children in institutional and community settings, including: *Dear Daughter* (RTÉ, 1996), *States of Fear* (RTÉ, 1999), *Cardinal Secrets* (RTÉ, 2002) and *Suing the Pope* (a BBC documentary broadcast in the UK and Ireland in 2002). These landmark programmes led to the setting up of the first inquiries into the church's handling of allegations of abuse (discussed in Chapter 3). Moreover, media coverage of child abuse prompted some survivors to come forward and provide testimony to the inquiry teams, for instance, for the Ferns Report (Murphy et al, 2005) and the Dublin Report (DJELR, 2009). The media also provided opportunities for survivors themselves to raise public awareness of the issue and campaign for change. Representatives from survivor organisations, such as One in Four, have participated in numerous television news programmes and panel discussions, provided interviews to journalists and convened press conferences, particularly in the aftermath of child abuse inquiries.

Notwithstanding the many positive aspects of the media's interest in child abuse, it must also be acknowledge that there are a number of drawbacks. According to Franklin and Parton (1991), media reporting of child abuse has been sensational, simplistic and often factually inaccurate. Moreover, the issue has been presented and framed within the parameters prescribed by dominant and traditional social values. Discussions of the rights of children and feminist critiques of patriarchy that seek to go beyond these narrow confines have been largely ignored. Fitzgibbon (2011) highlights the increasingly intrusive and voyeuristic manner in which abuse is reported. She contrasts the 'computer-assisted voyeurism' that attended the death of Baby P (in 2007) with the more 'respectful' coverage of the earlier Colwell case: 'If Maria's death was a tragedy, a family gone wrong, Baby Peter's is sadistic torture in which the lurid descriptions with their macabre visual aids add up to an emotional horror movie populated by monsters and helpless victims' (Fitzgibbon, 2011: 24). Kitzinger (2004: 47) raises concerns around the 'new identity of victimhood being pedalled by discussion shows' and the way in which the media have 'psychopathologised' survivors. Media reporting has also been criticised for scapegoating the professionals (usually social workers) connected with child abuse cases (Franklin and Parton, 1991). In particular, the British tabloid press have launched a series of personal attacks on those practitioners implicated in major child abuse inquiries (Fitzgibbon, 2011). Moreover, the tabloids' preoccupation with attacks perpetrated by strangers ('stranger danger') may divert attention from the fact that most abuse is perpetrated by individuals already known to the child. According to Silverman and Wilson (2002), the explosion in media interest in child sex offences has also helped to fuel a 'moral panic' at a time when there is no evidence to suggest that these offences are on the increase. It can be seen, therefore, that while the media has undoubtedly played a key role in raising awareness of child abuse, this has sometimes been a mixed blessing.

Child abuse and changing constructions of childhood

In the course of this chapter we have seen how public awareness of child abuse was transformed in western societies, particularly over the last 50 years. To understand *why* child abuse emerged as a major social issue, we must situate it in the wider context of changing conceptions of childhood itself. How we define child abuse varies across cultures and over time, and depends in large part on how we socially construct the child and define the characteristics and needs of childhood. The contemporary western concept of childhood innocence, for example, is central to how sexual assaults against children are interpreted. Thus the media often report child sexual abuse in terms of 'lost innocence', while the perpetrator is represented as an animal or other non-human being (beast, monster, fiend) in the tabloid press. Moreover, the profound transformation that occurred in the *social value* of children during the 20th century has made the mistreatment of children increasingly unacceptable to the public. As children were removed from the labour market (through compulsory education and age restrictions on employment) they gained a new sentimental value, becoming economically 'worthless' but emotionally 'priceless' (Zelizer, 1994). Recent developments around children's rights – particularly in light of the UN Convention on the Rights of the Child 1989 –

have also served to redefine our understanding of child abuse. This was particularly evident in the 'pindown' scandal, which, as we saw earlier, was primarily a civil rights issue. The changing conceptions of childhood – and how this shapes our understanding of child abuse – will be considered in later chapters.

TWO

The public child

> The term 'public child' refers to a child whose private
> life has in some sense become public business. (Robbie
> Gilligan, 2009)

Over the last 40 years, public inquiries into welfare practice have
become a familiar feature of western democracies, particularly in the
field of child protection. While some of these are destined for relative
obscurity, others become landmark cases, shaping policy and providing
a benchmark for future inquiries. They become defining moments
in our understanding of social issues, living on in popular memory
long after the events themselves (Kitzinger, 2004). In this chapter, the
discovery of child abuse in Ireland is explored through the lens of the
Kilkenny incest case, which became a defining event in changing public
discourse. We adopt Robbie Gilligan's (2009) concept of 'the public
child': the child whose life becomes public business in a 'reluctant state'.

The Kilkenny incest case, in which a man was found to have
physically and sexually abused his daughter over a 15-year period,
achieved a notoriety similar to that of the Maria Colwell case in the UK.
Virtually overnight the issue of family violence and child care policy
was catapulted to the top of the political agenda. Following the trial,
the Minister for Health immediately announced an inquiry to establish
why action to halt the abuse was not taken earlier. Legislation to
increase the maximum sentence for incest was rushed through the Dáil
and, following the publication of the inquiry report, the government
announced plans to release £35 million to implement the Child Care
Act 1991. The level of public interest in the case was unprecedented,
with record numbers of people contacting the Department of Justice
to express their revulsion and complain about the perceived leniency
of the seven-year sentence given to the abuser.

The manner in which the story was reported in the media played a
key role in sensitising the public and politicians to the issue of extreme
child abuse (Ferguson, 1993). From the outset the story was reported
extensively in the Irish media, with a degree of frankness not previously
seen. The victim's interview with Raidió Teilifís Éireann (RTÉ)
(2 March 1993) was particularly powerful and became an important

reference point for public debate around the case. Moreover, there were dire warnings that this might only be the tip of the iceberg and that many more children were at risk of abuse. From being a barely acknowledged social problem, child abuse suddenly appeared to be endemic within Irish society.

The aim of this chapter is to provide a critical perspective on the public debates surrounding the Kilkenny case, an area that has hitherto been largely overlooked in academic research. First, we will consider the central issue of whether the inquiry team, the media and key stakeholders attributed responsibility for 'why action to halt the abuse was not taken earlier' to the individual practitioners involved in the case (doctors, police, social workers) or to the system and structures within which they operated. Comparisons will be made with the UK, where a number of high profile inquiries ascribed responsibility for professional 'failures' to individual practitioners who were subsequently pilloried in the media (Fitzgibbon, 2011). Second, we will consider the controversy surrounding the sentencing of the abuser. While the focus of public anger in high-profile child abuse scandals is often on social workers and child protection procedures, in the Kilkenny case much of the initial outrage was targeted at the judge and the criminal justice system. Indeed, Judge Carney was one of the few people involved in the case to be named in the media, and his photograph became ubiquitous in the national press following the trial and the publication of the report. Third, we will explore the 'emblematic' features of the case – what appeared to be the wider implications of the Kilkenny case for Irish society at that time? Our research suggests that while recent child abuse scandals in the UK have been seen to represent the breakdown of the traditional family (Fitzgibbon, 2011), in Kilkenny it was the sanctity of the institution that was seen to be problematic, as it discouraged disclosure of abuse and outside intervention.

Development of child protection in Ireland

To understand the significance of the Kilkenny Incest Inquiry, it is important to appreciate something of the historical context from which it emerged. For much of the 20th century there was little or no social work or statutory involvement in services for deprived or vulnerable children in Ireland (Skehill, 2004: 61). This was in keeping with a more general reluctance on the part of the state to intervene on social matters. Irish social policy during this period was guided by the Catholic principle of subsidiarity, which held that the state should not be responsible for providing supports or services that individuals, families and other associations were in a position to provide for themselves. Where a family was considered unable to meet the needs of its members, it was believed that church-run institutions and voluntary agencies were in the best position to provide assistance. As a result, much of Irish social provision was under the control of the Catholic Church or voluntary organisations, with the state having a much lesser role. Orphaned or abandoned children or those who were neglected or ill-treated by their parents were often placed in industrial schools. Virtually all of these residential services were managed by religious orders, while the National Society for the Prevention of Cruelty to Children (NSPCC), or later the Irish Society for the Prevention of Cruelty to Children (ISPCC),[1] had primary responsibility for matters relating to child care and protection within the community (Ferguson, 1993, 1995). The state appeared equally reluctant to legislate on behalf of children: The Children Act 1908 continued to provide the main legal framework for child care for much of the 20th century (Gilligan, 2009).

From the 1970s onwards this situation began to change, due in part to a growing awareness of child abuse in western countries (discussed in Chapter 1). In her history of the development of child protection in Ireland, Caroline Skehill (2004) identifies a number of key milestones, most notably the introduction of the Health Act 1970, which led to the restructuring of the health services and the subsequent employment of social work teams within the community care services. The newly established health boards took over primary responsibility for the provision of child care services. In the same year, the Kennedy Report (CIRISS, 1970) on the reformatory and industrial schools was published, signifying 'the emergence of a growing awareness of the needs of deprived children' (Skehill, 2004: 60). The key message of the report was that large scale institutional care for children was no longer a viable option within a modern welfare system. The report also made significant recommendations in relation to the training of child care staff within residential units, the development of aftercare services for children in care, and the closure of a number of reformatory and remand schools. The Kennedy Report signalled the demise of the industrial school system. The momentum for change was continued with the setting up of a task force to review child care services in Ireland, the

---

[1] The first Irish branch of the NSPCC was founded in Dublin in May 1889, with branches founded in Cork and Belfast in 1891. In 1956, the Irish Society for the Prevention of Cruelty to Children was founded as a successor to the National Society for the Prevention of Cruelty to Children, which had operated in Ireland from 1889 to 1956.

findings of which were published in 1980. Skehill argues that although a considerable time lag existed between the publication of the report and the subsequent administrative and legislative change, it nevertheless represented 'the embodiment of many ideals of the reformers of the late 1960s and early 1970s and gave full expression to the developmental model of child welfare' (Skehill, 2004: 82).

The introduction of the Child Care Act 1991 is generally acknowledged as a key moment in the development of the child protection and welfare system in Ireland (Ferguson, 1995; Lavan, 1998; Skehill, 2004). Up until that point, the precise role and duties of the Irish state and its professionals in child care had been unclear in many crucial respects. According to Ferguson (1995), a vital overall function of the 1991 Act was to clarify the nature and scope of the powers and duties of health boards in child care practice. Crucially, the Act placed a duty on health boards 'to promote the welfare of children in its area' and required each board to 'take such steps as it considers requisite to identify children who are not receiving adequate care and protection and coordinate information from all relevant sources relating to children in its area'. Under the provisions of the act the legal definition of a 'child' was also extended to 18 years. However, the implementation of the legislation moved slowly: by May 1993, just 16 of the 79 sections had been implemented, none of which involved new responsibilities and procedures regarding child protection (Ferguson, 1993-4: 407). While the government had indicated that implementation of the act would be on a phased basis, the amount of time taken certainly seemed to suggest that it was not seen as a priority. Moreover, while there might have been a growing awareness of child abuse within certain *professional* groups (mainly social workers), the level of *public* awareness and media interest was still minimal at this time. As Ferguson (1993-4: 393) argues, the Irish situation had 'lacked a powerful symbolic event to focus public and political interest on the social problem of child abuse and men's violence to women'. In 1993, that symbolic event was provided in what became known as the Kilkenny incest case.

The Kilkenny incest case

Details of the case first came to public attention on 1 March 1993, when a Co. Kilkenny father-of-two was sentenced to seven years imprisonment at the Central Criminal Court in Dublin, having pleaded guilty to charges of rape, incest and assault against his eldest daughter (McGuinness, 1993: 9). The abuse began in 1976 when 'Mary' (as she was later referred to in the inquiry report) was aged 10 and continued until she finally left home in 1991. She became pregnant by her father and had a son at the age of 16. At the court hearing it emerged that the victim had had a number of hospital admissions over the years for the treatment of serious physical injuries and had been in contact with the gardaí and with health professionals, including doctors, social workers and public health nurses. The case immediately attracted huge public attention, with politicians, interest groups and media commentators expressing outrage at the perceived leniency of the sentence and bewilderment at how the abuse could have been allowed to continue for so long.

The government responded swiftly, announcing an inquiry that was to be headed by Senior Counsel, Catherine McGuinness. Its terms of reference were 'to carry out an investigation, insofar as the health services are concerned, of the circumstances surrounding the abuse ... and in particular to establish why action to halt the abuse was not taken earlier, and to make recommendations for the future investigation and management by the health services of cases of suspected child abuse' (McGuinness, 1993: 11). In accordance with instructions from the Minister of Health, Brendan Howlin, the investigation was to be held on an informal basis and would not be a statutory inquiry. At a press conference to announce the inquiry, McGuinness cautioned that it would not be a search for a 'scapegoat' – a comment no doubt inspired by some of the critical media coverage of the case at this time.[2]

Published on 18 May 1993, the Kilkenny Report had an important influence on the direction of child protection policy and practice in Ireland (Ferguson, 1993-4; Lavan, 1998: 43, Kilkelly, 2012: 8). Key recommendations included the full implementation of the Child Care Act 1991 and the overhaul of the existing Child Abuse Guidelines (McGuinness, 1993: 95-7). The report also recognised the importance of liaison between health boards and the gardaí, something that had been singularly lacking in the Kilkenny case where 'each aspect of the health services dealt with the individual manifestations of Mary's abuse and her various illnesses entirely separately and without interdisciplinary communication and cooperation' (McGuinness, 1993: 87). It recommended the establishment of policies and written protocols to ensure 'effective interagency communication' as well as the provision of specially trained officers to act as contact persons in child protection cases (106). Recognising the 'complex, challenging and emotionally charged' nature of child protection work, the report also made a number of recommendations in relation to staff training

---

[2] *Irish Independent* 7 March 1993 'Incest case probe "not hunt for scapegoat"'.

and supervision. More controversially, the report recommended the introduction of mandatory reporting of all forms of child abuse by designated persons (eg, doctors, teachers, welfare officers) to the Director of Community Care.

While acknowledging certain shortcomings in professional practice, the Kilkenny Report did not attribute 'blame' to particular individuals involved in the case. Moreover, it took into consideration the wider context in which professionals worked at that time. As Ferguson (1993-4) argues, the Kilkenny Report is exceptional in terms of its attempt to make an assessment on the basis of an appreciation of what it was possible for professionals to think and do in Kilkenny as the case unfolded over the years. Actions that were or were not taken were 'placed in the context of the law, procedures, available resources and knowledge of the time' (Ferguson 1993-4: 394). The report stresses, for example, that the social work services of the Eastern Health Board did not become aware of Mary's abuse until *after* she reached the age of 16, by which time they had no statutory powers to protect her under the existing legislation (McGuinness, 1993: 88). In dealing with adults, social workers' powers were largely limited to persuasion and the offering of options, such as leaving home, seeking a barring order or making a complaint to the police (78), though the report also acknowledged that it may be difficult for those in abusive families to take up these options (86). In addition, the report notes that in the late 1970s and early 1980s (when Mary first came into contact with health professionals for various injuries) general awareness of child abuse as an issue would 'not have been high' (74-5). Specific guidelines in relation to child abuse only became available in 1980 and these made no reference to sexual abuse. Moreover, the extent of the circulation of those guidelines within the health board and to people outside was 'questionable'.

In a key passage, the inquiry team state:

> We conclude that each individual responded to the best of his or her abilities to the presenting symptoms of Mary's abuse. There was however a lack of the necessary effective probing of the nature and causes of the problem which could have been achieved both from an inter-disciplinary and inter agency approach and a better understanding on all sides of the nature of family violence and sexual abuse. This must be viewed in the context of the knowledge and limited legal powers available at the time and in the context of community attitudes. (McGuinness, 1993: 89)

Looking back many years later, McGuinness would reiterate the point that 'the major fault lay in the system, or rather lack of system, rather than with the individuals involved, each of whom did what they believed was the best they could for the girl at the centre of the story' (McGuinness, 2012: 52). While the Kilkenny Report was generally well received, this apparent refusal to hold individuals to account proved to be one of its more contentious elements, with a small but vocal group describing it as a 'whitewash' – an issue that we will return to later in this chapter.

The media's coverage of the Kilkenny case

For much of the 20th century there was little media coverage of any sexual issues relating to children and the language of disclosure was 'imprecise, vague and euphemistic' (Coldrey, 1996: 371). The Kilkenny case represented a major turning point. The case was extensively reported, with graphic details emerging from accounts provided by Mary herself. Particularly important was Mary's televised interview with RTÉ's legal affairs correspondent, Kieron Wood, which was broadcast on the RTÉ Six and Nine O'clock News, on 2 March 1993 – the day after her father was convicted and sent to jail. In the course of the interview, she spoke about some of the worst instances of abuse, as well as commenting on her father's sentence and on the conduct of the professionals (doctors and social workers) involved in the case. The following day, the interview was reported extensively in the press, including verbatim extracts and detailed analysis. The case was also discussed in the Dáil, where the Minister for Health, Brendan Howlin, claimed that: 'Everyone who watched last night's television interview with her has been deeply upset by her harrowing account of the dreadful suffering she endured. I watched it in the Dáil studio and I was weakened by the experience' (*Dáil debate* 3 March 1993).[3] Similarly, Fine Gael TD (Teachta Dála/Member of Parliament) Alan Shatter described watching 'with great distress' the televised interview 'with the tragic victim of the Kilkenny case' (*Dáil debate*, 10 March 1993). Meanwhile, members of the public expressed their anger by phoning the Department of Justice in record numbers to complain about the perceived leniency of the sentence, prompting the government to

---

[3]   This is a parliamentary debate. The National Parliament of Ireland (Oireachtas) consists of two Houses: Dáil Éireann (House of Representatives) and Seanad Éireann (the Senate).

introduce legislation increasing the maximum sentence for incest (discussed later in this chapter).

The response to Mary's television interview is indicative of the considerable influence of the media in the Kilkenny case. Mary also provided interviews to the *Irish Press*, the *Irish Independent* and British Broadcasting Corporation's (BBC) Radio 4. She collaborated with Kieron Wood to produce a book, which was published in the same week as the inquiry report itself (Wood, 1993). Narrated in the first person, this book provided a highly accessible account of the tragic circumstances of her life and personalised the Kilkenny case in a way that the more formal tones of an inquiry report could not hope to do. It became an instant bestseller, and it almost certainly reached a wider audience that the actual Kilkenny Report itself at that time.[4] The book also attracted further media attention to the case, with reviews, extracts and discussions of its contents appearing in the national press.[5]

From the beginning, a diverse range of stakeholders contributed to the public debate around the Kilkenny case, including professional associations, the health board, the gardaí, politicians from across the political spectrum and various voluntary groups representing women and children (eg, the ISPCC, Barnardo's, the Rape Crisis Centre, Council for the Status of Women). Expert opinion was also provided by psychologists and social workers in the field of child protection. Therefore, in considering media coverage of the Kilkenny case, we will also be exploring the reactions of key stakeholders and the wider public debate surrounding the case. Newspaper editors and broadcasters would, of course, stamp their own identities on these stories by giving prominence to certain viewpoints and by sidelining or challenging

[4] It ranked number two in the paperback nonfiction best-seller list at the end of May and throughout June in 1993. The number one slot during this period was occupied by Brian Keenan's *An Evil Cradling*. See *The Irish Times* 29 May and 5, 12, 19 and 26 June for lists).

[5] The book is discussed in: *The Irish Times* 17 May 1993 'Incest victim expected to respond to report', *The Irish Times* 18 May 1993 'Book depicts long agony of Kilkenny incest victim's life'; *The Irish Times* 18 May 1993, 'Howlin expected to seek £30m for child care'; *Irish Independent* 17 May 1993 'Incest case girl criticises social workers'.

others.[6] Nonetheless, the variety of voices and viewpoints featured in the media's coverage meant that there wasn't a 'monolithic media message' comparable to that which was seen during recent abuse investigations in the UK (Fitzgibbon, 2011: 20). Different newspapers approached the case differently, and even within the *same* newspaper a number of viewpoints could sometimes be aired.

The focus of our analysis of media coverage is primarily on newspapers, including the four main daily newspapers at that time (*Irish Independent*, *The Irish Times*, *Irish Press* and the *Irish Daily Star*) and two Sunday newspapers (*Sunday Independent*, and *Sunday World*). Two time periods are covered: 1–15 March (the period following the sentencing of Mary's father and the announcement of the inquiry) and 15–30 May (the period immediately leading up to and following the publication of the inquiry report). Also included in the analysis are: RTÉ news broadcasts for 1 and 2 March, including Mary's televised interview; Dáil and Seanad debates (March 1993); and the book *The Kilkenny Incest Case as told by Kieron Wood* (1993).

The story breaks: media representations of the trial and sentencing

Much of the initial controversy surrounding the Kilkenny case centred on the seven-year jail sentence given to Mary's father by Judge Carney at the Central Criminal Court on 1 March 1993. In the days following the trial, a number of organisations, politicians and members of the public expressed disbelief and outrage over the perceived leniency of the sentence. The most important intervention into this debate came from Mary herself. In the course of her television interview on RTÉ on 2 March, Kieron Wood asked her if she was 'happy with the sentence' her father had received, to which she replied:

> "I don't want revenge or anything like that. I think he is sick. He needs help. But I don't think seven years is long

---

[6] *The Irish Times*, for example, reported the ISPCC's critique of the Kilkenny report, but on the same day published an article by the paper's social services correspondent disputing some of the ISPCC's claims. Similarly, on 19 May 1993, the *Irish Independent*'s editorial criticised the Kilkenny report for not attributing blame to the individual professionals involved in the case, while also featuring an article by Kieran McGrath (from the Irish Association of Social Workers) supporting this decision.

enough. I had to go through hell and the only thing that kept me going was that I had to look after my son."

[Wood: "What will happen when your father gets out of prison?"]

"He will come looking for me, I know that. After you have lived with him for so long you know the person really well. He will have it all bottled up inside him – that I put him there, my mother helped me. The two of us won't be safe when he comes out. And the upsetting part of it is that we didn't do any wrong, so why do we have to run?"

The next morning her comments received widespread coverage in all four national newspapers with headlines such as: 'Incest victim fears release of father' (*Irish Press*); 'I live in fear of his release' (*Irish Independent*) and 'He'll come looking for me' (*Irish Daily Star*). In interviews with the *Irish Press*[7] and the *Irish Independent*,[8] Mary reiterated her fears of retaliation once her father was released and expressed her disappointment in the criminal justice system: 'I was told that when it got to court, justice would be done' (*Irish Press*, 3 May); '... because I'm a poor person the law just doesn't care' (*Irish Independent*, 3 May). In these and in other articles, Mary is presented as a young woman who continues to be victimised by fear of her father's release.

A number of organisations highlighted the broader implications of the seven-year sentence and their views were also widely reported in the press, adding further momentum to the story. Representatives from the ISPCC, the Rape Crisis Centre and the Irish Country Women's Association protested that the sentence had trivialised incest and domestic violence.[9] Avril Molloy, chairperson of the Fine Gael Women's Group, queried whether the judiciary in sexual abuse cases took sufficient note of the traumas experienced by the victims,[10] while the Chairwoman of the Council for the Status of Women asked: 'how many more women have to suffer ... before these crimes are dealt

[7] *Irish Press* 3 March 1993 'Daughter in "pure hell" believes father will seek revenge'; 'Incest victim fears release of father'.
[8] *Irish Independent* 3 March 1993 'Rape victim's son learns father's identity'
[9] *Irish Press* 4 March 1993 'One-third of Irish Women Abused'; *Irish Daily Star* 3 March 1993 'Brute could have been locked up for life'.
[10] *Irish Press* 3 March 1993 'Real trauma for victims'.

with as severely as they deserve?'[11] Writing in the *Irish Times*, Kieran McGrath (from the Irish Association of Social Workers) noted that incest was treated as a 'misdemeanour' in Irish law and that this 'reflects our own ambivalence about domestic violence'.[12] Parallels were drawn with an earlier, high-profile case in which a man convicted of rape had received a suspended sentence. The victim in that case, Lavinia Kerwick, publicly criticised the outcome of the Kilkenny trial, claiming that there was 'no justice in what happened'.[13] The public statements made by these organisations and individuals not only helped to keep the issue of sentencing in the public eye but elevated it to a symbolic level – it came to represent the judiciary's (and society's) ambivalence towards violence within the family.

As well as reporting the views of these various stakeholders, national newspapers provided their own particular views on the issue of sentencing, through their editorials and commentaries. Both the *Irish Press* (3 March 1993) and the *Irish Daily Star* (3 March 1993) questioned the adequacy of the sentence in their editorials, while *The Irish Times* was more reticent, noting only that the father 'may well serve no more than four years of a seven-year sentence for incest'.[14] Outspoken commentators, such as John Donlon in the *Irish Daily Star*, provided more sensational criticism, describing the sentence as a 'sick joke' and endorsing chemical castration as a more suitable punishment for crimes of this nature:

> Thankfully [the victim's father is] now locked up. And it's difficult to argue with TD Brendan McGahon who says this type of sex offender should be chemically castrated. As to the six-and-a-half year sentence, it's a sick joke.
>
> This man will be out in four years, given good behaviour. Unless he goes through some incredible transformation or rehabilitation, he will make his daughter's life a hell again.[15]

The sentencing in the Kilkenny case quickly became politicised, with members of the Dáil and Seanad discussing the implications of the case for the justice system. While members of both houses were prohibited from criticising sentences in specific cases (a rule that sometimes proved

[11] *Irish Press* 3 March 1993 'Women's group angry at "lenient" sentence.
[12] *Irish Times* 3 March 1993 'A misdemeanour – how the law regards incest'
[13] *Irish Press* 3 March 1993 'Lavinia slams "rule of rapist"'.
[14] *The Irish Times* editorial on 3 March 1993.
[15] *Irish Daily Star* 8 March 1993 'Neighbours stay silent'.

difficult to enforce), they were able to discuss the *laws* relating to sentencing for incest. As the controversy showed no signs of abating, the Minister for Justice, Màire Geoghegan-Quinn, found herself in an increasingly difficult position. On the one hand, she could not appear to be interfering in the decisions of the judiciary, but on the other, public anger at the Kilkenny case meant that the government was under pressure to take some action. In the days following the trial, the Justice Department had been inundated with callers angered by the perceived leniency of the sentence.[16] According to the minister herself, the Department had never before had this kind of reaction from members of the public.[17] Speaking on RTÉ's *Primetime* programme, she noted that '... we expect law-breakers to have no respect for the law but we get worried when law-abiding citizens and victims of crime lose respect for the law.'[18]

The Justice Department's response was two-fold. Firstly, Màire Geoghegan-Quinn and Willie O'Dea (a junior minister) distanced themselves, and the justice department, from the judge's decision, making clear that this was his responsibility alone and that a much tougher sentence could have been imposed even under the *existing* legislation. In a series of statements to the Dáil and the media, they pointed out that the crime of rape, to which the man had pleaded guilty, carried a maximum sentence of life, as did incest with a female under the age of 15. These assertions were widely reported[19] so that the media spotlight was (to some extent) deflected back onto Judge Carney. The government's second line of action was to rush through legislation which enabled 'unduly lenient' sentences to be reviewed by the Court of Criminal Appeal and which increased the maximum

---

[16] *Irish Independent* 5 March 1993 'Public fury at Kilkenny jail term'.

[17] *Irish Times* 8 March 1993.

[18] Extract from RTÉ programme *This Week*, reported in the *Irish Independent* 8 March 1993 'Health care role in family cases sought'.

[19] See, for example, *Irish Independent* 5 March 1993 'Public fury at Kilkenny jail term'; *Irish Times* 4 March 1993 'Government refuses Dáil time for FG incest bill', 'Inquiry ordered into failure of health services in incest case', 'Geoghegan-Quinn promises action following Kilkenny case'; *Irish Daily Star* 8 March 1993 'Minister quizzed about controversial sentence'; *Irish Press* 3 March 1993 'Statement from the Minister for Justice', Incest Victim Fears Release of Father; *Irish Press* 4 March 1993 'Longer maximum jail terms are called for in Dáil Debate', 'He could have been given life sentence'; *Irish Press* 15 March 1993 'Minister may meet judges on sentencing'.

sentence for incest from 7 years to 20.[20] While the legislation was welcomed,[21] there was also criticism that the government had failed to introduce measures to review lenient sentences earlier in the wake of the Lavinia Kerwick case, and that politicians appeared to act only in response to public outcry.[22]

While tougher sentencing was the dominant theme, there were also calls for abusers to receive some form of therapy while in prison. According to an article in the *Irish Independent*, the Council for the Status of Women had demanded 'compulsory therapy' for convicted sex offenders,[23] and even the *Irish Daily Star* (which took a tough stance on sentencing) acknowledged that sex offenders should not simply be 'left to rot', if only because they were more likely to re-offend on their release (*Irish Daily Star*, 8 March 1993).

While much of the initial controversy in the Kilkenny case was concerned with the sentence, the judicial system and Judge Carney, attention soon moved on to those professionals with whom Mary met over the years when she was being abused by her father.

Who is to blame? Media representation of professionals in the Kilkenny case

In the UK, a number of high-profile child abuse inquires have attributed responsibility for professional 'failures' to individual practitioners, leading to widespread criticism in the media (Ferguson, 1993-4: 389; Fitzgibbon, 2011). While there are generally a number of professionals involved in these cases (police, teachers, health visitors, doctors), social workers often bear the brunt of public censure. According to Franklin and Parton (1991), the media's representation of child protection social workers in such cases falls into two main categories: (1) social workers as naïve, incompetent and easily fooled by abusers; or (2) social workers as authoritarian and prone to intervene unnecessarily into family life. While the press gave a relatively sympathetic – or at least non-judgemental – hearing to the social workers involved in the UK's *first* major inquiry (into Maria Colwell's death), coverage of subsequent inquiries has become progressively more hostile (Fitzgibbon, 2011).

---

[20] *Dáil debate* 10 March 1993.

[21] See *Irish Independent* editorial 11 March 1993; *Irish Press* editorial 11 March 1993; *Irish Daily Star* 15 March 1993 'Waiting for the Outcry'.

[22] *Irish Daily Star* 15 March 1993 'Waiting for the outcry'; *Irish Press* editorial on 8 March 1993.

[23] *Irish Independent* 4 March 1993 'Compulsory therapy "essential"'.

The Irish media's representation of the various professionals involved in the Kilkenny case was generally quite mixed, both before and after the publication of the inquiry report. National newspapers expressed shock and bewilderment at the apparent inaction of the doctors, gardaí and social workers who had come into contact with Mary over the years and who must (it was assumed) have had some knowledge of the abuse. At the same time, the press acknowledged the difficulties and restraints under which these professionals worked. Social workers were sometimes singled out for particular criticism, but (as we shall see later in this chapter) this was due largely to *Mary's* comments to the media, rather than emanating from media commentators themselves. Indeed, in some instances editors and other contributors defended the position of the social workers involved in the Kilkenny case. Moreover, public debate went beyond an examination of the professionals immediately involved in the Kilkenny case to consider the inadequacies of the current child protection system and the legislative framework within which it operated.[24] The government was, for example, roundly criticised for not having implementing the Child Care Act 1991, under which key changes could have been made to child protection.[25]

Questions about the professionals involved in the Kilkenny case first came to public attention in the course of the father's trial. According to Counsel Barry White (defending), the 'greatest tragedy' was that the assaults had been going on for a number of years to the knowledge of the medical profession and a social worker. If something had been done at an early stage, he asserted, a lot of suffering and denigration would have been avoided.[26] In the following days, as further details emerged, various commentators expressed a sense of bafflement that professionals and members of the community could have known about the abuse and not taken action to end it. *The Irish Times* editorial (3 March 1993), for example, described it as 'extraordinary' that this young woman, who had come into contact with the health services on several occasions, did not receive the kind of attention that would have uncovered her true circumstances and led to her having the protection she needed. 'No one, lay, clerical or professional, in her small place,

---

[24] See, for example, *The Irish Times* 26 May 1993 'Incest report assailed for failure to attach blame'.

[25] See, for example, *The Irish Times* 18 May 1993 'Howlin to seek £30m for child care'; *The Irish Times* 19 May 1993 'A salutary case'; *The Irish Times* 1 June 1993 'Do Irish children need a change in the constitution?'.

[26] *Irish Independent* 2 March 1993 'Father jailed for daughter's 16-year incest rape horror'.

saw fit to ask the awkward questions that would have elicited the information that should have set the official responses in motion.' On a similar note (though in more sensational terms), the *Irish Daily Star* editorial (3 March 1993) asked: 'How did the savagery of this beast escape the notice of the social workers and the Gardaí for so long?' Even after the publication of the inquiry report, the same kinds of questions were occasionally raised by journalists who continued to be baffled by the circumstances surrounding the case.[27]

More explicit criticisms appeared in some of the commentary and features pages of the national newspapers. The seeming ineptitude of those professionals who met Mary over many years was contrasted with the tenacity and patience of Garda (police officer) Agnes Reddy, who eventually persuaded Mary to leave home for good and press charges against her father. Writing in the *Irish Press*, Kate Shanahan asserts that 'So many people were seeing Mary for various reasons, yet until Ban-gharda Agnes Reddy sat by her hospital bedside no one saw fit to give her the kind of support she so desperately needed'.[28] In another article she speculates that had Garda Reddy 'not taken a keen interest' in the case 'then the horror that overtook one young woman for 17 years might have remained undetected'.[29] Similarly, Mary Holland (*The Irish Times* 11 March) described the reactions of the police, the medical profession and the social workers involved in the case as being 'desperately inadequate' and suggested that the inquiry team consider why it was that Garda Reddy succeeded where others had so obviously failed. While expressing incomprehension as to how the abuse was allowed to go on for so long, Holland also asserts that for those who have experience in dealing first hand with the victims of domestic violence it came as no surprise at all that the various agencies involved 'failed' this young woman. The *Irish Independent* also alluded to professional failure, comparing the apparent indifference of professionals and community members with the 'kind and compassionate Garda Agnes Reddy' to whom the victim could 'reveal the full extent of the horror with which she had lived for 16 years'.[30]

From the outset, Mary herself was the most vocal and influential critic of the social workers involved in the case. In the course of her RTÉ

---

[27] See, for example, *Irish Independent* 20 May 1993 'Why didn't someone shout stop?', *Irish Independent* 22 May 1993 'No hope here'.

[28] *Irish Press* 19 May 1993 'Nobody shouted stop'.

[29] *Irish Press* 2 March 1993 'A woman's agony'.

[30] *Irish Independent* 22 May 1993 'No hope here'.

interview (2 March 1993), Kieron Wood asked whether she blamed the doctors or social workers, to which she replied:

> "I blame the social worker. She could have got me out a lot earlier but she just wouldn't interfere into it. I don't blame the doctors. I mean a doctor might think he knows what's behind it all but unless you tell him there's nothing he can do about it."

Particularly damning was Mary's allegation, made in the course of interviews with the *Irish Press*, the *Irish Independent* and BBC Radio, that she had disclosed details of the abuse to a social worker while in hospital giving birth to her son, and that she had been told that it was a 'family matter' and that she [the social worker] could not get involved.[31] It was also alleged (in the *Irish Independent* article) that the social worker had urged her to give up the child for adoption. However, the Health Board disputed this version of events and Mary, in her own evidence to the Kilkenny Inquiry, 'clearly stated that this did not occur' (McGuinness, 1993: 77). Nonetheless, the story had by then been in circulation in the media for some time and the allegation that Mary had been advised to have her child adopted was repeated in her bestselling book, written with Kieron Wood. In the publicity surrounding the publication of the book, social workers were again thrust into the media spotlight, with the *Irish Independent* (17 May 1993) featuring a front-page headline: 'Incest case girl criticises social workers'.

As noted earlier, the Kilkenny Report eventually concluded that 'each individual responded to the best of his or her abilities to the presenting symptoms of Mary's abuse' (McGuinness, 1993: 89). Ironically, this outcome appeared to have the effect of hardening attitudes towards the professionals involved. While there had been general agreement that the inquiry should not be a witch-hunt or a scapegoating exercise, it soon became clear that the apparent exoneration of all those involved was not seen, by some commentators, as an appropriate outcome either. The *Irish Independent*, in particular, objected to the report's reluctance to attribute blame to individuals. According to its editorial (19 May 1993):

---

[31]   *Irish Independent* 6 March 1993 'But he never saw me cry'. The BBC interview is referred to in the *Irish Independent* 15 May 1993 '£30 million for child care "far short of Kilkenny probe target", and in *The Irish Times* 15 May 1993 'Policy against child abuse is needed, incest inquiry told'.

If the report has a fault it is that it places the burden of blame on the institutions and shortage of funds rather than on people. Yet over a period of many years it was people, not institutions, who made the judgements which consigned Mary to her fate. People in positions of responsibility, again and again, failed to identify the symptoms of abuse. And some of them failed to act properly even when they did identify these symptoms.

The most outspoken criticism of the report came from the Chief Executive of the ISPCC, Cian O'Tighearnaigh, whose views were reported prominently in all four national newspapers.[32] In these articles, O'Tighearnaigh stated that he was at a loss to understand how Health Minister Brendan Howlin, the Health Board or the investigation team could accept that the professionals involved in the case had been 'exonerated' or 'did their best'. To say that would be 'sick-making', he added, when the victim had over a hundred contacts with professionals in different services. Moreover, O'Tighearnaigh disputed the idea that the South Eastern Health Board could not intervene because Mary was over 16 when the abuse became known to its staff – the board was still in a position to have both Mary and her child made wards of court. He concluded that the facts of the case 'represented a litany of missed opportunities to protect the victim, poor professional judgement, poor staff supervision, failure to act, weak administration and denial of the girl's problems'. These comments were immediately challenged by the Health Minister[33] and Catherine McGuinness, the Chair of the Kilkenny Inquiry.[34] However, on the following day, Conor Cruise O'Brien (former Editor in Chief of the *Observer*), writing in the *Irish Independent*, defended O'Tighearnaigh's right to speak out and made clear his own views on those professionals whom he refers to as 'delinquent individuals' who had 'got away with it':

---

[32] *Irish Independent* 19 May 1993 'Ordeal of mother ignored'; *Irish Independent* 20 May 1993 'Incest Report shows 'series of failures' to protect girl'; *The Irish Times* 19 May 1993 'Corps of specially trained gardaí sought'; *The Irish Times*, 20 May 1993 'ISPCC attacks Howlin over Kilkenny case'; *Irish Daily Star* 20 May 1993 'Child care experts slam incest report'.

[33] *Irish Independent* 21 May 1993 'Incest outrage: "too little co-ordination"'.

[34] *Irish Independent* 20 May 1993 'Incest Report shows "series of failures" to protect girl'.

> [The Minister for Health] was wrong to dismiss the objections of the ISPCC chief executive concerning the apparent exoneration, through the report, of all the individuals concerned in the long failure to protect an abused person. That doesn't send the right message. The right message is that, while it is expedient to close the book, delinquent individuals have been lucky to escape punishment and no one can so behave in future with impunity ... But those who complain about people who have been remiss and got away with it should be, at least, treated with respect.[35]

Liz O'Dowell, Progressive Democrats (PD) spokeswoman on health and social welfare, also made a scathing attack on the Kilkenny Report, describing it as a 'whitewash' and arguing that it was simply not good enough that nobody was held accountable.[36] In addition, she called into question the inquiry team's acceptance of the explanations given by the health care agencies, suggesting that the non-statutory, 'informal' status of the inquiry had 'hindered its capacity to determine the truth of the case'.[37]

While concerns were raised in the media about the behaviour of professionals involved in the Kilkenny case, these were, nonetheless, quite restrained, particularly when compared with the vitriolic media coverage of some inquiries in the UK (Parton, 1991; Fitzgibbon, 2011). None of the professionals involved were named in the national press, for example, nor were there calls for their resignation. Even the *Irish Independent*, one of the more critical voices following the publication of the inquiry report, only commented on a lack of staff training and support that needed to be redressed. Moreover, an article published in its sister-paper (*Sunday Independent* 23 May 1993) praised the Kilkenny Report for not attributing blame to individuals, arguing that this would have simplified matters 'beyond meaning'.[38] It is also noteworthy that the editors of the other three national dailies did not dispute the inquiry's conclusions, and that *The Irish Times* social services correspondent, Padraig O'Morain, challenged the ISPCC's critique of

---

[35]   *Irish Independent* 22 May 1993 'Wrong message given on incest'.

[36]   *The Irish Times* 26 May 1993 'Incest report assailed for failure to attach blame'.

[37]   *Irish Independent* 19 May 1993 'Timetable of tragedy'.

[38]   *Sunday Independent* 23 May 1993 'When the law is offside'.

the Kilkenny Report on the grounds that it ignored the complexities of the situation and was 'wise only with the benefit of hindsight'.[39]

In addition, most national newspapers were willing to consider events from the perspective of the social workers, doctors and gardaí involved in the case. Both *The Irish Times* and (to a lesser extent) the *Irish Independent* featured articles and statements from Kieran McGrath (editor of the *Irish Social Worker*) and Harry Ferguson (then a lecturer in Social Studies at Trinity College Dublin). McGrath presented a robust defence, emphasising that the health board could only have legally intervened in the case up until Mary had reached the age of 16, at which point the abuse had not yet been disclosed,[40] a point that was reiterated by the Chief Executive of the South Eastern Health Board on several occasions prior to the publication of the Kilkenny Report.[41] In addition, McGrath questioned the remit of the inquiry, which only took into consideration the health services and did not extend to the gardaí and other areas: 'This is in spite of the fact that the local health board's legal responsibilities had ceased when the girl in question became 16 years of age, before knowledge of the abuse became known'.[42] Following the publication of the report, McGrath challenged those (particularly Cian O'Tighearnaigh) who felt that the professionals involved had been treated 'too softly', arguing that Mary could not have been made a state ward under the laws at that time.[43] Writing in the *Irish Independent*, he acknowledged and addressed some of the criticisms that Mary herself had levelled at social workers, drawing attention to the inconsistencies between her account of when she first reported the abuse to social workers and the findings of the Kilkenny Inquiry:

> Mary has stated and restated that she was let down by a great many people, family neighbours, teachers, plus health and social services professionals. She has singled out social workers for particular criticism, saying that she told social workers when she was in hospital at the time of the birth of her child that her father was 'raping' her. She claims that

[39]   *The Irish Times* 20 May 1993 'Kilkenny case: ISPCC is wise only with benefit of hindsight'.

[40]   *The Irish Times* 3 March 1993 'A misdemeanour – how the law regards incest'.

[41]   *Irish Independent* 3 March 1993 'Domestic Violence Move'; *The Irish Times* 3 March 1993 'Garda unable to act on incest without "reliable accusations"'.

[42]   *Irish Independent* 11 May 1993 'Long delay on child care measures'.

[43]   *The Irish Times* 26 May 1993 'Kilkenny ire should take realities into account'.

she was told it was 'a family matter' and nothing could be done to help her. The investigation committee could find absolutely no evidence that she was seen by a social worker in hospital at that time. Indeed, she told the committee that no such meeting took place ... In all, Mary met with over a dozen professionals who knew, in one way or another, about the abuse before it became possible to take steps to intervene effectively. The fact that the investigation has not made any significant criticisms of the individuals in any particular aspect of the management of the case means that 'professional error' cannot be blamed for the abuse. This means that the focus must return to the structure within which those child protection workers were functioning. [44]

Interestingly, this article appeared on the same day as the *Irish Independent*'s editorial criticising the Kilkenny Report's failure to attribute blame, and this is indicative of the media's willingness to represent different perspectives on the case. Both McGrath and Harry Ferguson argued that if a scapegoat had been found in the Kilkenny case it would have deflected attention from the need for wider changes in the system.[45] They also drew attention to the enormous impact that such an inquiry would have on the staff concerned, regardless of whether or not they were vindicated, and dismissed the notion that practitioners had 'gotten off lightly'.[46]

Another major line of defence presented in the course of public discussions was that the professionals involved could do little to help Mary or her mother unless they were willing to cooperate, for example, by making a formal complaint to the police and providing full and

---

[44] *Irish Independent* 19 May 1993 'A charter for caring: neither promises nor scapegoats will protect our children's rights'.

[45] *Irish Independent* 19 May 1993 'A charter for caring: neither promises nor scapegoats will protect our children's rights'; *Irish Independent* 21 May 1993 'Incest inquiry was no whitewash'.

[46] *Irish Independent* 19 May 1993 'A charter for caring: neither promises nor scapegoats will protect our children's rights'; *Irish Independent* 21 May 1993 'Incest inquiry was no whitewash'; *Irish Times* 8 March 1993 'Incest inquiry likely to increase social workers' anxiety; *The Irish Times* 15 May 1993 'McGuinness report a useful step forward'.

frank accounts to doctors and social workers.[47] As one representative from the gardaí told *The Irish Times*: 'There is very little we can do if the injured party isn't prepared to cooperate and make an official complaint.' Similarly, the CEO of the South Eastern Health Board, John Cooney, is reported in the *Irish Independent* as saying that the social workers involved in the case could not make Mary press charges against her father or force her to leave home: 'She was a young adult at this stage. Our only powers in that regard were powers of persuasion'.[48] Some media commentators clearly sympathised with these arguments. On the same day that Mary's interview with Kieron Wood (in which she criticised social workers) was widely reported in the media, the *Irish Press* editorial (3 March) defended their position:

> The sad fact of the matter is that, if the victims are unwilling to accuse the perpetrator and stand by their accusations in a court, there is very little that anyone can do to help under present law. The most diligent social worker or doctor is helpless in the face of a family's silence.

Writing in *The Irish Times*, Padraig O'Morain argued that, while there may have been some shortcomings in professional practice, Mary's reluctance to make a formal complaint to the authorities hindered efforts to end the abuse: 'In this and other respects – explaining away her injuries to doctors and failing to show up for meetings with social workers – Mary appears to have been a difficult person to help'.[49] John Donlon, the *Irish Daily Star* columnist, took a slightly different approach, criticised the neighbours for not coming forward to the authorities, noting that 'Gardaí and social workers need some sort of evidence before they can investigate'. What these and other accounts have in common is a recognition of the fact that without the willing engagement of those at the centre of the case (Mary, her mother and neighbours) there was a limit to what the authorities could do.

Overall, the level of coverage afforded to representatives from the professions involved – particularly in *The Irish Times* – ensured that there were a number of different viewpoints and that some of the

[47] See, for example, *The Irish Times* 3 March 1993 'Sexual abuse – not just a family matter'; *The Irish Times* 3 March 1993 'Garda unable to act on incest without "reliable accusations"'.

[48] *The Irish Times* 3 March 1993 'Garda unable to act on incest without "reliable accusations"'.

[49] *The Irish Times* 19 May 'Concealment hindered efforts to help'.

criticisms of professionals (particularly those made by the ISPCC) could be addressed. Moreover, the Kilkenny case was also considered in the much wider context of Irish society at that time: professionals certainly were not seen as the only ones to 'blame' for what had happened, as we shall see later in this chapter.

Mea culpa: the emblematic status of the Kilkenny case

Butler and Drakeford (2008) argue that some high-profile child abuse scandals achieve an 'iconic' status. They have significance 'beyond the professional communities of interest and private individuals around which the scandal is built' and connect 'to more general "social commentaries" or moral and sociocultural concerns' (p 369). The deaths of Maria Colwell and Baby P, for example, sparked a debate about the decline of the family unit and of 'traditional values' in Britain (Fitzgibbon, 2011). With the growing influence of neoliberalism from the 1980s onwards, some social commentators would also attribute child deaths (including that of Baby P) to the emergence of a 'feral underclass' of welfare dependents, opening the way to a wider critique of the welfare state and the 'leftist progressive intelligentsia' that supported it (Fitzgibbon, 2011: 22).

In Ireland, the Kilkenny incest case also gave rise to a wider social commentary, beyond the events of the case itself. As one contributor to the *Irish Times* (10 March 1993) letters page rightly observed, 'we are in the midst of a national mea culpa'. Much of this soul-searching concerned the status of the family within Irish society. However, while in the UK child abuse is often seen to be symptomatic of the *breakdown* of the family unit and of the erosion of 'traditional' values, in Ireland it was the *inviolability* of the family that was seen to be problematic. The crux of this argument was that the family occupied a privileged position within Irish society, making it difficult for 'outsiders' (whether professionals or members of the community) to intervene, even in cases of domestic violence and abuse. Consequently, there was a 'culture of silence' around incest and an ambivalence towards domestic violence: it was tolerated in a way that other forms of violence were not. TD Frances Fitzgerald (former chairwoman of the Council for the Status of Women and future Minister for Children and Youth Affairs) was one of the most vocal commentators on the social implications of the

Kilkenny case. Her views are summed up in the following extract from a Dáil debate (3 March 1993), which was widely reported in the press:[50]

> I am afraid this case forces us to ask some very uncomfortable questions about ourselves. We are horrified as a society by this crime, yet there is a deep ambivalence in Ireland to anything that is seen as an attempt to interfere with the family. We have a tendency to idealise the family. We must ask ourselves if we are prepared to stand up and be counted on this issue. I do not think we yet want to believe that such horrific crimes can take place in our midst and within the family. The courage of this woman in speaking out last night, and the courage of Lavinia Kerwick last year, and the Minister's inquiry could do much to turn the tide of this issue. We still have a tendency to deny that these things can happen in our society. (Francis Fitzgerald *Dáil debates* 3 March 1993)

In a Seanad debate (4 March 1993), Senator David Norris put the case in more forceful terms:

> "When we consecrate the family we should examine its reality instead of holding it up as an icon or totem. There are many things wrong with Irish families. There is not only incest but rape within marriage, drunkenness and wife battering. Before we fall down and worship the golden calf of Irish marriage we ought to examine that institution and try to correct what is wrong."

Similar views on the status of the family (and the subordinate position of children and women within it) were expressed by media commentators, politicians, professionals and organisations that worked with women and children.[51] While recognising that an unwillingness to 'interfere

---

[50] *Irish Independent* 4 March 1993 'Inquiry to probe official inaction'; *The Irish Times* 4 March 1993 'Geoghegan-Quinn promises action'; and *Irish Press* 4 March 1993 'Longer maximum sentence are called for in Dáil Debate'.

[51] See, for example, *The Irish Times* 26 May 1993 'Incest report assailed for failure to attach blame'; *The Irish Times* 15 March 1993 'When a parent's love turns to lust …'; *The Irish Times* 3 June 1993 'Next time there has to be someone who can say "Well, I tried. I did my best"'; *The Irish Times* 3 March 1993 'Sexual abuse – not just a family matter'; Seanad Éireann, 4 March 1993 – various speakers.

with the sacredness of the family' was a feature of many societies,[52] some argued that this tradition was particularly strong in Ireland due in part to the privileged position of the family under the Irish Constitution. Under Article 41, the state 'recognises the family as the natural primary and fundamental unit group of society, and as a moral institution possessing inalienable and imprescriptible rights, antecedent and superior to all positive law'. However, while the Constitution gives great powers to the family, it does not include any articles specifically giving rights to children (other than to the unborn) and this may have serious repercussions in child abuse cases.[53] Writing in *The Irish Times* (3 March 1993), Kieran McGrath argues that until we start to recognise that children themselves have rights 'it will remain difficult for the "helping" services to intervene' in cases of suspected abuse. Similarly, in a Seanad debate (4 March 1993), Senator Kelly described children as being little more that the 'property' of the family, with no rights of their own under the Irish Constitution. The Kilkenny Inquiry team appeared to share these concerns: one of their main recommendations was that the Constitution be amended to include a statement of the rights of children.

The *Irish Times* was one of the more vocal critics of the 'sacred' position of the family in Irish society and its privileged position in the Irish Constitution. The proposed constitutional amendment was therefore warmly welcomed, as the following editorial illustrates:

> One of the reasons for the reluctance of many who became aware of her plight to take action on behalf of the beaten, raped and deeply wounded child, was the legal and constitutional framework which protects the family even, as in this instance, at the expense of the health and happiness of one of its members.
>
> From [Article 41] flows a vision of the family and an understanding of its rights which have long informed official thinking in the State. The vision is that of a particular time, the 1930s, and of a cast of mind which owes more to the version of Catholic social teaching then in vogue, than to any profound understanding of the social and psychological conditions experienced by a majority of people. It is

---

[52] *The Irish Times* 15 March 1993 'When a parent's love turns to lust …'.

[53] *The Irish Times* 3 March 1993 'A misdemeanour – how the law regards incest'; *The Irish Times* 19 May 1993 'Child Care Act makes a number of important changes in law'.

altogether inappropriate that it should remain in the 1990s
an unreformed influence on social legislation or on the way
in which those in the public service approach their work.
(*The Irish Times*, 19 May 1993)

Catholic social teaching is also implicated in an earlier article in *The
Irish Times* (10 March 1993), in which Fintan O'Toole (a long-standing
critic of the institutional church) argues that 'it is the basic precept of
Irish Catholic conservatism that the state and its institutions should
not interfere in the life of the family'. While acknowledging that
it would be 'absurd' to blame church and state for the actions of an
abuser, nonetheless, he argues, 'it is the passivity of the community
as a whole, and not the active malevolence of the abuser, that is at
issue here, and in that context it is foolish to ignore the fundamental
attitudes embedded in the traditions of Church and State which see the
family as its own little State-within-a-State, policed and controlled by
its fountain of authority, the father'. Similarly, another columnist from
The Irish Times asserts that professionals working on the health boards
or in related agencies are still influenced by the Catholic social thinking
of the 1930s: 'Before anyone crosses a threshold to save a child from
degradation, it is necessary to think first of the rights of the family'.[54]

While *The Irish Times* provided some of the most outspoken social
criticism, concerns around the inviolability of the family were also
raised in the *Irish Independent* and the *Irish Press*, both before and after
the publication of the Kilkenny Report. The *Irish Independent* featured a
series of articles from social commentators, including Harry Ferguson,
Bruce Arnold and Conor Cruise O'Brien. While Ferguson sets out
a measured analysis of the state's traditional reluctance to intervene
in the family,[55] Arnold provides a more stinging critique, suggesting
that Ireland's 'emotional, religious and constitutional respect for the
family' sometimes borders 'on connivance in wrong-doing' (19 May
1993). Similarly, Conor Cruise O'Brien attests that '"traditional family
values", backed strongly by the State, could be a shield for child
abusers'. In another article he attacks the Catholic Church for not
doing more to address the problem of incest – an article that resulted
in a series of angry letters to the editor. A few of the *Irish Independent*'s
other columnists also highlighted the need for a change in attitude to
the family, although the issue of constitutional change is not mooted

54   Dick Walsh writing in *The Irish Times* on 22 May 1993.
55   *Irish Independent* 3 March 1993 'Constitutional concerns may be limiting
     interventions'.

in these articles. In addition, on the day after the publication of the Kilkenny Report, the *Irish Independent*'s editorial makes no mention of the proposed constitutional amendment to recognise the rights of children – a recommendation that dominated the editorial in *The Irish Times*.

In the course of this public discussion on the nature of the Irish family, tensions began to emerge between some of its more outspoken critics and organisations with a 'pro-family' agenda. Speaking in the Seanad (4 March 1993), Senator David Norris criticised 'the deafening silence' on the Kilkenny case from 'all rightwing moralistic groups', including Family Solidarity: 'Where are they when they are needed to talk about a case of cruelty and family misery?' he asked. The implication here would seem to be that these groups choose to ignore the negative side of family life, as evinced in the Kilkenny case, because this did not support their own particular agenda. In *The Irish Times*, Fintan O'Toole (10 March 1993) argued that many of the campaigns for 'family values' (by Family Solidarity, the Responsible Society and others) have given explicit or implicit endorsement to the view that each family is 'an independent republic', which should be free from outside intervention. This attitude, as was indicated earlier in this chapter, was implicated in creating a culture of silence around familial abuse. Following the publication of the Kilkenny Report, Dick Walsh (columnist at *The Irish Times*), wrote disparagingly of how the state's 'cultural defenders' were planning to resist the proposed amendment to the Constitution because they feared that it might undermine 'traditional family values' (22 May 1993).

Soon after, Family Solidarity *did* express reservations about the proposed amendment to the Constitution, arguing that it was unnecessary because children were protected under the existing legal and constitutional framework.[56] In the same article, Alice Glenn (former TD, well-known social conservative and one of the 'cultural defenders' identified by Walsh) provided a more robust and ideologically explicit defence of the Constitution. She argued that the Kilkenny case was an aberration that did not reflect Irish family life and that a constitutional amendment to recognise the rights of children could undermine the status of the family, allowing social workers and other professionals to go 'rampaging through the homes of Ireland':

"I think an amendment to the Constitution would be a retrograde step. The Constitution already provides for

---

[56] *The Irish Times* 1 June 1993 'Do Irish children need a change in the Constitution?'.

anyone at risk within the family, and I have reservations about upsetting the balance between parent and child. After all, the family is the basic unit of Irish society. The Kilkenny case is a horrific account of what could happen in a family, but the family is not typical in Ireland. It is not an Irish family. Without the Grace of God there is a strong inclination to evil. Luckily Ireland is a very Christian country, a country where parents make legendary sacrifices for their children.

An amendment to the Constitution would allow the State to trample on the Irish family. I have a vision of an army of social workers, community nurses and gardaí rampaging through the homes of Ireland, making false accusations, and damaging the fragile fabric of the family."

Her comment that 'it is not an Irish family' is presumably in reference to the fact that the family in the Kilkenny case were from England and were therefore not to be seen as representative of Irish families.[57] Senator Farrell, another defender of 'traditional family values', asserted that 'this type of crime would not have happened in years gone by'. In a speech to the Seanad (4 March 1993), he bemoaned the loss of respect for traditional authority (teachers, priests and gardaí) and the emergence of a more affluent and indifferent society in which abuse could remain undetected. He also spoke approvingly of how in the past 'if an unmarried mother had to go into a convent the nuns would have investigated and found out her story' – a particularly ironic comment given the scandals that later enveloped some of the church-run institutions for single mothers and their children.

After Kilkenny

There have been only three other major inquiries into familial abuse since the Kilkenny case, the most recent being the Roscommon Inquiry (Gibbon, 2010), which explored the circumstances surrounding the neglect and abuse of children by their parents over a number of years. Looking at the media's coverage of this case, it becomes clear that there have been a number of significant changes from the early 1990s. Firstly, the proliferation of tabloids (the *Irish Sun*, the *Irish Daily Mirror* and the

[57]   Interestingly, the nationality of the family is rarely referred to in the newspapers, apart from the first day when, in reporting on the trial, the father is identified as English.

Irish Daily Mail, along with the long-established *Sunday World* and the *Irish Daily Star*) has resulted in a more 'sensationalist' style of reporting of abuse cases. The *Irish Sun*, in particular, presented the parents in the Roscommon case in demonic terms; for example, the parents were referred to as the 'fiend father and incest hag mother' (28 October 2010). The case itself was routinely referred to in the tabloids as the 'house of horrors'. While the demonisation of abusers in the tabloid press has become a commonplace, it has been criticised for giving a misleading impression that abusers are in some sense 'outsiders', separate from mainstream society (Kitzinger, 2004).

Writing soon after the Kilkenny Inquiry, Harry Ferguson (1993-4: 406) noted that there were heightened expectations that such a case 'won't happen again' and predicted 'that if, or when, it does it is doubtful than an inquiry will be as reluctant to criticise individual professionals and the relevant government departments'. Certainly, media coverage in the Roscommon case was far more critical, with some tabloids calling for the dismissal of social workers. Perhaps one of the most striking differences is that while in the Kilkenny case a number of viewpoints from different organisations were represented, this was largely absent in Roscommon. In one of the few articles to consider the perspective of the social workers involved in the case, the source is referred to obliquely as someone 'close to the Kilkenny case' (*Irish Sun*, 30 October 2010). The hardening of attitudes towards the professionals involved in abuse cases is probably due in part to heightened expectations – there had been several inquiries, followed by reforms to the child protection system, so that the media, politicians and the public may have become less tolerant of perceived failures in the health services. But this hardening of attitudes may also be due to the changed social and economic climate at the time. By 2010, the Irish economy was in free-fall and there was a degree of hostility in the media, spurred on by some politicians, towards public servants who were seen as overpaid and a drain on the country's already limited resources. Moreover, there was a sense of anger that various organisations, both in the public and private sector had precipitated a national crisis but appeared to be unaccountable for their actions. The anger directed at social workers in the Roscommon case needs to be considered within this wider context of distrust in public institutions (in this instance the Health Service Executive, or HSE) and a growing hostility towards public servants.

Conclusion

Inquiries are often a focus for public anger, which in the Kilkenny case reached extraordinary proportions, and they also provide politicians with the basis of a rhetoric that something is 'being done' (Ferguson, 1993-4: 389). A central issue is whether the inquiry (or the media) attributes responsibility to individuals or to the wider structures and systems within which they operate. The Kilkenny Report is unusual, not only in its focus on the system (or the lack of a system, as McGuinness later noted in 2012) but also for its recognition of the need for broader changes in people's attitudes to children, to the family and to domestic violence. This was reflected in particular in the recommendation for a change in the Constitution.

The media's reaction to the Kilkenny case was mixed. While there was bewilderment and some anger at the apparent inaction of some professionals involved in the case, there was also recognition that there were limits to what they could do within the existing legislation. Significantly, the press considered the case in the much wider context of Irish society, with some commentators arguing that it was the reverence for the institution of the family and a clinging to outdated ideas that was at the root of the problem exposed through the Kilkenny case. Similarly the anger over the sentencing was not only interpreted as a failure of the judge or the judicial system but as being indicative of society's tolerance of domestic violence.

Kilkenny represented a landmark in terms of the development of child protection, but equally it marked a turning point in media coverage and public attitudes to child abuse. It paved the way for further inquiries not only into familial but also clerical abuse (see Chapter 3).

THREE

The Catholic Church, scandal and media

> When all the numbing details of the [Dublin] report are absorbed, we have to reassemble the big picture of the institutional church's relationship with Irish society. And we have to say that relationship itself has been an abusive one. The church leadership behave towards society with the same callousness, the same deviousness, the same exploitative mentality and the same blindly egotistical pursuit of its own desires that an abuser shows towards his victim. (Fintan O'Toole, *The Irish Times* 28 November 2009)

Over the last 25 years, revelations of child sexual abuse by Roman Catholic clergy have given rise to one of the greatest institutional scandals of modern history. Sexual abuse by Catholic clergy has been reported across all five continents, though the countries that have received most attention are located in the 'First World', including the United States, Canada, Australia, the United Kingdom and Ireland, and more recently, Germany, Belgium, Austria, the Netherlands, France, Malta, Italy and Switzerland (Keenan, 2012: 3). The media played a key role in raising awareness of clerical child abuse in these countries by bringing this hitherto taboo subject to a mass audience and by campaigning for public inquiries into the church's handling of allegations. Moreover, in decrying the 'evils' of child abuse, the media acted as society's moral arbitrator, a role previously occupied by the church itself.

In this chapter we explore the role of the media in exposing clerical child abuse in Ireland, focusing in particular on how a series of television documentaries paved the way for two major inquiries (Ferns and Dublin) and on the media's subsequent coverage of the inquiry reports. We look at how the controversy surrounding the clerical child abuse inquiries embodied key features of an 'institutional scandal': social norms were transgressed leading to moral outrage; the actions of individuals brought the Catholic Church as a whole into disrepute; and allegations of institutional 'cover-ups' proved to be as damaging as the acts they sought to conceal. The process of 'scandal inflation', whereby the media keeps a story alive by finding new 'angles' and 'unveiling even more bizarre or aberrant behaviours' (Butler and Drakeford, 2003) is also considered in relation to media coverage of the inquiries. In the case of Ferns, media reporting quickly turned to speculation on the possible scale of clerical abuse elsewhere in the country (with a number of dire predictions) while in the Dublin case much of the media's focus was on the need for high-level resignations – a common reaction to scandals in public life, which nonetheless signified the shifting balance of power between church and media in Ireland.

While our focus will be on Ireland, the issues raised in this chapter are of international significance: child abuse inquiries have been a feature in several western countries, with profound consequences for the Catholic Church and for those agencies charged with the protection of children.

Our analysis of the media's coverage of the two inquiry reports is set within the wider context of contemporary media scandals. In order to elucidate why clerical child sex abuse became one of the greatest scandals of the late 20th century, we will first explore the meaning and significance of this concept.

What is scandal?

One of the defining features of scandal is that it involves actions or events that transgress accepted values, norms, or moral codes. According to Lull and Hinerman (1997: 3), scandal occurs 'when private acts that disgrace or offend the idealised, dominant morality of a social community are made public and narrativised by the media, producing a range of effects from ideological cultural retrenchment to disruption and change'. A transgression assumes added significance when the individuals involved, by virtue of their position or affiliations, have formerly espoused or represented the values and norms that they themselves violate. In such instances, there is an element of double-standards, whereby the protagonist is revealed as having failed to practice what he/she preaches to others (Soukup, 1997). Public figures, notably politicians, religious figures and others who actively promote certain values or lifestyles, may be particularly vulnerable in this regard. During the 1990s, for example, several senior members of the Conservative party in the UK found themselves at the centre of a media storm when it was revealed that they had had extra-marital liaisons, despite belonging to a party that supported 'traditional' family values. In Ireland, the disclosure in 1992 that the popular and charismatic bishop of Galway, Eamon Casey, had had a long-term relationship (and fathered a son) with an American divorcee became one of the greatest scandals of recent Irish history. Not since the late 19th century – when the leader of the Irish Home Rule Party, Charles Stuart Parnell, was revealed as having an adulterous relationship – had there been a scandal of similar magnitude.

Transgressions of a value or norm can give rise to a scandal only if the value or norm has some degree of moral force in society. However, at a time of increasing diversity in terms of lifestyles and personal behaviour, it cannot be assumed that different sections of society will be united in what they find 'scandalous'. Values and norms are often contested features of social life, adhered to by some individuals and groups and rejected (or simply ignored) by others. Despite this diversity there are still some issues that provoke 'a solid moral consensus', most notably paedophilia, which has become an issue of growing public concern – even 'moral panic' – in western countries (Furedi, 2013: 7).

Certain people are more vulnerable to scandal than others. This differential susceptibility to scandal is linked in part to the degree of visibility of the individuals concerned: politicians and celebrities from the worlds of sport, music and acting are far more visible than others and therefore more vulnerable to scandal in the event of transgressing a norm (Thompson, 1997: 40). Indeed, in the age of global media, scandal has become almost an occupational hazard for those in the public eye. Other scandals occur when individuals associated with a particular *institution* transgress accepted norms, thereby bringing the institution itself into disrepute: 'Their indiscretions become scandalous because these persons represent not only themselves, but the institutions in which they are professionally situated' (Lull and Hinerman, 1997: 20). However, not all institutional scandals can be attributed to the actions of a few 'bad apples' that can be duly purged. In some instances the transgression may be so widespread and established that it is seen to be endemic to the culture of the institution: the police forces in the UK and the US, for example, have at various points been accused of institutional racism. Similarly, the practice of falsifying expense claims was found to be so pervasive among MPs across all political parties in the UK that it brought the House of Parliament itself into disrepute.

Many scandals involve what Thompson (1997) describes as 'second-order transgressions' whereby attention is shifted from the original offence to a series of subsequent actions that are aimed at concealing it. Indeed, attempts to 'cover up' a transgression may become more significant than the original transgression itself, 'giving rise to an intensifying cycle of claim and counter-claim that dwarfs the initial offence and fuels a scandal that escalates with every twist' (Thompson,

1997: 42). Recent US history provides a number of examples of how botched cover-ups have become more notorious than the events that they sought to conceal, most notably the Watergate scandal in which the Nixon administration attempted to conceal its involvement in a break-in at the Democratic National Committee headquarters. More recently Bill Clinton's denial of a relationship with a young intern (Monica Lewinsky) prolonged the scandal and proved to be hugely politically damaging for the President, culminating in his impeachment trial on charges of perjury and obstruction of justice.

A key element of scandal is that the transgression becomes widely known: there can be no scandal without disclosure. In this respect the media plays a crucial role. According to Lull and Hinerman (1997), the revelations must be widely circulated via communications media where they are effectively narrativised into a story that inspires widespread interest and discussion. The authors emphasise the importance of the concept 'story' when analysing scandals:

> The need for stories is basic to all societies, even pre-literate ones. A scandal is not just a logical reporting of damaging facts, no matter how shocking they may be. In a scandal, the story triumphs over the facts at some point, and in doing so takes on a life of its own. The scandal story arouses the curiosity of a substantial audience who encourage the media to continue 'telling the story'. The scandal continues as long as the public remains interested in the story. Closure requires some kind of social consensus, which often demands a final 'truth', 'moral lesson', or 'justice served'. Terms of closure rest ultimately with the public. (Lull and Hinerman, 1997: 14)

As suggested in this extract, scandals, like all stories, need an ending – 'maybe not a "happy ending", but at least a satisfactory one' (Lull and Hinerman, 1997: 15). So the story not only reports the events that have transpired but calls out for *future* action in order to bring about closure, for example, the resignation or dismissal of the wrong-doer, the payment of compensation to those wronged, the initiation of institutional reform, public apologies and so on. Key stake holders (eg, civil society organisations) can play an important role in campaigning for change following institutional, financial or political scandals. Moreover, the media often goes beyond simply reporting transgressions to campaigning for change. Following the murder of Sarah Payne, for example, the *News of the World* campaigned vigorously for the introduction of legislation in the UK that would allow people to find out if a convicted sex abuser was living in their area.

The Catholic Church and scandal

The revelations of clerical child abuse, from the 1980s onwards, formed the basis for one of the greatest and longest running scandals of modern history. The clerics who abused children not only breached a social taboo, they violated norms and values that they themselves passionately espoused. The Catholic Church is known for its strict moral code on all matters relating to sexual behaviour (including abstinence before marriage and a prohibition on homosexual behaviour) and the control of reproduction (opposition to contraceptives and abortion). For Catholic priests to sexually abuse *children* was therefore an almost unimaginable breach of the church's own values and teachings. The scandal was made considerably worse by allegations of cover-ups that reached the highest echelons of the church hierarchy.

Revelations of sexual abuse by priests came primarily from adults who had been sexually abused as children and who sought civil claims and criminal charges against their offenders (Keenan, 2012: 17). Some wrote books detailing their suffering. Disclosures of clerical abuse also came from investigative reporting by national and international reporters, resulting in numerous articles, news reports and documentaries. Once the floodgates had been opened, there was an avalanche of publicity surrounding the issue (Keenan, 2012: 17).

Child sexual abuse scandals in Ireland

In Ireland, over the space of just 15 years, clerical child abuse moved from being a taboo subject to a major area of media reporting. Donnelly and Inglis (2010: 8) argue that as the power and symbolic dominance of the Catholic Church in Irish society gradually diminished, clerical sex abuse changed from being a topic that was not talked about or reported on to being a topic that was increasingly disclosed by victims, with reports becoming commonplace in Irish media.

The first major clerical child abuse scandal in Ireland concerned the case of Brendan Smyth, a priest with the Norbertine Order, who in 1994 pleaded guilty to 72 charges of indecent and sexual assault and was sentenced to 12 years in prison (Keenan, 2012). One of the most shocking revelations was that the abuse had gone on for decades, with the knowledge of at least some of Smyth's superiors. Chris Moore, a reporter with Ulster Television's[1] *Counterpoint* programme, found that the clerical authorities had known for years of Smyth's crimes, but dealt with it by moving him on and essentially covering up his actions (Ferguson, 1995: 247). The Brendan Smyth affair became especially significant when it emerged that the Irish State had failed to extradite Smyth from the Republic of Ireland to answer sex abuse charges in Northern Ireland. A request from the Royal Ulster Constabulary (RUC) for Smyth's extradition had lain dormant in the offices of the Irish Director of Public Prosecutions for seven months (Donnelly and Inglis, 2010). The controversial handling of the extradition led to the resignation of the then Taoiseach (prime minister), Albert Reynolds, and the President of the High Court, Harry Whelahan who had been attorney general at the time. It also led to a serious rupture within the Fianna Fáil/Labour coalition and the eventual fall of the government. Three key elements of the Smyth case – clerical abuse, institutional cover-up and state collusion – would become recurring themes in later inquiries into child abuse.

One of the lasting legacies of the Smyth scandal was that it brought the issue of clerical child sexual abuse into the open for the first time in Ireland. Up until the 1990s, the church had managed to prevent either the media or the state from interfering in the affairs of the church (Donnelly and Inglis, 2010). However, the disclosure in 1993 of Bishop Casey's relationship with a divorced woman, followed closely by the Brendan Smyth's conviction for child abuse, delivered a major blow to the church's reputation and legitimacy. As Keenan (2012) points out, the Smyth scandal cleared the way for further revelations: case after case of abusing priests who had held positions in orphanages, parishes and schools began to emerge. The church responded by introducing new policies and procedures relating to the handling and reporting of clerical child abuse, including the stipulation that where it is known or suspected that a child has been, or is being, sexually abused by a priest or religious the matter should be reported to the civil authorities. These policies were set out in the document *Child Sexual Abuse: Framework for a Church Response*, which will be referred to by its more generally known name in this chapter – the *Framework Document* (Irish Catholic Bishops' Advisory Committee on Child Sexual Abuse by Priests and Religious, 1996).

[1]   Ulster Television changed its name to UTV in 2006

The media and clerical child abuse

The media – through a series of television documentaries and investigative reporting – played a major role in raising public awareness of clerical child abuse and in pressurising the Irish government to take action over the issue. Particularly significant was the British Broadcasting Corporation's (BBC) documentary *Suing the Pope*. It reported on the allegations of abuse against Father (Fr) Sean Fortune and the mishandling of the case by the (still serving) Bishop of Ferns, Brendan Comiskey. First broadcast on the BBC in March 2002, *Suing the Pope* was later shown on Raidió Teilifís Éireann (RTÉ) (Ireland's national broadcaster) and was the subject of a *Primetime* (current affairs) programme and extensive press debate. The ensuing controversy led to the resignation of Bishop Comiskey and the initiation of a preliminary investigation by George Birmingham, Senior Counsel (SC), into allegations of child abuse in the diocese of Ferns, which in turn led to the setting up of the Ferns inquiry. The crucial role of the BBC documentary in setting in motion this series of events is acknowledged in the Ferns Report (Murphy et al, 2005: 6). Significantly, some of the revelations of clerical sexual abuse that were broadcast in *Suing the Pope* were *already* in the public domain: it was known that Fr Sean Fortune had been facing criminal charges but had committed suicide before his trial in 1999. However, it was only when the issue was broadcast in all its shocking detail (including first-hand accounts from several of Fortune's victims) to a national and international television audience that the Irish government decided to take action.

Similarly, RTÉ's documentary series *States of Fear* (1999) played an important role in highlighting the issue of institutional abuse (in industrial and reformatory schools) and the Irish government came under considerable pressure to respond. On 11 May 1999, the day on which the final *States of Fear* programme was broadcast, the government issued a public apology to victims of child abuse and announced the establishment of the Commission to Inquire into Child Abuse (Donnelly and Inglis, 2010: 14) that later reported its findings in the landmark Ryan Report (CICA, 2009). Commenting on the setting up of the commission, Donnelly and Inglis (2010: 15) argue that 'the government was predominantly motivated to investigate the inadequacies of church and state facilities for children in response to media pressure'.

RTÉ broadcast another key programme during 2002, *Primetime: Cardinal Secrets*, which included allegations of sexual abuse within the Dublin archdiocese and the church's repeated failure to act on these allegations. The Archbishop of Dublin, Cardinal Desmond Connell, came in for particular criticism. Survivors of clerical abuse, as well as their families, were interviewed as part of the programme. In addition, Fr Tom Doyle, a canon law expert and 'international expert on clerical child sexual abuse', provided damning commentary on the Diocese's handing of child abuse allegations. He asserted that there had been a 'cover-up' and 'collusion' among clergy *at all levels* to not report clerical sexual abuse, concluding that there was 'something radically, radically wrong' within the archdiocese. The visual imagery of the documentary was particularly striking in evoking the apparent duplicity of the church. In one scene, for example, victims recount their ordeals against the backdrop of Archbishop Connell performing mass, dressed in all his episcopal regalia and blessing celebrants as he leaves: the pomp and ceremony of the church contrasts with the harsh reality experienced by some of its youngest members.

Following the broadcast of *Cardinal Secrets* in 2002, a major police investigation was undertaken into clerical child sexual abuse complaints, including those relating to clerics in the Archdiocese of Dublin (DJELR, 2009: 84). The controversy surrounding the allegations of abuse in this programme also paved the way for the setting up of the Dublin Archdiocese Commission of Investigation.

The media undoubtedly played a key role in helping to instigate the first clerical child abuse inquiries in Ireland. In the following pages we will examine the findings of two of these inquiries – Ferns and Dublin – followed by a detailed analysis of the media's coverage of their findings, based on an analysis of press and television news coverage.

The Ferns inquiry

The Ferns inquiry was set up in March 2003 to investigate allegations and complaints of child sexual abuse by members of the clergy in the Diocese of Ferns and to consider the appropriateness of the response of the church and state authorities, 'judged in the context of the time when the complaint or allegation was made' (Murphy et al, 2005: 2). It was chaired by Justice Francis D. Murphy, a former judge of the Supreme Court, and covered a period of approximately 40 years up to April 2002. The inquiry identified over 100 complaints made against 21 priests under the aegis of the Diocese of Ferns. Over 40 of those complaints related to two priests only. Ten of the priests complained against were deceased at the time of the inquiry, three had been laicised and the remaining eight priests were no longer in active ministry (Murphy et al, 2005: 6). The gardaí (police) investigated complaints of child sexual abuse by eight priests of the Diocese and proceedings were instituted by the Director of Public Prosecutions in three of those cases (246).

The major findings of the Ferns Report are concerned with the leadership of Bishop Donal Herlihy (Bishop of Ferns from 1964 to 1983) and Bishop Brendan Comiskey (Bishop of Ferns from 1984 to 2002), both of whom were found to have acted inappropriately in dealing with allegations of child sexual abuse against priests during their terms of office. The inquiry found that during the 1960s and 70s Bishop Herlihy moved two priests, against whom allegations were made, to the Diocese of Westminster 'without taking any steps to protect other children' from the dangers that these men presented (Murphy et al, 2005: 250). Moreover, both priests were later allowed to return to Ferns, having served their 'penance', and to assume positions of authority where they would have had unsupervised access to children and young adults.[2] When allegations of sexual misconduct were made against two other priests in the early 1980s, Bishop Herlihy's response was to send the alleged perpetrators for psychological assessment, a course of action that, the inquiry notes, was 'entirely appropriate' and reflected the developing understanding of the nature of child sexual abuse (Murphy et al, 2005: 250). However, Bishop Herlihy failed to act on the 'extremely unfavourable reports' that he received and both priests were appointed to curacies in the Diocese of Ferns, where they worked without any effective monitoring or control.

Bishop Herlihy's responses to allegations of child abuse during his term of office are explained by the Ferns inquiry in terms of a lack of understanding on his part of the recidivist nature of child abuse and its effect on victims:

> The inappropriateness and inadequacy of responses by Bishop Donal Herlihy are, in the opinion of the Inquiry, explained by the failure of the Bishop to appreciate the very serious psychological damage which could be and was caused by the sexual abuse of children by adults, particularly adults in positions of authority and respect. An additional factor was the failure to anticipate the likelihood that an abuser having once abused a child was likely to repeat the offence. It is the view of the Inquiry that Bishop Herlihy

---

[2]   One of the 'offending priests' was appointed as principal of St Peter's College, while the second held managerial positions in local schools before being transferred abroad.

focussed on the moral aspects of the allegations made to
him to the exclusion of criminal and social aspects of the
conduct alleged. (Murphy et al, 2005: 54)

The inquiry's comments here resonate with arguments made by some
church leaders that they were on a 'steep learning curve' and that
mistakes made in the handling of abuse complaints were due to sheer
ignorance on their part and a general lack of awareness about the
prevalence of child sexual abuse (Keenan, 2012: 207). Nonetheless,
the Ferns Report notes that some of Bishop Herlihy's actions were
'inadequate and inappropriate even by the standards of the time'
(Murphy et al, 2005: 132).

Herlihy's successor, Bishop Brendan Comiskey, accepted that the
appropriate response to an allegation of child sexual abuse was to
have the accused priest step aside from active ministry pending a
determination of the allegation made against him. However, the
Ferns inquiry found that the bishop 'consistently failed to achieve this
objective' (Murphy et al, 2005: 251). Where an allegation of child
sexual abuse was made against a priest of the diocese and denied by
him, as happened in the majority of cases, Bishop Comiskey attempted
to institute or conduct some form of enquiry to satisfy himself of the
guilt or innocence of the accused. In most cases these enquiries and
investigations 'were protracted and inconclusive and in all cases failed
to meet the standard of proof required by the Bishop' (p 48). Where
psychological assessments were availed of, Bishop Comiskey was 'unable
or unwilling to implement the advice which he received' (p 251).
Moreover, the inquiry received some evidence that the bishop did not
fully inform these medical experts of the full history of priests against
whom previous allegations had been made (p 251).

The Ferns inquiry concluded that Bishop Comiskey had failed
to remove from active ministry priests against whom allegations of
abuse were made, 'primarily because of his belief that he could not
and should not take an action that would necessarily damage the
reputation of one of his priests without convincing evidence of their
guilt. He did not prioritise child protection in his response' (Murphy
et al, 2005: 255). While condemning Comiskey's misplaced priorities,
the report also expresses a degree of sympathy with the bishop's
motives, noting that he was 'rightly conscious of the need to protect
the good name and reputation of his clergy' (p 251) and appears to
reject 'sinister' explanations for his actions, proffered by some of those
who appeared before the inquiry (p 254). Moreover, the possibility
that the bishop might have acted to protect the institutional church –

not just individual priests in Ferns – receives only a fleeting mention in the conclusion to the report. Overall, Comiskey is represented as misguided and ineffective rather than unscrupulous or manipulative. Later media reports would focus largely on Comiskey's failures and alleged weaknesses, but he is not vilified in the manner of some of the hierarchy involved in the Dublin inquiry (discussed later in this chapter).

While critical of the response of church authorities to allegations of clerical abuse, the Ferns Report is nonetheless measured in its criticism, particularly when compared with the later Dublin Report. Crucially, the inquiry team stops short of accusing either Bishop Herlihy or Comiskey of having perpetrated a deliberate 'cover-up' of child abuse. Moreover, while the conclusion acknowledges that 'a culture of secrecy and a fear of causing scandal informed at least some of the responses' (Murphy et al, 2005: 256), this issue is not explored in any detail or highlighted as one of the significant findings of the report. As we shall see in the next section, the Commission of Investigation into clerical abuse in the Archdiocese of Dublin was to be far more outspoken in its critique of the institutional church and its role in the cover-up of allegations of clerical child abuse.

The Dublin Report (2009)

The Dublin Archdiocese Commission of Investigation was established in 2006 'to report on the handling of Church and State authorities of a representative sample of allegations and suspicions of child sexual abuse against clerics operating under the aegis of the Archdiocese of Dublin over the period 1975 to 2004' (DJELR, 2009: 1).[3] Like the Ferns inquiry, the Dublin Commission did not set out to establish whether or not child sexual abuse actually *took place* but rather to record the manner in which complaints were dealt with by the relevant authorities (DJELR, 2009: 1). Nonetheless, the Dublin Report concluded that it was 'abundantly clear … that child sexual abuse by clerics was widespread throughout the period under review' (DJELR, 2009: 2).

In the course of its investigation, the Dublin Commission, which was chaired by Judge Yvonne Murphy, encountered a number of set-backs to its work, including a legal challenge by Cardinal Connell, the

---

[3]   The commission received information about complaints, suspicions, or knowledge of child sexual abuse in respect of 172 named priests and 11 unnamed priests, 102 of whom came under the commission's remit. It sampled 46 cases and carried out an in-depth investigation into complaints made against these priests (Dublin Report, 2009: 2-3).

details of which are set out in its report (DJELR, 2009: 35-42). Of particular note was the commission's unsuccessful attempt to obtain documents from the Congregation for the Doctrine of the Faith (CDF) in Rome and from the Papal Nuncio. A number of written requests went unanswered, though the CDF did contact the Department of Foreign Affairs stating that the commission had not gone through appropriate diplomatic channels (p 37). The commission subsequently chose not to pursue the diplomatic route because it saw itself as 'a body independent of government' (p 37). Although this unfruitful correspondence with the CDF and the Papal Nuncio takes up only a few paragraphs of the Dublin Report, it attracted considerable media attention and speculation as to the possible reasons for the apparent noncooperation of these authorities.

The Dublin Report provided a damning account of the handling of allegations of clerical child sexual abuse by both church and state authorities. A key finding, in line with the Ferns Report, was that priests accused of abuse were moved into other areas where the cycle of abuse often began again. Where priests were sent for psychiatric or psychological treatment, full information was not always given to the professionals about the priests' history. This inevitably resulted in 'useless reports', which were nonetheless sometimes used 'as an excuse to allow priests back to unsupervised ministry' (DJELR, 2009: 19). The report is scathing in its assessment of the four archbishops who served in the Archdiocese during the period under review (McQuaid, Ryan, McNamara and Connell), all of whom were found to have handled child sexual abuse complaints 'badly' (p 10). In the case of Archbishop McQuaid, the commission found that his dealings with one priest in 1960 were 'aimed at the avoidance of scandal and showed no concern for the welfare of children' (p 11). His successor, Archbishop Ryan, failed to properly investigate complaints, ignored professional advice given in relation to one priest (who was later convicted of a serious sexual assault) and pursued a 'deliberate policy to ensure that knowledge of the problems was as restricted as possible' (p 11). Archbishop McNamara, who was appointed Archbishop of Dublin in 1984, was found to have restored priestly faculties to one cleric despite his having pleaded guilty to charges of child sexual abuse in 1983 and despite the fact that there were suspicions about him in relation to numerous other children. In the case of Archbishop Connell, the commission's findings are mixed. While the commission recognises that he put in place the current structures and procedures, it also notes that he was slow to recognise the seriousness of the situation when he took over in 1988. Moreover, in spite of his knowledge of the recidivist nature of abusers,

Cardinal Connell allowed one priest to continue in ministry when the complaint against him became known in 1991 (DJELR, 2009: 12).

A number of auxiliary bishops were also found to have dealt 'badly' with allegations of abuse, particularly Bishops O'Mahony, Kavanagh and Murray (DJELR, 2009: 13). Bishop Murray – whose handling of one case was described as 'inexcusable' – would come under intense media scrutiny following the publication of the commission's findings (DJELR, 2009: 14).

While the findings of the Dublin Commission are in some respects similar to those of the Ferns inquiry (eg, with regards to the relocation of priests and the dubious use of psychiatric assessments) there are notable differences in the conclusions and tenor of the two reports. Unlike its predecessor, the Dublin Commission explicitly accuses church authorities of perpetrating a *cover-up* in order to protect the institution's reputation and assets. In one passage, under the heading 'cover-up', it states that 'complainants were often met with denial, arrogance and cover-up and with incompetence and incomprehension in some cases' (DJELR, 2009: 10). Moreover, the state authorities were found to have 'facilitated the cover up' by not fulfilling their responsibilities to ensure that the law was applied equally to all and by allowing the church institutions 'to be beyond the reach of the normal law enforcement processes' (p 28). The self-serving nature of the church's responses to allegations of abuse are asserted at various points in the Dublin Report – it is noted, for example, that the complainants and their families often 'behaved in a much more Christian and charitable way than the Church authorities did' (p 27). The following passage, in particular, was much cited in the media:

> The Dublin Archdiocese's pre-occupations in dealing with cases of child sexual abuse, at least until the mid 1990s, were the maintenance of secrecy, the avoidance of scandal, the protection of the reputation of the Church, and the preservation of its assets. All other considerations, including the welfare of children and justice for victims, were subordinated to these priorities. The Archdiocese did not implement its own canon law rules and did its best to avoid any application of the law of the State (DJELR, 2009: 4).

Another significant difference between the Ferns and Dublin Reports is that the latter is dismissive of the notion that church authorities were on a 'learning curve' and did not appreciate the extent or seriousness of the problem (DJELR, 2009: 4). The commission notes that allegations of abuse were known to Archbishop McQuaid in the 1950s and 1960s and that Archbishop Ryan later showed a clear understanding of both the recidivist nature of child sexual abuse and its effect on victims (pp 5-6). The authorities in the Archdiocese of Dublin who were dealing with complaints of child sexual abuse were 'all very well educated people' – some of whom had qualifications in canon and civil law – and this, the commission asserts, 'makes their claims of ignorance very difficult to accept' (DJELR, 2009: 5). Moreover, the church's decision to take out insurance to deal with claims of clerical child abuse was viewed by the commission as 'an act proving knowledge of child sexual abuse' that was 'inconsistent with the view that Archdiocesan officials were still "on a learning curve" … or were lacking in an appreciation of the phenomenon of clerical child abuse' (DJELR, 2009: 6). While Bishops Herlihy and Comiskey are represented in the Ferns Report as misguided leaders who got their priorities wrong, those at the centre of the Dublin inquiry are constructed as more Machiavellian figures who appear to have systematically covered up the actions of suspected child abusers in order to safeguard the interests of the church. In this respect, the Dublin Report can be seen to be significantly more scandalous and more damaging to the reputation of the church than its predecessor in Ferns.

Media reporting of the Ferns and Dublin inquiries

The issue of clerical child sexual abuse dominated news coverage in the days following the publication of the Ferns and Dublin reports. In the following pages we will explore how the scandal unfolded, based on an analysis of news coverage in the main broadsheet (*The Irish Times*, *Irish Independent*) and tabloid (*The Irish Sun*, *Irish Daily Mirror*, *Irish Daily Star*) newspapers and in the RTÉ television news. We do not set out to provide an account of *all* media reporting of the inquiries (the representation of state authorities is not included, for example) but rather to present an in-depth qualitative analysis of key themes relating to the church and scandal.

Moral outrage: victims and villains in media reporting of inquiries

One of the defining features of scandal, as outlined earlier in this chapter, is that it involves actions or events that transgress values, norms or moral codes. Despite significant changes to social attitudes over the last few decades, the taboo surrounding child abuse remains firmly in place and has, if anything, grown stronger (Furedi, 2013). This sense of moral outrage around child abuse pervaded much of the media's coverage of the Ferns and Dublin reports, with commentators expressing shock, horror and revulsion at the revelations. Headlines in the *Irish Independent* and the *The Irish Times*, for example, spoke of the 'appalling horror of Ferns abuse', 'horrific abuse over 40 years' and a 'catalogue of cruelty'. The most strident commentary on the 'evils' of clerical child abuse was provided by the tabloids – *The Irish Sun*, the *Irish Daily Mirror* and the *Irish Daily Star*. In these publications, clerics accused of abusing children were often represented as animals (eg, 'beasts') or some other nonhuman, malevolent beings (eg, 'monsters') who 'prey' on defenceless children and who should be 'hunted down' (*The Irish Sun* 27 November 2009). A range of pejorative terms (vile, depraved, perverted, sick, twisted, paedo) are deployed to convey a sense of outrage and revulsion, and the idea that child abusers are different from the rest of humanity, the 'other' living in our midst who must be duly cast out. Certain priests – most notably Fr Sean Fortune – are singled out for particular vilification. The following is a typical example of tabloid reporting on the Fortune case:

20st beast's reign of evil knew no limits

Depraved Father Sean Fortune was the most notorious child abuser in the Ferns diocese, this week's shocking report reveals. The 20st beast began raping and assaulting children before he was ordained – but he was still allowed to become a priest. He continued his campaign of terror north and south of the border for 20 years …The vile pervert was just 23 and training to be a priest when the first complaint against him was made.[4]

In reporting clerical child abuse, the newspapers – particularly the tabloids – would also draw on another set of references, namely the language and imagery of the Christian tradition itself (albeit in its more punitive and moralising forms) with references to 'evil', 'sin', 'devils' and 'hell'. Newspaper headlines following the publication of the Ferns Report labelled child abusers as 'The Devil's Disciples'[5];

[4]   *The Irish Sun* 27 October 2005.
[5]   *Irish Daily Star* 26 October 2005.

'Guilty Sinners'[6] and 'Devils of the Church'[7]. Ferns itself is described as 'the most evil diocese in the world',[8] while the inquiry report is compared to a 'Horror from [the] book of revelations'.[9] The double standards of the offending priests is summed up in phrases such as 'the men of God who did Satan's work'.[10] Similar headlines appeared again just over four years later in the tabloid's coverage of the Dublin Report, during which abusers were described as 'Servants of Satan', 'Devil's Disciples',[11] 'the Devil's Servants'[12] and 'sinners'.[13] Hell awaited these wrong-doers, according to editorials and articles in these papers:

> ...for those who escaped justice in this life, remember this – in the next life you will burn in HELL for all eternity. (*The Irish Sun*, 27 November, 2009)

> The Catholic Church preaches that there is a hell where the wicked go and if that is true it's inhabited by priests and bishops and even archbishops (*Irish Daily Mirror*, 27 November 2009).

> It's enough to make you pray that there is a hell – with a particularly hot spot for those priests who abused children and those who let it happen over and over again. (*Irish Daily Star*, 1 December 2009)[14]

In similarly strident mode, the front page of the *Irish Daily Star* features the heading 'CRUCIFY THEM' – a reference in this case to the Justice Minister's plans to (in the words of the *Irish Daily Star*) 'bring pervert priests to justice'.[15] Tabloid headlines such as this are indicative of the changing position of church and media: it is the latter that now

---

[6]   *The Irish Sun* 28 October 2005.

[7]   *Irish Daily Mirror* 26 October 2005 (and subsequent days).

[8]   *The Irish Sun* 26 October 2005.

[9]   *Irish Daily Star* 26 October 2005.

[10]   *Irish Daily Mirror* 26 October 2005.

[11]   *The Irish Sun* 27 November 2009.

[12]   *Irish Daily Star* 27 November 2009.

[13]   *Irish Daily Star* 30 November 2009.

[14]   *Irish Daily Star* 1 December 2009 'Murray defender Willie Walsh did not even read child sex abuse report'.

[15]   *Irish Daily Star* 27 November 2009 'Crucify them: now minister says it's time for justice'.

stands in judgement, as the moral arbiter with the right to condemn and cast-out wrong-doers. In their reporting, *The Irish Sun*, the *Irish Daily Star* and the *Irish Daily Mirror*, deliver the tabloid equivalent of a 'hell-fire and brimstone' sermon on the evils of child abuse, and the punishments that face perpetrators, either in this life or the next. While the broadsheets generally avoided demonising abusers, the *Irish Independent* occasionally strayed into this territory with references to 'paedophile wolves in clerical clothing',[16] 'pervert priests',[17] 'depraved animals'[18] and 'evil young paedophile priests'.[19]

Juxtaposed with this image of abusers as evil monsters/devils is that of the child victims of abuse who are routinely described in terms of their vulnerability, innocence and damaged lives. The notion of 'innocence' has become central to contemporary constructions of childhood in western societies (Furedi, 2013), and it is therefore not surprising that the theme of lost innocence should feature so prominently across all media coverage (including tabloids and broadsheets) and in statements made by politicians, senior clergy, victim support groups and other key stakeholders. In the press, childhood innocence is described in terms of something precious that has been 'violated', 'stolen', 'damaged' or 'destroyed'. The following is a typical example:

> The personal stories of abuse [in the Ferns Report] are harrowing. Each tale of horror is unique but all tell the same story: how priests used their power and position in society to rob children of their most precious gift – their innocence.[20]

In the Dáil debate that followed the publication of the Dublin Report, politicians spoke of 'the destruction of the innocence and lives of vulnerable children'; 'assaults on the innocence of children'; and 'the groping hands of predators on the innocence of young children'. Similarly, Archbishop Martin, in his public response to the report,

---

[16] *Irish Independent* 28 November 2009 'The long black shadow of John Charles McQuaid'.

[17] *Irish Independent* 27 November 2009 'Long line of leaders who failed to act'.

[18] *Irish Independent* 26 October 2005 'Tea and sympathy in towns and hamlets without prince'.

[19] *Irish Independent* 1 December 2009 'Our mob law cowardice is to blame for legacy of abuse'.

[20] *Irish Daily Mirror* 28 October 2005 'We must listen to our children'.

apologised to survivors of abuse for 'the theft of childhood' and 'the damage done to their innocence'.[21]

Catholic iconography was also used to evoke the suffering of abuse victims. Images of Christ on the cross appeared as a backdrop in news features on child abuse, thereby linking the suffering of Christ to that of the children.[22] There were allusions to the special position of the child within the Christian tradition (eg, statues and images of children, including the infant Jesus with his mother) that underlined the duplicity and betrayal of trust perpetrated by clerical abusers and those who shielded them.[23] In one picture, a child is shown hunched as the foot of the cross, combining the imagery of childhood suffering and divine martyrdom.[24] The media's use of images of the crucifixion could also be seen as symbolising the notion of sacrifice – children were sacrificed to protect the church's reputation and position. This was to be an important theme in the media's representation of the church's 'cover-up' of abuse. While the abuse of children by priests is the source of moral outrage, some of the most outspoken media criticism was directed at their superiors who are accused of allowing the abuse to continue.

The 'cover-up' of clerical child abuse

Cover-ups can sometimes be as scandalous as the original events themselves (Thompson, 1997). This was certainly the case with media reporting of the clerical child abuse inquiries in Ireland where much of the coverage was focused on the handling of complaints and allegations of abuse by the church hierarchy. In the case of Ferns, the nuance and measured tone of the report itself is often lost in press reporting. Even though the Ferns Report never explicitly accused Bishops Herlihy and Comiskey of having perpetrated a deliberate cover-up of abuse, this assertion is made in a number of newspaper articles. According to a front-page *Irish Independent* article, for example, 'church leaders repeatedly lied and covered up', turning the diocese of Ferns into 'a haven for priests intent on abusing children'.[25] Their actions are

---

[21] Cited in *The Irish Times* 27 November 2009 'No words of apology will ever be sufficient, says archbishop'.

[22] See, for example, *The Irish Sun* 28 November 2009; *Irish Independent* 26 October 2005; *The Irish Times* 29 October 2005.

[23] See, for example, *The Irish Times* 28/29 November 2009.

[24] *Irish Daily Mirror* 23 November 2009.

[25] *Irish Independent* 26 October 2005 'The terrible truth'.

located in the wider context of 'the cover-ups and the determination of dioceses across the world to resist exposure'.[26] In another *Irish Independent* article, Conor Cruise O'Brien, a long-standing critic of the Catholic Church, asserts that 'both Rome and the Irish bishops have been systematically and habitually covering up the abuse for many years'.[27] Similarly, Colm O'Gorman, then director of the victim support group One in Four, refers in an article in the *Irish Daily Star* to 'cover up after cover up in the name of protecting a church that was supposed to be about truth'.[28] In other articles Herlihy and Comiskey's actions are described with little or no explanation so that a cover-up may be implied, if not explicitly stated. Nonetheless, the bishops at the centre of the Ferns scandal fared better than their counterparts in Dublin. While Bishop Comiskey was often presented in the press as a rather weak, ineffectual leader who was overwhelmed by the scale of the abuse problem,[29] the archbishops in the diocese of Dublin are constructed as calculating figures who put the reputation of the church and its assets above the protection of children.

The media was damning in its critique of the church hierarchy in Dublin. Quoting extensively from the Dublin Report itself, the press highlighted the fact that what happened in the archdiocese was in no way due to oversight or ignorance but was the result of a carefully planned, systematic cover-up, perpetrated by those at the highest levels of the Catholic Church in Ireland. In the *Irish Independent*, for example, the church hierarchy is accused of presiding over 'a systematic calculated perversion of power' and of 'creating the closed, secret environment' in which child abuse could thrive.[30] Writing in *The Irish Times*, Mary Raftery (producer of the documentary *Cardinal Secrets*) compared the church leadership with the *Cosa Nostra* (mafia), asserting that 'the organised, premeditated pattern of secrecy and concealment of crime is worthy of the world's most notorious criminal fraternity'.[31] The repeated use of terms such as 'conspiracy', 'covered

26 *Irish Independent* 26 October 2005 'Horror upon horror'.
27 *Irish Independent* 29 October 2005 'I must hope that we are now witnessing the advent of a post-Roman society ...'
28 *Irish Daily Star* 26 October 2005 'It must never happen again'.
29 See, for example, *The Irish Sun* 27 October 2005 'Cowards in frocks'; *The Irish Star* 27 October 2005 'Stop hiding you drunken bishop'; *The Irish Star* 29 October 2005 'Bishop runs for cover'.
30 *Irish Independent* 27 November 2009 'A cruel conspiracy'; *Irish Independent* 3 December 2009 'Moral compass must point towards justice for victims'.
31 *The Irish Times* 27 November 2009 'Bishops lied and covered-up'.

up' 'colluded', 'lied', and 'connivance' in press headlines conveyed a sense of the underhandedness of the hierarchy's response to allegations of abuse. Moreover, the Dublin Report itself provided some choice quotes, which needed little embellishment on the part of the media to create a sense of moral outrage. The commission's assertion that the Archdiocese was preoccupied with 'the maintenance of secrecy, the avoidance of scandal, the protection of the reputation of the church, and the preservation of assets' was reported extensively in the media, as were other critical comments on the handling of individual cases (eg, 'inexcusable', 'catastrophic', 'disastrous', 'unacceptable' 'haphazard and desultory').[32]

Newspaper editorials on the day after the publication of the Dublin Report were particularly damning in their criticism of the former archbishops and auxiliary bishops, and their role in the cover-up, as the following extract illustrates:

> 'Repulsive' is a word that comes to mind in considering the response by former Dublin bishops and archbishops to clerical child abuse. As charted by the Murphy commission, the complaints of parents and their children were ignored and other families placed in immediate danger as prelates from John Charles McQuaid onwards suppressed scandals and took refuge in canon law to protect offenders at the expense of innocent children. The vast majority of uninvolved priests turned a blind eye. (*The Irish Times* 27 November 2009)

The editorial in *The Irish Sun* (27 November 2009) put the issue in even starker terms:

> The Catholic Church tolerated the rape of countless children by paedophile priests because its image was more important than the protection of innocence. This is the damning finding of the report by the Dublin Archdiocese Commission of Investigation. It found that high-ranking clergy, including former Archbishop Desmond Connell, were involved in a deliberate cover-up of abuse because they wanted to avoid a scandal. They repeatedly ignored

---

[32] See, for example, *The Irish Times* 27 November 2009 'Abuse continued for years due to protection of priests'; and *The Irish Times* 1 December 2009 'Bishop failed to protect children'.

abuse claims and moved pervert priests around dioceses. The Catholic Church in Ireland cared nothing for the welfare of children, the commission noted – and the actions of its leaders allowed priests to **CONTINUE** to abuse kids with impunity. What a scandal. What a horror. What an injustice to the weakest and most vulnerable in our society – our children.

As these extracts suggest, one of the most damaging aspects of the cover-up of child abuse was that it was seen as *allowing* the abuse to continue. From this point of view, some commentators – in the media and survivor groups – would argue that those responsible for the cover-up were as culpable as the abusers themselves.[33] In media reporting there are repeated references to children being 'sacrificed',[34] a term with particular significance within the Christian faith, which holds that Jesus Christ sacrificed his life for mankind's salvation. The children in the clerical abuse cases were sacrificed (by the church itself) for more self-serving reasons. Thus Mary Raftery, writing in *The Irish Times* (27 November 2009), asserts that 'Children were blithely sacrificed to protect priests, the institution and its assets'.[35] Similarly the *Irish Independent* claims that 'Catholic children were crushed because Catholic archbishops offered them as sacrifices to the false god called protecting the Dublin Archdiocese's reputation'.[36] Elsewhere there are references to abusers being given 'licence' to continue, to 'a systematic collaboration *with* abusers'[37] [authors' emphasis] and of abuse being 'facilitated and perpetuated' by the actions of senior clerics.[38] According to John Kelly, of Survivors of Child Abuse, 'Not only did they know, they could have prevented hundreds of other children being abused. That's the crime'.[39] Abuse victims themselves provided moving

[33] See, for example, *Irish Independent* 27 November 2009 'Survivors: prosecute those who covered up'.

[34] See, for example, *Irish Daily Mirror* 27 November 2009 'Prosecute them'.

[35] Raftery also claims that some bishops, 'Pontius Pilate-like, washed their hands' while others actively protected the criminals in their midst: *The Irish Times* 27 November 2009 'Bishops lied and covered up'.

[36] *Irish Independent* 27 November 2009 'New light on a dark history reveals church's false gods'.

[37] *The Irish Times* 28 November 2009 'Church relationship with Irish society has itself been abusive'.

[38] *Irish Daily Mirror* 4 December 2009 'Church still to convince disillusioned'.

[39] *Irish Independent* 27 November 2009 'Prosecute those who covered up abuse'.

accounts of how other children might have been spared if allegations of abuse had been acted on.[40] Writing in the *Irish Independent*, Andrew Madden recalls what happened after his abuse (by Fr Ivan Payne) was reported to the Archdiocese:

> Fr Payne was moved to his new parish in Sutton. The Murphy report finds that he abused at least seven more boys after that time, though a total of 31 people made allegations against him. This, for me, is the worst single fact that has come out of this report. Whether they manipulated information and medical professionals to get favourable medical reports or wrote letters of reference for paedophile priests moving to other dioceses, they are absolutely responsible for the abuse of every child after that.[41]

Following the publication of the Dublin Report, there were fulsome apologies from all quarters of the church for what had happened and promises to change. However, these apologies were met with a degree of cynicism in the media and by survivors themselves. Writing in the *Irish Independent*, Bruce Arnold was dismissive of the 'predictable platitudes and statements of horror' (28 November 2009), while Andrew Madden accused the church of orchestrating a 'damage limitation exercise'[42] (a view that was reiterated in *The Irish Times*).[43] It was argued that the church had only publicly acknowledged and addressed the issue of abuse when forced to do so, and this cast doubt over the hierarchy's protestations of shock and sorrow at the revelations of the Dublin Report.[44] In a damning indictment, one abuse victim, Marie Collins, told the commission that within the institutional church there had been 'no change of heart only a change of strategy' (DJELR, 2009: 647), a claim that was widely reported in the media and raised in a Dáil debate on the report.[45] Particular significance was attached

[40] See, for example, *Irish Independent* 27 November 2009 '"All I got was lies, I was bullied and threatened"'.

[41] *Irish Independent* 28 November 2009 '"My abuser then went on to molest at least seven other boys."'

[42] *Irish Independent* 2 December 2009 'Martin demands answers to satisfy Sunday congregations'.

[43] *The Irish Times* 1 December 2009 'The bishops close ranks'.

[44] See, for example, *Irish Daily Mirror* 2 December 2009: Mervyn Rundle's comments in 'Abuse Report – a victim speaks'.

[45] Dáil debates, 3 December 2009.

to the fact that only one bishop had unequivocally admitted to the Dublin Commission that he had dealt badly with allegations. While senior clerics subsequently apologised for their failings, they were not willing to admit that they had deliberately *covered up* abuse to protect the church. The bishops had still not accepted their own culpability, according to Mary Raftery, and had 'focused on the crimes of the abusing priests while conveniently ignoring their own heartless and cynical betrayal of children through their cover-up'.[46] Survivor groups and media commentators argued that words of sorrow and regret were no longer sufficient – the bishops implicated in the cover-up had to be made accountable for their behaviour. It was at this point that the issue of resignations began to take centre stage, and they came to dominate the coverage of the Dublin Report.

Resignations and prosecutions

Following on from major scandals in public life there are usually calls for resignations, dismissals or (where criminal activity is involved) prosecutions. In the case of the child abuse scandals, it was accepted that those accused of abusing children should face the full brunt of the law, regardless of their status. As Justice Minister Ahern so forcefully put it, 'A collar will protect no criminal'.[47] But what of the bishops who had in the past failed to adequately protect children or been complicit in a 'cover-up'? What should happen to them? This question would occupy much of the media coverage following the publication of the Dublin Report. The Ferns case was largely exempted from this debate. By the time the Ferns Report was published, Bishop Comiskey had already resigned as bishop and had by all accounts disappeared from public life. His predecessor, Bishop Herlihy, had died some years earlier and by 2006 the diocese of Ferns was in the seemingly capable hands of Bishop Eamonn Walsh, therefore the issue of resignations did not arise. The situation with regards to the Dublin Report was somewhat different. Although the four archbishops at the centre of the scandal were dead or (in the case of Cardinal Connell) retired from the position of archbishop, several of the former auxiliary bishops were

---

[46] *The Irish Times* 3 December 2009 'Every auxiliary bishop had some knowledge of crimes'; *Irish Mirror* 4 December 2009 'Church still to convince disillusioned', p 10: this article argues that the church's response has been 'woeful' and Murray's continuation as bishop is evidence of this.

[47] His comments were widely reported in the media, see for example *The Irish Independent* 27 November 2009 '"No protection behind a collar" warns Ahern' .

still in active service and occupying senior positions in different parts of the country. In light of the revelations of the Dublin Report, it was argued by survivor support groups and the media that the position of these bishops within the church was no longer tenable and they should either resign or be dismissed by the pope.

In the weeks following the publication of the Dublin Report, Donal Murray (who was by then Bishop of Limerick) found himself at the centre of this controversy around resignations. He was among the former auxiliary bishops who were found by the Dublin Commission to have dealt 'badly' with allegations of child sexual abuse, and his handling of the Fr Naughton case was described as 'inexcusable' – a comment that appeared repeatedly in media coverage of the case. On the day the Dublin Report was published, Bishop Murray issued a statement expressing his 'deepest regret' but also insisting that he had 'never deliberately or knowingly sought to cover up or withhold information'.[48] When asked, the bishop said that he was not planning on resigning his post. However, in the following days and weeks the pressure on Bishop Murray to step aside intensified. Daily reports on the RTÉ news and damaging press headlines helped to keep the issue of resignation firmly in the public eye.[49] While most of these headlines conveyed a sense of mild disapproval or surprise at the bishop's continued tenure ('Prelate in no mood to resign *despite* report revelations'[50] (authors' emphasis); 'Bishop refuses to quit over abuse')[51] some were openly hostile, for example: 'bishop should go now before the Vatican gives him his P45';[52] 'clerics at fault must go'[53] and 'Pray he quits'.[54] Several victims of clerical abuse and their families also called for the bishop's resignation, and their comments were widely reported

---

[48] *The Irish Times* 27 November 2009 'Bishop expresses regret but says he will not resign'.

[49] See, for example, RTÉ Six One News 2 and 3 December 2009. Articles on Murray appeared almost daily in most newspapers, both tabloids and broadsheets.

[50] *The Irish Times* 28 November 2009.

[51] *The Irish Sun* 2 December 2009.

[52] *Irish Independent* 1 December 2009.

[53] *The Irish Sun* 2 December 2009.

[54] *The Irish Sun* 7 December 2009.

on the television news and in the press.[55] Bishop Murray was accused of arrogance, of bringing the church into disrepute and of causing further distress to abuse victims. According to the *Irish Daily Mirror*, he had 'needlessly prolonged the agony for the victims'[56] while *The Irish Sun* accused him of 'continuing to rub their noses in it by refusing to take responsibility for his action'.[57] One of the most stinging critiques of the Bishop's intransigence appeared in the *Irish Independent* on 1 December 2009:

> Most certainly Donal Murray should resign as Bishop of Limerick and respect the state judicial finding of the Murphy commission that his mishandling of the complaints against the notorious paedophile cleric Thomas Naughton was 'inexcusable'. Dublin-born Bishop Murray, a leading academic theologian, finds himself in public disgrace and an embarrassment to his Church.

The controversy surrounding Bishop Murray (and other former auxiliaries) soon extended beyond the bishops themselves to encompass politicians and senior members of the hierarchy who were urged to take a stand on the issue. In an unprecedented move, Enda Kenny, leader of the Fine Gael party, appeared to call for the resignation of those implicated in a cover-up: 'In my view, from the point of personal leadership ... people who were in positions and are still in positions should not continue in those positions'.[58] While Enda Kenny's comments were widely reported and praised in some sections of the press,[59] the then Taoiseach, Brian Cowen, was criticised for not demanding episcopal resignations. According to the *Irish Independent*,

---

[55] RTÉ Six One News 3 December 2009; *Irish Independent* 2 December 2009 'Archbishop turns up heat over abuse'; *Irish Independent* 2 December 2009 'Martin demands answers to satisfy Sunday congregations'; *The Irish Times* 28 November 2009 'Bishop of Limerick urged to resign as victim's family speaks out on abuse'; *The Irish Times* 2 December 2009 'Church engaged in "damage limitation" exercise'; *Irish Daily Mirror* 1 December 2009 'Abuse report: a victim speaks'; *The Irish Sun* 2 December 2009 'Clerical disgrace'.

[56] *Irish Daily Mirror* 4 December 2009 'Church still to convince disillusioned'.

[57] *The Irish Sun* 7 December 2009.

[58] *Irish Independent* 28 November 2009 'Outcry from opposition but no comment from Taoiseach'.

[59] *Irish Independent* 1 December 2009 'Go now, bishop, before the Vatican sends you a P45'.

he was still living in the deferential era of the 1950s, while the *Irish Daily Mirror* claimed that the government had lost its 'moral compass'.[60] Outside of the political arena, Archbishop Diarmuid Martin was also criticised for not demanding resignations, something that he consistently refused to do on the grounds that it was up to their individual conscience.[61]

Murray responded to the growing controversy by declaring that he would consult with parishioners and priests in the Diocese of Limerick and be guided by them as to whether he should continue as their bishop.[62] Within days, a group of 80 were reported to have expressed their support.[63] However, media coverage continued to be critical. Writing in the *Irish Independent*, John Cooney was particularly scathing of Murray's actions and the lack of genuinely representative channels within the Catholic Church: 'Bishop Murray knows that the channels for absolving him will be cardboard box entries such as deaneries, priest councils and pastoral assemblies, all reflective of the voice of their diocesan master rather than the broad sweep of public opinion that is scandalised by his clinging to office'.[64] Similarly, a prominent Church of Ireland figure was reported as saying 'that a bishop should not cling to office on the basis of some opinion poll, some "X-Factor" vote, some popularity contest among his clergy and their parishioners'.[65] One in Four's Andrew Madden publicly queried Murray's decision to fall back on the support of his parishioners, and even Archbishop Diarmuid Martin expressed dissatisfaction with how those bishops named in the Dublin Report had responded to the allegations against them. In what might be seen as a thinly veiled criticism of Murray, the archbishop contended that those implicated

---

[60] *Irish Independent* 1 December 2009 'Go now, bishop, before the Vatican sends you a P45'; The editorial of the *Irish Daily Mirror* 30 November 2009.

[61] Writing in the *Irish Independent*, for example, John Cooney claimed that Archbishop Martin's 'semi-criticism, semi-defence of Cardinal Connell – and his refusal to speak his own mind as to the resignation of Bishop Murray is putting at risk the public's appreciation of his colossal work of disclosure to the commission'; *Irish Independent* 30 November 2009 'Cardinal Connell must come clean without 'reservation'.

[62] *Irish Independent* 30 November 2009 'Embattled cleric places his fate in hands of the faithful'.

[63] *The Irish Times* 2 December 2009 'More consultation on future of Bishop Murray'.

[64] *Irish Independent* 1 December 2009 'Go now bishop, before the Vatican sends you your P45'.

[65] *The Irish Times* 3 December 2009 'Bishop should not "cling to office"'.

in the Murphy Report were answerable to the people of Dublin, not just those of their current diocese.[66]

As the pressure for a resignation increased, a few voices cautioned against making Bishop Murray into a scapegoat, including the family of one abuse victim.[67] The most high-profile intervention came from Bishop Willie Walsh who, in an interview on RTÉ Radio 1's *Morning Ireland*, claimed that there had been "a gross misreading" of the Dublin Report in relation to Bishop Murray, and cautioned against seeking "a head on a plate". His comments were widely derided in the national press (particularly in light of the fact that Bishop Walsh was reported to have not actually read the report) and proved to be largely counterproductive.[68] By providing a new and controversial angle to the story, Bishop Walsh had inadvertently helped to keep the issue of Bishop Murray's resignation in the headlines. Moreover the fact that Walsh was a well-respected bishop appeared to make his intervention all the more damaging. Writing in *The Irish Times*, Fintan O'Toole asked 'if Willie Walsh doesn't get it, what hope is there for the rest of the institutional church?'.[69] The *Irish Daily Mirror* editorial described Bishop Walsh's defence of Bishop Murray as 'utterly outrageous' and suggested that those who supported him should themselves resign,[70] a view that was shared by the *Irish Daily Star*.[71] In the face of vehement press criticism, Bishop Walsh apologised for his comments. The

[66] *The Irish Times* 2 December 2009 'Archbishop Martin not satisfied with response of some bishops'; *Irish Independent* 2 December 2009 'Martin demands answers to "satisfy Sunday congregations"'; *Irish Daily Mirror* 3 December 2009 'Arch-enemies'.

[67] *The Irish Times* 3 December 2009 'Story being used "to get at" Bishop Murray'; *The Irish Times* 1 December 2009 '"Scapegoating" of bishop will not help healing process'.

[68] *The Irish Times* 2 December 2009 'Avoiding resignations is same as evading accountability – FG'; *The Irish Times* 1 December 2009 'Bishop failed to protect children'; *The Irish Times* 1 December 2009 'An abysmal abdication of responsibility'; *The Irish Times* 1 December 2009 'The bishops close ranks'. *The Irish Star* 1 December 2009 'They can't be saved'.

[69] *The Irish Times* 1 December 2009 'An abysmal abdication of responsibility'. On the same day, *The Irish Times* editorial accused the bishops of closing ranks: see *The Irish Times* 1 December 2009 'The bishops close ranks'.

[70] *Irish Daily Mirror* 1 December 2009 'Bishop Walsh out of touch with people' (editorial).

[71] *The Irish Star* 1 December 2009 'Murray defender Willie Walsh did not even read child sex abuse report'.

incident is perhaps indicative of how difficult it was – particularly for members of the church hierarchy – to challenge the media consensus on the need for resignations.

While the focus in the *Irish Independent* and *The Irish Times* was largely on the issue of resignations, the tabloids also demanded tougher action against those accused of covering up abuse, including criminal investigations and prosecutions. According to the *Irish Daily Mirror*, those who 'shielded vile perverts' from prosecution should themselves be 'brought to justice'.[72] The editorial in *The Irish Sun* was even more strident, arguing that anyone who covered up abuse should 'be dragged before a judge and face the punishment they deserve'.[73] Gardaí investigations into the handling of child abuse allegations were reported with enthusiasm in all three tabloid newspapers under headings such as: 'Top Cop to Nail Cover-up Bishops'; 'Top Cop: Justice will be served'; and 'Nowhere to hide: all involved in cover up will face charges'. The most powerful case for prosecutions was presented by the victim support group One in Four, which argued that those implicated in a cover-up were as culpable as the abusers themselves.[74]

Despite the tabloids' optimism about 'top cops' nailing errant bishops, other reports indicated that the chances of prosecution were unlikely under existing laws. Perhaps in consequence, the pressure on Bishop Murray to quit appeared to intensify during the first week of December 2009, with articles appearing on a near daily basis in both the broadsheets and tabloids. The saga was finally brought to a close when Bishop Murray announced his resignation, though the pressure on other former auxiliaries continued. While survivors of clerical abuse welcomed Bishop Murray's departure, they also called on other bishops named in the Dublin Report to follow his example.[75]

Clearly, the issue of Donal Murray's resignation had a significance above and beyond the bishop himself – it was presented by the media as a test of whether the church hierarchy had truly accepted the findings of the Dublin Report and wanted to make recompense. The fact that the Bishop of Limerick had remained in his position for more than two weeks following the publication of the report was taken as further evidence that the church was 'out of touch' and only took action when forced to do so under public scrutiny. Moreover, the issue of

---

[72]   *Irish Daily Mirror* 28 November 2009 'A shameful past never to be forgotten'.

[73]   *The Irish Sun* 27 November 2009 'Hell's too good for paedo priests'.

[74]   *The Irish Times* 27 November 2009 'Call for prosecutions of those behind cover-ups'.

[75]   See RTÉ Six One News 17 December 2009.

resignations and prosecutions of those in high office may have had an added significance at this particular point in Irish history. Over the previous 12 months, powerful interest groups – including bankers, property developers and politicians – had been accused of corruption and of causing the financial crisis that unfolded in Ireland from 2008 onwards. There was public anger that many of those who were seen to be at fault had not been made accountable for their actions. Given the political and economic climate at that time, Bishop Murray's reluctance to quit despite his 'inexcusable' behaviour (and the church's seeming inability or unwillingness to force him out) became all the more controversial and unacceptable.

Role of the Papal Nuncio

The further up the hierarchy an institutional scandal goes, the more scandalous it becomes. The controversy surrounding the child abuse inquires in Ferns and Dublin had, as we have seen, extended from the lower ranks of the clergy to encompass members of the hierarchy, including bishops and archbishops. But it did not stop there. Following the publication of the two inquiry reports, the media spotlight also fell on the Papal Nuncio and the Vatican. In their coverage of the Ferns inquiry, both the *Irish Daily Star* and *The Irish Times* published articles by Colm O'Gorman that were critical of the Vatican. Moreover, the *Irish Daily Star*, in an outspoken editorial on 26 October 2005, criticised the Ferns inquiry for not investigating the role of the Vatican in dealing with allegations of abuse and even casts aspersions on Pope Benedict:

> And by this omission, it begs the obvious questions – did the Papal Nuncio know, was he informed, and as a result, was the Vatican aware of the abuse and what was or was not being done about it? Indeed, the ultimate question must be – did the Vatican orchestrate the entire response to these allegations of abuse when they came to light? Why were these questions not asked? Why did Judge Frank Murphy not pose these questions to the office of the current Papal Nuncio – or if he did, did he get an answer and what was it? For example, did the current Pontiff, Pope Benedict XVI known of what was going on when he was Cardinal Ratzinger? We must know the answers to these vital questions. Because as it stands on receiving this report we still only know half the story.

Four years later, there was more extensive media coverage of the Dublin Commission's dealings with the Papal Nuncio and the Vatican's CDF. As outlined earlier, the commission's requests for information had met with no reply, while the CDF informed the Department of Foreign Affairs that the proper diplomatic channels had not been used to make these requests. The general consensus in the media was that the Papal Nuncio and CDF had been remiss in their dealings with the Murphy commission. It was accepted that the church authorities had, at the very least, shown a lack of respect for the commission's work and a misplaced adherence to diplomatic protocol. In the press, the CDF's behaviour towards the commission was condemned as patronising and 'contemptuous'.[76] The fact that the Vatican initially remained silent on the findings of the Murphy Report added to the controversy: it appeared that church authorities in Rome (and their envoy in Dublin) had effectively washed their hands of the crisis unfolding in Ireland.[77] The most outspoken commentary was provided by *The Irish Times*, which ran a series of damning articles criticising the CDF's intransigence and lack of respect for the commission's work.[78] More controversially, *The Irish Times* suggested that the Vatican chose not to cooperate with the commission because it wanted to protect its already 'tattered image'[79] as well as its financial assets:

> Vatican analysts point out that while the Catholic Church is very centralised when it comes to issues like church appointments, it is contrastingly decentralised when it comes to day-to-day, local church financial administration. Put simply, this means that bishops are appointed in Rome but damages are paid in Dublin. For the nuncio or indeed the CDF to respond directly to the commission might have implied acceptance of a certain Vatican responsibility or indeed culpability with regard to Irish affairs.[80]

In an even more pointed attack, the editorial in *The Irish Times on* 3 December 2009 implicates the Vatican in an international cover-

---

[76] See for example *Irish Daily Star* 30 November 2009 'Sinners must go'.

[77] *Irish Independent* editorial on 30 November 2009.

[78] *The Irish Times* 27 November 2009 'Cult of loyal obedience at heart of lies and cover-up'.

[79] *The Irish Times* 27 November 2009 'A legacy of abuse and cover up'.

[80] *The Irish Times* 27 November 2009 'Holy See keeps its distance from Irish abuse problem'.

up of clerical child abuse ('we know this because the approach to allegations of child abuse was consistent ... around the world') and accuses it of refusing to take responsibility for the consequences of its own actions. The Papal Nuncio's and the CDF's failure to cooperate with the Murphy commission must be seen within this wider context of self-preservation:

> The Vatican does not do things lightly. When it refused to deal with the commission except through diplomatic contacts at the level of one state to another, it was not being precious. It was asserting a claim that is crucial to its efforts to avoid the consequences of its own policies. The insistence on being treated as a state rather than as a church is the key to its claim of sovereign immunity. The context for this claim is a case in the US in which the circuit court of appeals ruled that the Vatican could be sued by victims of an Irish priest. The US supreme court is currently considering whether to hear an appeal from the Vatican, which is hoping to avoid a wave of lawsuits from victims in the US. (Editorial: *The Irish Times* 3 December 2009)

As this extract suggests, the controversy surrounding the Vatican and the Papal Nuncio had clear diplomatic and political implications. While the Taoiseach could legitimately claim that the government had no grounds to demand the resignation of bishops, it could take action to register its displeasure with the actions of another state (ie, the Vatican). There were calls – reported primarily in *The Irish Times* – for the Papal Nuncio to be expelled or, at the very least, summoned to the Department of Foreign Affairs to provide an explanation.[81] However, Brian Cowen decided on a different course of action. During a Dáil debate (1 December 2009) on the Dublin Report, he appeared to defend the Vatican's dealings with the commission and even sought to dispel any 'impression [that] the Holy See was refusing to co-operate with the commission'. Under questioning from the opposition leader, Enda Kenny, the Taoiseach contended that the Vatican's response had been 'consistent with international law' and that the information

---

[81] *The Irish Times* 30 November 2009 'Call for expulsion of papal nuncio' and 'Call to extend commission's inquiry to every diocese'; *The Irish Times* 1 December 2009 'Department rejects call to expel nuncio'; *The Irish Times* 2 December 2009 'Call for expulsion of papal nuncio' and 'Meeting urged'.

requested by the commission might well have been forthcoming, had the correct diplomatic channels been used:

> "It is not unreasonable to assume the Holy See was open to responding to a further approach through formal diplomatic channels. Neither is it unreasonable to assume that when the papal nuncio received correspondence from the commission in February 2007 and earlier this year, both the present and previous papal nuncios believed the matter was more properly addressed by the diplomatic note … It is regrettable that the failure to acknowledge either letter has given rise to the impression the Holy See was refusing to co-operate with the commission." (Dáil debate: 1 December 2009)

In this extract, Cowen seems to imply that the impasse between the commission and the Vatican was the result of some unfortunate misunderstanding. Continuing in this placatory approach, the Taoiseach asserts that while the desired outcome might not have been achieved, neither party was at fault: "The commission and the Holy See, it appears, acted in good faith in this matter, even if the best outcome was not achieved".

However, Cowen's intervention on behalf of the church authorities proved to be entirely counterproductive (much like Bishop Willie Walsh's defence of Bishop Murray) and only served to further undermine his own already poor public image. In the *Irish Independent*, the Taoiseach was mocked for his apparent inability to take decisive action against men 'whose actions wrought various degrees of suffering on the citizenry', including bankers, financiers, developers, speculators and clerics' (2 December 2009). The *Irish Daily Star* accused Cowen of 'acting as an apologist for the Vatican' and urged him to show greater leadership: 'Mr Cowen must get up off his bended knee in front of the Church and assert his authority as the leader of a sovereign republic'.[82] Again, some of the fiercest criticism came from *The Irish Times*. In a strongly worded article, religious affairs correspondent Patsy McGarry expressed astonishment at Cowen's 'sanguine' attitude towards an institution 'whose officer class oversaw the mass cover-up of rape and abuse of children in this State'. Cowen had, by his defence of the Vatican, shown himself to be 'second an Irishman and first a

---

[82] *Irish Daily Star* 2 December 2009 'Stop bowing to Vatican'.

Catholic'.[83] On the same day, the editorial in *The Irish Times* poured scorn on the Taoiseach's 'painfully deferential statement', arguing that 'this submissiveness is entirely inappropriate to the leader of a republic, some of whose most vulnerable citizens have been grievously harmed by the policies and practices of the Holy See'[84].

There was general agreement in the media that the Papal Nuncio and CDF were at fault for not releasing information to the commission. Only one article, published in the *Irish Independent*, appeared to suggest that the Minister for Foreign Affairs and the Dublin Commission itself might share at least some of the blame for the impasse because they had not sought a diplomatic solution.[85] Moreover, the author expresses surprise at the commission's refusal to channel its requests through a department of state: 'This raises the question as to whether the commission was so protective of its independent status that it did not entrust its communications to the Government that appointed it!' He concludes that the controversy was the result of 'a diplomatic cock-up rather than conspiracy by the Government, the commission, the Vatican and the nunciature'.

The controversy over the Vatican's role in relation to the handling of child abuse allegations would resurface in 2010, with the publication of the Cloyne Report (discussed later in this chapter).

Scandal inflation: media speculation on the extent of abuse

The media's coverage of both the Ferns and Dublin inquiries was characterised by what Butler and Drakeford (2003) describe as 'scandal inflation', a process whereby the media keeps a story alive by finding new 'angles' and 'unveiling even more bizarre or aberrant behaviours'. As we have seen earlier in this chapter, the issue of resignations and prosecutions provided a new and fruitful 'angle' to the reporting on

---

[83] McGarry is here adopting a phrase first used by former Taoiseach John Costello, who in 1951 declared "I am an Irishman second, I am a Catholic first, and I accept without qualification in all respects the teaching of the hierarchy and the church to which I belong." This statement was made following the government's decision to drop the 'mother and child scheme', which the Catholic Church, led by Archbishop McQuaid, had strongly opposed. *The Irish Times* 3 December 2009 'Cowen shows he is "second an Irishman, first a Catholic"'.

[84] *The Irish Times* Editorial 3 December 2009.

[85] *Irish Independent* 2 December 2009 'Unholy row with the Papal Nuncio is an affront to us all'.

the Dublin inquiry. In the Ferns case, media coverage quickly moved beyond the findings of the report itself to encompass a number of other potentially damaging allegations concerning clerical abuse in other parts of the country. Stories began to appear in the press on a daily basis of priests who were under investigation or had been convicted for child abuse or (in one case) of accessing child pornography.[86] One of the most high profile media exposés concerned a priest who was under investigation for rape (alleged to have taken place 20 years earlier) and was still in active ministry. [87] While the alleged attack was carried out on an *adult*, it was nonetheless reported in the context of the Ferns inquiry into child abuse, thereby tapping into the moral outrage surrounding that case. In a clear indication of the media's growing power, the Archbishop of Tuam immediately asked the priest in question to step aside in order to protect the reputation of other priests in the parish who had come under suspicion in the wake of the *Irish Independent*'s revelations.

Following the publication of the Ferns Report there was also considerable *speculation* as to the scale of clerical abuse in the rest of the country. Patsy McGarry, the Religious Correspondent for *The Irish Times*, pointed out that no one would have believed the scale of abuse in Ferns before the inquiry was set up, adding:

> 'You have to wonder just what has been going on in the other 25 Catholic dioceses in Ireland where the clerical child sex abuse issue is concerned? What would a State inquiry unearth if it was to investigate?'[88]

---

[86] See, for example, *The Irish Sun* 28 October 2005 'Child sex shame of Omagh Bomb Priest'; *Irish Daily Star* 1 November 2005 'Priest leaves his post over abuse allegations'; *Irish Daily Star* 2 November 'Priest quits in abuse inquiry'; *Star Sunday* 30 October 2005 'Gardai probe Dublin priest'; *Irish Daily Mirror* 28 October 2005 '1 yr jail for child porn surfing'; *The Irish Times* 31 October 2005 'Priest in Elphin steps aside pending inquiry' (the nature of the allegations in this case is not specified).

[87] *Irish Independent* 27 October 2005 'Rape probe priest is still practicing'. The *Irish Independent* provided extensive coverage of the story, arguing that the church was taking a 'protective attitude' towards the priest.

[88] *The Irish Times* 26 October 2005 'Report begins Herculean task of exorcising child sex abuse'.

In a similar vein, Maurice Hayes noted that 'the trouble is wider than Ferns ... who knows what lurks under stones elsewhere'.[89] There were already dire predictions of what the Dublin Commission was likely to find. Speaking in the Dáil, the leader of the Labour party declared that 'Some of the allegations in the Dublin diocese are if possible more horrific and ghoulish than the allegations made in Ferns'.[90] It was taken as given that the Ferns case was not unique and that it was in all probability indicative of what was happening elsewhere in the country.[91]

In the face of mounting speculation, several bishops made public the details on the numbers of priests who had been accused of child sexual abuse within their dioceses and the compensation payments made to victims. While these revelations may have been made with the hope of 'clearing the air', they almost certainly contributed to a growing moral panic about clerical abuse. Articles appeared in the press reporting both the national picture (eg, 'clerical child sex abuse: diocese by diocese';[92] '241 clerics accused of sex abuse over four decades'),[93] as well as more detailed accounts on individual dioceses where the numbers of accused priests were found to be higher.[94] The archdiocese of Tuam again found itself at the centre of unwanted media scrutiny when it was revealed that 27 priests had had allegations made against them.[95] The story was reported in sensationalist terms in the *Irish Independent* where a front page headline on 31 October 2005 declared that there was a 'New Abuse Timebomb'. The article goes on to assert that the diocese was facing a scandal 'even worse than Ferns':

[89] *Irish Independent* 27 October 2005 'Church's authority damaged by failure to confront evil abusers'.

[90] Cited in: *The Irish Times* 26 October 2005 'Dublin abuse inquiry "will go ahead"'.

[91] See, for example, Colm O'Gorman writing in *The Irish Times* 26 October 2005 'A diocese which ignored horrific abuse over 40 years'.

[92] *The Irish Times* 29 October 2005 'Clerical child sex abuse: diocese by diocese'.

[93] *Irish Independent* 28 October 2005 '241 clerics accused of sex abuse over four decades'.

[94] See, for example, *Irish Independent* 28 October 2005 'Claims brought against 26 priests in one diocese, but only one convicted'; *The Irish Sun* 28 October 2005 'Limerick's 10 abuse claims'; *Irish Sunday Mirror* 28 October 2005 '10 priests accused of sex abuse'; *Irish Sunday Mirror* 29 October 2005 'Diocese's €250k bill for abuse'.

[95] *The Irish Times* 31 October 2005 'Allegations against 27 priests in Tuam'; *The Irish Times* 1 November 2005 'More details emerge of sexual abuse cases involving priests'.

> A child abuse timebomb is ticking away in another Catholic archdiocese. Allegations have been recorded against a shocking total of 27 priests who have served in the archdiocese of Tuam. The Ferns scandal involved 21 priests. Astonishingly, eight clerics have left the priesthood in Tuam after a 'reasonable suspicion' that child abuse had taken place was established.' Three clerics have already been convicted of horrific child sex abuse charges. Last night Colm O'Gorman, Director of One in Four, said the claims in Tuam were 'on a par' with Ferns, given the similarity of the population of each diocese.

With stories like this, the Catholic Church appeared to be drowning under what one church source later referred to as a 'tsunami' of clerical child abuse (McGrady, cited in the Dublin Report [DJELR, 2009: 3]). Moreover, newspapers speculated that the actual incidence of abuse was likely to be much higher than had been revealed. There were widespread calls – particularly from support groups and media commentators – for further inquiries of one form or other. Taken together, the emergence of new abuse cases, the release of figures relating to previous cases of abuse, and the calls for further investigations helped to escalate the crisis surrounding the Catholic Church and clerical abuse, following the Ferns Report.

Clerical child abuse in social context

Butler and Drakeford (2003) have argued that scandals concerning the institutional abuse of children often ignore the wider social context in which the abuse was allowed to take place. The institution and its residents are seen as separate from the wider community and issues such as the powerlessness of all children are overlooked. Much the same might be said of the media's representation of clerical child abuse in the wake of the Ferns and Dublin reports. The Catholic Church, as we have seen, was roundly criticised, as were certain state authorities. But the broader social context within which these institutions are located is largely exempted from the analysis. This is in contrast with the media's coverage of the earlier Kilkenny Report (McGuiness, 1993) where there was considerable soul-searching around the public's attitudes to domestic violence, the subordinate position of children in Irish society and the need for a constitutional amendment to assert children's rights (see Chapter 2). These wider social issues barely receive a mention in the reporting of clerical child abuse, with the media spotlight remaining firmly on the offending clerics, the church and the state authorities.

There were a few exceptions. In an article in the *Irish Independent*, a representative from the Irish Society for the Prevention of Cruelty to Children (ISPCC) pointed out that the Ferns case was 'not unique': 'It is another stark example of how Irish society has traditionally failed to deal adequately with the exploitation of children'.[96] In the same article, the Ombudsman for Children called for increased rights for children, noting that victims were only listened to when they were *adults*. Writing in *The Irish Times*,[97] Fintan O'Toole, also located clerical abuse of children within a wider social context, in which children have few rights:

> The church's response to child abuse was collusive and the State's utterly negligent, and both need to undergo a stringent process of institutional and legislative reform. But such reforms will not work unless we also address the more uncomfortable question of the wider culture that facilitates the exploitation of children. In a context where the Constitution makes no mention of children's rights, where services for vulnerable kids are still massively under-resourced and where one Irish child in seven lives in consistent poverty, can we really claim that the era in which children were not our first priority is over?

Fintan O'Toole is also critical of the way in which Irish Catholics themselves 'helped to corrupt their priests by obedience, indulgence and easy absolution'.[98] He is particularly scathing in his commentary on lay Catholic organisations, noting that 'when the issue of child sexual abuse began to surface in Ireland from the 1980s onwards, the most aggressive attacks on attempts to acknowledge the problem and do something about it came not from bishops and priests but from lay Catholic organisations'.[99] Similarly, Ian O'Doherty, writing in the *Irish Independent*, berates 'a complicit and craven society' for doing little or

---

[96] *Irish Independent* 26 October 2005 'Professionals must be obliged to whistle-blow, says Barnardo's'; *The Irish Sun* 26 October 2005 '"We're at fault for ignoring torment"'.

[97] *The Irish Times* 29 October 2005 'The strut of power gave them a sense they could do whatever they liked, whenever they liked'.

[98] *The Irish Times* 1 November 2005 'A culture that failed to see evil'.

[99] *The Irish Times* 1 November 2005 'A culture that failed to see evil'.

nothing to address clerical child abuse even though 'everyone knew'.[100] Significantly, O'Doherty acknowledges that journalists themselves were among those who allowed the abuse to continue, through their silence. However, this is a rare moment of self-reflection in the media's coverage of clerical child abuse: while church and state are roundly condemned for 'covering-up', the possibility that they might have done so with media collusion is rarely broached.

Following on from Ferns and Dublin: the Cloyne Report

Towards the end of its remit, in March 2009, the Irish Government asked the Dublin Archdiocesan Commission of Investigation to carry out a similar investigation into the Catholic Diocese of Cloyne. During the Cloyne investigation, the commission examined all complaints, allegations, concerns and suspicions of child sexual abuse by relevant clerics made to the diocesan and other Catholic Church authorities and public and state authorities in the period from 1 January 1996 to 1 February 2009 (DJELR, 2011: 1). Virtually all of the allegations reported to the Cloyne diocese during the period covered by the commission were historical allegations (ie, made by adults who claim to have been abused as children) though the procedures that apply in respect to such allegations are the same as those for current or recent abuse (pp 2 and 62).

The context of the Cloyne Report differed significantly from the context of the *Report into the Catholic Archdiocese of Dublin*, in that it deals with allegations made *after* 1996, the year in which the Catholic Church in Ireland put in place detailed procedures for dealing with child sexual abuse, and two years after the state had been 'convulsed' by the Fr Brendan Smyth case (DJELR, 2011: 1-2). According to the Cloyne Report (p 2), 'This meant that the so-called "learning curve" that it was claimed excused very poor handling of complaints in other dioceses in the past could not have had any basis or relevance in Cloyne'.

The key finding of the Cloyne Report (DJELR, 2011: 4-5) was that the church authorities in the diocese were not fully or consistently implementing the Catholic Church's own procedures for dealing with allegations of child sexual abuse, as set out in the *Framework Document*. The *Framework Document* required, among other things, that allegations of clerical child abuse be reported to the civil authorities. The commission found that the person charged with responsibility for dealing with child abuse allegations in Cloyne – Monsignor

---

[100] *Irish Independent* 31 October 2005 'You church-bashing load of hypocrites'.

O'Callaghan – was not fully supportive of the procedures and consequently they were never properly implemented (DJELR, 2011: 71). In letters obtained by the commission he expressed the view that the church's role in such cases should be pastoral, and that it was the responsibility of the complainant – rather than the clergy – to report abuse to the police (DJELR, 2011: 7 and 13). However, the 'primary responsibility' for the failure to implement procedures in the diocese lay with Bishop Magee (p 5). The commission found that he 'adopted a "hands off" approach' to cases of clerical child sex abuse and failed to properly monitor Monsignor O'Callaghan's implementation of the *Framework Document* (p 71). The commission also found that the Vatican had expressed reservations about the *Framework Document*, and this led the commission to conclude that 'this gave comfort to those, including Monsignor O'Callaghan, who fundamentally disagreed with the policies of the document' (p 72).

While highly critical of Monsignor O'Callaghan, the Cloyne Report also acknowledges that he arranged counselling, that he put 'an enormous amount of time and effort into dealing with complainants' and that 'he was personally kind in many respects' (p 20). Moreover the commission did not find evidence of priests being moved around in order to cover up abuse, as was the case in the Archdiocese of Dublin. A number of priests against whom allegations were made were "retired" or in some cases their ministry was restricted (DJELR, 2011: 16). Significantly, the commission also found that, with a few exceptions, the Gardaí 'carried out their tasks well and did so while treating the complainants with compassion and dignity' – this contrasts with the Dublin Report where serious concerns had been raised in relation to the Gardaí's handling of clerical child abuse (pp 17-18). Of course, given that the Cloyne Report investigated a relatively recent period of Irish history – during which awareness of clerical child abuse had increased exponentially – this is perhaps not surprising.

While the Cloyne Report was certainly damaging for the church, it did not initially appear to be as controversial as its predecessors in Ferns and Dublin. However, events in Cloyne became significantly more newsworthy when the Taoiseach, Enda Kenny, in his response to the publication of the report, berated the Vatican for its attitudes towards clerical child abuse. Speaking in the Dáil (20 July 2011) he asserted that the culture of the Vatican was dominated by "dysfunction, disconnection and elitism" and that:

> "The rape and torture of children were down-played or managed to uphold the primacy of the institution, its power,

standing and reputation. Far from listening to evidence of humiliation and betrayal with St. Benedict's "ear of the heart", the Vatican's reaction was to parse and analyse it with the gimlet eye of a Canon lawyer. This calculated, withering position is the polar opposite of the radicalism, humility and compassion on which the Roman Church was founded."

The Taoiseach's statement to the Dáil was seen as a landmark moment in church–state relations in Ireland, and it received extensive media coverage, both nationally and internationally.

Conclusion

As we have seen in the course of this chapter, the issue of clerical child abuse embodied key elements of 'scandal', most notably the violation of social norms and values espoused by the church itself and the alleged 'cover-up' of these transgressions by the hierarchy. While sexual abuse by Catholic clergy has now been reported in numerous countries – particularly in North America, Europe and Australia – the shock to the public psyche in Ireland was arguably much worse because of the central position of the Catholic Church in Irish society and history.

The media played a key role in raising awareness of clerical child abuse in Ireland by bringing this hitherto taboo subject to a mass audience. For much of the 20th century, the church had effectively been beyond public criticism. However, the Fr Smyth case proved to be a turning point and from this time onwards the church became subject to increasingly hostile media scrutiny. Just as in the United States, Australia and Britain, television documentaries – notably *Suing the Pope*, *Cardinal Secrets* and *States of Fear* – played a large part in bringing the issue of clerical child abuse into the open. Moreover, following the publication of the abuse inquiry reports, the media provided damning commentary on the findings. As the moral standing of the church declined, the media appeared to take on the role of moral arbiter, condemning the abuse of children and those who colluded to keep it secret and calling for further investigations, policy changes and the resignation of senior church figures implicated in a 'cover-up'. In this respect, the media played an important part not only in reporting clerical child abuse but also in instigating change. The 'first estate' is now increasingly being called to account by the fourth in a radical redistribution of power. Arguably, this reversal of fortunes was made possible by the gradual secularisation of Irish society from the 1980s onwards (Donnelly and

Inglis, 2010; Inglis, 1998), a process that has no doubt been accelerated by the ongoing revelations of clerical child sexual abuse.

FOUR

The Ryan Report and
the charity myth

> The Report of the Commission to Inquire into Child Abuse
> is the map of an Irish hell. It defines the contours of a dark
> hinterland of the State, a parallel country whose existence
> we have long known but never fully acknowledged. It is
> a land of pain and shame, of savage cruelty and callous
> indifference. The instinct to turn away from it, repelled
> by its profoundly unsettling ugliness, is almost irresistible.
> We owe it, though, to those who have suffered there to
> acknowledge from now on that it is an inescapable part of
> Irish reality. We have to deal with the now-established fact
> that, alongside the warmth and intimacy, the kindness and
> generosity of Irish life, there was, for most of the history
> of the State, a deliberately maintained structure of vile and
> vicious abuse. (*The Irish Times,* 21 May 2009: 19)

The publication of the *Report of the Commission to Inquire into Child
Abuse* (which will be referred to here as the Ryan Report) during 2009
was a seminal event, not only in the vindication of the human rights
of survivors of child abuse in Irish reformatory and industrial schools,
but also in the journey towards truth-telling about child abuse. The
Ryan Report is 2,600 pages in length and is composed of five volumes.
It contains the testimony of over 1,500 witnesses and when it was
published it exposed a mephitic hole in Irish society. It is a powerfully
revelatory document that stands as a unique testament to child suffering
in the modern world. However, in terms of truth-telling it is arguably
a flawed document because the alleged perpetrators of abuse (living
and dead) have been given anonymity following legal action, but, on
the other hand, the danger of a witch-hunt was avoided by taking
this approach. Furthermore, the original Chair of the Commission
to Inquire into Child Abuse (CICA), Justice Mary Laffoy, resigned in
2003 because of an alleged lack of official cooperation, notably on the
part of the Department of Education (Arnold, 2009: 98–109). She was
replaced by Justice Sean Ryan. The Ryan Report reveals that child
abuse was endemic in the industrial and reformatory school system

in Ireland. The shocking revelations it contains have been reported around the world, exposing the failure of Ireland's human rights record in relation to children to critical international scrutiny. The alleged crimes against children described in the Ryan Report are on a systemic scale and involve a degree of sadistic cruelty that is difficult to comprehend in a developed society. Public reaction has been one of shock and horror, but, perhaps inevitably, media interest was transient and sensational. There was and continues to be an unwillingness to confront the deep, underlying human rights issues, and there remains an urgent need to respond to the challenge of developing a culture of civility and civicness that informs and guides the rhetoric of children's rights. Ireland has been slow to develop a cultural literacy of human rights. This chapter seeks to explain the background, context and political response to the Ryan Report. It is argued that there were two phases – in the form of distinctive campaigns for children's rights – leading up to the investigatory process into industrial and reformatory schools that produced the Ryan Report in 2009.

The background

There are varying estimates of the number of children who were incarcerated in Irish industrial and reformatory schools. According to Raftery and O'Sullivan (1999), 150,000 children were placed in industrial schools between 1869 and 1969 and 15,000 children in reformatory schools between 1858 and 1969. The Ryan Report (CICA, 2009: 1: 3.01-3.04) estimates that during the period 1936 to 1970 'a total of 170,000 children and young persons (involving about 1.2% of the age cohort) entered the gates of the 50 or so industrial schools'. The annual inmate population peaked in 1946 at 6,800 and steadily declined thereafter to 4,300 in 1960 and 1,740 in 1970. In the case of reformatory schools the numbers were much lower, amounting to approximately 2,000 to 3,000 children and young persons. The discrepancies between these estimates are not easy to account for but seem to be primarily due to an overestimation on the part of CICA, which appears to have used the stock figure rather than the flow figure in estimating the number of children in industrial schools. In relation to reformatory schools, the divergence between the two estimates can be accounted for by the closure of the majority of Ireland's ten reformatory schools by the early 20th century, when they were reduced to only two. The Cussen Report (CIRISS, 1936: 67) estimated that there were only 77 children left within the reformatory school system in 1934. However, the reality was more complex because industrial and reformatory schools began to merge into a common system; Letterfrack Industrial School in the West of Ireland was being described as a junior reformatory in 1954, and 76% of the child inmates came from Dublin (Barnes, 1989: 42).

Raftery and O'Sullivan (1999) have argued that the industrial and reformatory school system was based upon an elaborate series of myths that served to justify its existence in the public mind. Bronislaw Malinowski (1948) has analysed the function of myths in society and the role they play in legitimating the social structure. In Ireland, the social power and moral authority of the Catholic Church depended on a series of myths that placed it above the civic law in a sanctified realm. This mythology enforced belief in the church's moral and social hegemony over Irish civil society and the state.

The chronology of events that led to the exposure of child abuse in industrial and reformatory schools dates from the 1950s and 1960s when a social movement began with the aim of achieving a thorough-going reform of the Irish social care system, based upon the twin principles of deinstitutionalisation and human rights. Its impact over the ensuing half century was to fundamentally alter the direction of social care in Ireland away from institutionalisation. It represented the voice of liberal civil society in Ireland – made up of minority counter-publics that questioned the human rights record of the Irish state in relation to the institutionalisation of children. Mainstream conservative civil society showed little or no interest in the fate of institutionalised children, other than to cooperate in returning absconders or to participate in the benefits of the local economy. Raftery and O'Sullivan (1999: 318) have drawn parallels between public attitudes towards victims in Nazi Germany with Ireland's attitudes to these institutionalised children: 'both Irish and German society shared a similar pattern of denial'.

O'Sullivan and O'Donnell (2012: 33) have analysed a paradigm shift in the use of coercive confinement (ie, institutionalisation) in Ireland during the half century between 1951 and 2002 based on:

1. the massive downsizing of the population in coercive confinement: from over 31,000 (1069 per 100,000) to just under 5,000 (126 per 100,000);
2. the narrowing of the range of sites: the number of institutions which coercively held unmarried mothers and their children has been reduced to zero;
3. the changing gender balance of those held in coercive confinement: from a majority of women to a minority;

4. the increasingly dominant role of the state: voluntary religious or non-profit agencies have virtually disappeared as providers of coercive confinement.

As a result of this transition, community care has replaced institutionalisation and the state has replaced the church as the custodians of care. This fundamental change in child care policy did not happen in a vacuum. It was the product of a protracted human rights campaign that was relentlessly resisted by church and state in the interests of what Inglis (1998) has called 'moral monopoly'.

The first campaign

The first impetus towards social reform came from liberal civil society during the 1950s and 1960s, inspired by the Joint Committee of Women's Societies and Social Workers (JCWSSW), founded in 1935 (Ferriter, 2009: 146). It was officially regarded as a 'prejudiced organisation that was engaging in unwarranted criticism of the reformatory and industrial schools system' (Raftery and O'Sullivan, 1999: 356-7). However, when the Organisation for Economic Co-operation and Development (OECD) Committee published the report *Investment in Education* (1966) that highlighted the issue of institutionalisation, it was clear that something needed to be done if Ireland was to pass the necessary tests on democratic citizenship and human rights for entry into the European Union, then known as the European Economic Community (EEC). Ireland's dark secret of institutional child abuse could have stopped Ireland's application on human rights grounds. Michael Viney wrote a series of insightful articles on young offenders in *The Irish Times* during 1966 that exposed the system's shortcomings. Outside the country, away from the pressures of censorship, the London branch of Tuairim (Opinion), an organisation of young intellectuals, produced a report entitled *Some of Our Children: A Report on the Residential Care of the Deprived Child in Ireland* (1966). This influential report included participation by survivors of the Irish industrial schools system. Peter Tyrell (2006), who had survived the controversial Letterfrack institutional regime in Connemara, had an input into the production of the report. However, the report was guarded in its criticism of the punitive regime in Irish industrial and reformatory schools (particularly the use of corporal punishment), which it suggested had been 'excessive' in the 'past' stressing the 'hypothetical' nature of the criticism (Tuairim, 1966: 39). An exasperated Peter Tyrell, despairing of the possibility of truth and justice in Irish public discourse, committed suicide. It is remarkable that an organisation of Tuairim's standing, which included some of the most liberal intellectuals in mid-20th century Ireland, should have been so restrained in its criticism of what were clearly very serious human rights violations. However, both the Tuairim report and the OECD report in 1966 were to prove highly influential. In the following year, 1967, the government reluctantly established an official inquiry into the industrial and reformatory school system, known as the Kennedy Committee Inquiry (discussed later in this chapter).

The state already knew about the conditions in industrial schools and reformatories. An unpublished inter-departmental committee report on Crime Prevention and Treatment of Offenders (Department of Education, 1963, cited in Raftery and Sullivan, 1999) had highlighted some of the core problems including: inadequate finance; ineffective inspection; poor clothing and dilapidated facilities seriously in need of repair; inappropriate location far away from populous urban centres; the need for matrons and nurses to care for the children's health and hygiene and the deficient system of education and training. All of its recommendations were rejected by the Department of Education, the agency responsible for the oversight of the system of industrial and reformatory schools (Raftery and O'Sullivan, 1999: 356-60). The Department of Education, according to Raftery and O'Sullivan (1999: 363), was primarily concerned about supporting the financial position of the religious orders, which were losing funding due to falling numbers. Their emphasis was on attempting to find ways in which more children could be detained in the schools rather than proposing an alternative method of care in the community. Proposals from the Irish Council for Civil Liberties (ICCL) advocating deinstitutionalisation were rejected out of hand by the Department of Education (Raftery and O'Sullivan, 1999: 364). But it was clear that the liberal tide of social reform was beginning to engulf both the power of the Irish state and the moral authority of the Catholic Church, and to question their maintenance of a system of institutional care that had begun to be investigated by the media on the grounds that there was evidence of endemic abuse within it. This included allegations of repressive institutional regimes that not only used corporal punishment but also used shaming practices, such as shaving children's heads. There were also concerns about sexuality, which at this point in time were not specified (Raftery and O'Sullivan, 1999: 365-67). The Ryan Report (CICA, 2009: 4: 3.107) refers to the 'iron curtain' that stifled media reporting on industrial and reformatory schools. Censorship repressed discussion of public issues in Ireland at this time. The hegemony of the church over the state was all pervasive during most of the 20th century (Blanshard, 1954; Whyte, 1980).

Liberal civil society responded to the challenge of child care reform. The Campaign for the Care of Deprived Children (CARE) was formed in 1970, and it put human rights at the centre of its agenda. During 1972, CARE published *Children Deprived: CARE Memorandum on Deprived Children and Children's Services in Ireland*. The first chapter (1972: 8) sets out the human rights case for reforming services for children and young people:

> In claiming from the public special attention for deprived children and a will to do better for them, CARE can make a case based on many principles. We would especially emphasise the principle of the rights of these children. We can distinguish between (a) children's rights as persons and as young citizens of the state and (b) children's special rights as children.

The CARE Memorandum (1972: 9) asserted that the Irish state had failed to vindicate the rights of the child:

> In Ireland too we have recognised the special rights of children, in word if not in deed. The first Dáil (Parliament) stated that the *first duty* of the Republic was to children. In the Constitution the state's special role in relation to children and other weak groups is spelled out.

While it is true that the Proclamation of 1916 promised 'to pursue ... happiness and prosperity ... cherishing all the children of the nation equally', this political and social goal had not been achieved. The highly respected writer and *Irish Independent* columnist, Bruce Arnold, in his book *The Irish Gulag* (2009: 39), has commented:

> The claim made in the 1916 Proclamation, about cherishing the nation's children equally, and repeated in the 1919 Dáil, was sacred in Irish political texts. It was offered up as a verbal sacrifice on the altar of independence whenever the public vindications of such social charges and obligations were being aired. It meant nothing at all. It was just 'air'. No constructive purpose was served by the repetitious hypocrisy of the child-cherishing mantra. Those who fought for Irish freedom knew that such rhetoric would

attract public support for their campaign of violence. Their true intentions were revealed when they came to power. As soon as the last British administrator departed from Dublin, the notion of children's rights – when children were seen as wrong doers, rather than criminals – was comprehensively dismissed.

Arnold's reference to 1919 is to the Democratic Programme, a socialist statement of the children's rights as paramount, which was quickly dropped on the basis it was 'Marxist' (Powell, 1992: 158-9). Furthermore, the social justice philosophy of the Children Act 1908 (Ireland's principal child care and juvenile justice statute for most of the 20th century) was completely ignored. It was called the Children's Charter and was the product of the UK's Liberal reforms at the beginning of the 20th century. No group of children could have been more in need of a charter of rights than the vast population of disadvantaged children across Ireland incarcerated in industrial and reformatory schools. The Irish state ignored their human rights. Instead, as Arnold (2009) persuasively argues, the political violence that created an independent state, based upon a crude appeal to populist nationalist sentiment, visited a regime of social violence on the unfortunate inmates of industrial and reformatory schools in a brutal project that denied children's most basic human rights. Arnold (2009: 2) asserts that 'together with certain other establishments for children who were euphemistically described as being "in care", these institutions in reality constituted an "Irish Gulag"'. A regime of political conservatism (state) and social conservatism (church) had created conditions totally hostile to children's rights. This was to have catastrophic consequences for the most vulnerable section of Irish society – the legacy of which continues to be felt right down to the present day by its victims. Arnold is correct in his assertion that political independence was a disaster for children's rights. In a state controlled by the Catholic Church, deprived children were reconstructed as a problem population and subjected to a moral regime of coercive institutionalisation at a point where this form of care had been condemned in the UK (*Report of the Inter-departmental Committee on Child Care*, 1896). Smart (1999) presciently observes that innocent children went through the process of institutionalisation through which they were reconstructed as 'moral lepers' and treated as child criminals.

The CARE Memorandum (1972: 29-30) vigorously put the arguments for reform of the child care system:

Are we prepared to tolerate this state of affairs? Must we accept that the present standard of provisions for deprived children is the best we can achieve? Do we content ourselves with praising the efforts of those working with various children's difficulties while ignoring our responsibilities as individuals and as a community? CARE strongly urges the case that we should not and cannot be complacent about the present situation, that for a number of reasons we must improve it. Firstly, for reasons of justice ... secondly, deprived children deserve a better deal for reasons of charity ... But if we are not moved by considerations of justice and charity there is a third argument which can be stated thus: the deprived children of today are the dependent adults of tomorrow, if we do not provide for them adequately today we will have to support them and their families tomorrow.

A second platform for children's rights was established in 1975; it was called Children First. Its campaign was carried out through a newsletter, correspondence in the press and the production by its chairman, Charles Mollan, of a book, entitled *Children First* in 1979. Mollan (1979: 6) took the 1937 Constitution to task: 'of course it is right that the state should seek to support the family: but the Constitution does not seem to take sufficiently into consideration the rights of the child'. The reality has been that since the inception of the Irish state in 1922, children have been denied basic human rights and are still within a welfare state that has been unable to articulate a secular value system based upon social justice principles. The 1937 Constitution vindicates the rights of the family at the expense of the rights of the child. Children (apart from the unborn) are constitutionally invisible.

The campaign for child care reform was supported by the other liberal civil society organisations such as the Irish Association of Social Workers (IASW) and the ICCL. The ICCL published a report in 1977 called *Children's Rights Under the Constitution* that called for a more equitable balance between the claims of parents and the rights of children. In the previous year, to mark National Children's Day, a protest march took place to Dáil Éireann (Irish Parliament) and a Proclamation on Children's Rights, 50 years after the Easter Rising (Irish Revolution), was read to the assembled protestors including: representatives of CARE, Children First, the Irish Society for the Prevention of Cruelty to Children (ISPCC), the IASW and many other organisations. The Proclamation of Children's Rights declared:

> We, the undersigned, representatives of organizations, concerned about the welfare of children, on this National Children's Day June 13, 1976, demand that the Government take necessary action to ensure maximum protection, security, and happiness for the children of the state. We demand that legislation be introduced to provide that in any case in which the care and custody of a child is at issue, the welfare of the child shall be the first consideration. In the event that the enactment of such legislation is thought to be repugnant to the Constitution, the Government should take steps to have the Constitutional issue decided, and, if repugnant, to make the appropriate constitutional amendment (Cited in Mollan 1979: 17-19)

The advocacy of a constitutional referendum on children's rights was a far-sighted proposal that was realised in 2012. It is clear that equality of rights for children is impossible without a constitutional referendum. While there have been two referenda in Ireland on the rights of the unborn child, advocated by the traditionalist pro-life movement, a referendum on children's rights had been resisted by both the state and conservative civil society, often opaque in its influence over social policy (O'Reilly, 1992).

Apart from its advocacy of a constitutional amendment on children rights, the Proclamation of Children's Rights made several specific recommendations:

1. The interests of a child require that he receives continuous loving care in a family. He should remain with this caring family, and it should get support where necessary. Particular attention should be paid to helping single parent families.
2. The state must protect the interests of the child where family cannot or will not provide the care he needs. To this end, a comprehensive child care system incorporating adoption, fostering, and residential care must be provided. Each child should receive the care that is appropriate to his own particular needs.
3. In order to support family care, the state should ensure that its policies, with regard to income maintenance, housing and education should take account of the special needs of children, particularly deprived and handicapped children.
4. Children should not be accountable under the criminal law. Any system for dealing with young offenders should protect their interests and take account of their needs as children.

5. In addition in a case in which a decision is taken about the welfare of a child, he should have appropriate representation in his own right. (Mollan, 1979: 17–19)

These were very progressive recommendations that amounted to a manifesto for child care reform in Ireland. The Proclamation of Children's Rights sought to challenge the Irish state to take action to vindicate children's rights. Both CARE and Children First represented a vibrant social movement committed to child care reform.

The state's response: 'a cover-up'

The initial response from the Irish state to the growing campaign for children's rights following the publication of the Tuairim and OECD reports in 1966 was the establishment of a committee to examine the role of the reformatory and industrial school system. The 1970 *Report of the Commission of Inquiry into the Reformatory and Industrial School System* (also known as the Kennedy Report) recommended the closure of the reformatory and industrial school system but failed to reveal the scale and extent of child abuse within these institutions, leading to accusations of 'cover-up' by recent commentators (Arnold, 2009). However, the Kennedy Report was generally welcomed at the time of its publication in 1970. Given the pervasive climate of censorship and the hostility of conservative civil society to reforming child care policy, it must be evaluated within the context of the time, while recognising that Bruce Arnold's criticism is absolutely correct and the consequences of the Kennedy Committee's failure to disclose the truth has seriously impacted on survivors.

Valerie Richardson (1999: 175) has described the Kennedy Report as 'a watershed in terms of child care policy' in Ireland. In essence, the Victorian system of institutional child care was to be replaced by community care. As Raftery and O'Sullivan (1999: 379) put it: 'The Kennedy Report sounded the death knell for the institutional model of child care which had remained remarkably resilient in this country for almost exactly 100 years'. It constituted a major proposal for social reform, upon which subsequent policy was built. The Kennedy Report (CIRISS, 1970: 6–7) made thirteen recommendations, which included the immediate closure of the boy's reformatory at Daingean and Marlborough House Remand Home, and the replacement of the system of reformatories by 'modern special schools'. It also recommended that 'all children in residential care or otherwise in care, should be educated to the ultimate of their capacities'. Educational neglect was part of the abusive system of care. A system of aftercare was recommended, which was largely absent despite long periods of institutionalisation. At a policy level, the Kennedy Committee recommended a new child care statute, the ending of capitation payments (which encouraged institutions to play a numbers game) by block grants and the vesting of responsibility for children's services within the Department of Health (CIRISS, 1970: 6-7).

Recent commentators have taken a much more critical view of the Kennedy Report. In Arnold's view there were three core policy issues that were not tackled by the Kennedy Committee. First, Arnold (2009: 71) states that 'the exercise of discipline was a physical tyranny' within the industrial and reformatory school system and the Kennedy Committee's decision not to address this issue was very serious: 'to ignore punishment was to bypass the most fundamental problem of all'. Second, Arnold (2009: 71-2) is concerned about the committal procedure used to send children to industrial and reformatory schools:

> ... central to the dreadful nature of the system, and not examined at all in the Kennedy Report, was the committal procedure by the Courts ... She [Justice Eileen Kennedy] knew that the system used was not only dreaded by the victims of it and by their parents, but it was also more widely feared by the public. She also knew that it was being administered illegally.

Third, Arnold (2009: 72) asserts 'District Justice Eileen Kennedy and her committee failed to examine the character, training and psychological capacities of those who did work within the industrial school system: these were the nuns, brothers and priests involved in the supervision and control of inmates'. Arnold's analysis of the Kennedy Report amounts to a very serious indictment of Justice Eileen Kennedy and her colleagues. Given the composition of the Kennedy Committee, it is not possible to assume that they were naïve or ill-informed. It would seem with hindsight that the Kennedy Committee, despite the many plaudits it received from contemporaries in the 1970s, opted for closure over disclosure. While its recommendation to close this system was admirable, its failure to disclose the human rights abuses (eg, corporal punishment) was reprehensible. Presumably, the social power of the Catholic Church was too great an obstacle to permit the Kennedy Committee to open up the issue of child abuse within the industrial and reformatory school system to public discussion. Its silence was to keep the issue of child abuse in industrial and reformatory schools repressed for another four decades. This silence was very damaging for the survivors of the system, who deserved justice and reparation long before they achieved it.

The entry of the Labour Party (with an agenda of social reform) into government in 1974 led to the allocation of responsibility for deprived children to the Labour Party leader, Mr Brendan Corish, in his roles as Tánaiste (Deputy Prime Minister) and Minister for Health. CARE (1974: 1) reacted enthusiastically, observing that 'from the very beginning we have said, and we still believe, that making one Minister, and one Department, responsible for planning in respect of deprived children and children's services was the first step towards the sensible and humane reforms demanded in this whole area'. Action followed swiftly in the form of a Task Force on Child Care Services, established in 1974 and mandated (1) to make recommendations on the extension and improvement of services for deprived children and children at risk, (2) to prepare a new Children's Bill to modernise the law and (3) to provide a basis for administrative reforms of the child care system (Task Force on Child Care Services, 1980: 26).

When the *Task Force on Child Care Services: Final Report* was eventually published in 1980, it proved to be a disappointment to those who supported fundamental child care reform. It was divided into a majority report (reflecting the dominant view of five civil servants) and a minority report (authored by the two surviving independent representatives – an academic and a social worker). While the final report offered a comprehensive analysis of the child care system, there were major divisions, notably in relation to juvenile justice, where the majority view was against fundamental reform. However, there was broad agreement among the membership of the Task Force (1980: 265-75) in their principal recommendations that children should be cared for in the community rather than in residential care and that a new statute was needed to replace the Children Act 1908. The main reason for public disappointment was that the Task Force's report had not produced the blueprint for childcare reform that had been expected, but it was to prove highly influential in terms of accelerating the process of deinstitutionalisation. In 1968–69, of the 4,834 children in care, three-quarters were placed in residential institutions. In marked contrast, of the 2,641 children in care in 1988, only one-quarter were in residential facilities, which had undergone substantial reform (Gilligan, 1991: 185). Manifestly, a step-change had occurred in Irish social policy in relation to the deinstitutionalisation of deprived children and young people in need of care and protection. There was a basis for a new child care statute, even if there wasn't agreement in relation to juvenile justice reform. But the official inertia towards social reform remained as a powerful obstacle to change. The 1980s was a period when the liberal agenda of social reform stalled and Catholic social teaching was once again in the ascendant (Considine and Dukelow, 2009: 63). It took another decade to enact a new principal child care statute to replace the Children Act 1908. While the Irish state had systematically ignored the welfarist orientation of the Children Act 1908, it had been historically unwilling to provide an alternative. Finally, reform had become inevitable. In 1991 the Child Care Act was passed, which finally updated Irish child care law after a century of inertia. But the Irish child care system continues to fail children. In response to growing public concern about the deaths of children in care, an editorial comment in the *The Irish Times* (5 March 2010) on the death of Tracey Fay declared:

> The State's obligations towards children who cannot be cared for by their families are clear. Health authorities have a positive duty under the Child Care Act 1991 to 'identify children who are not receiving adequate care and protection' and to provide them with suitable protection. The crushing reality, however, is that social services are operating against a backdrop of scarce resources, staff shortages and heavy caseloads.
>
> This crisis in child protection services is not helped by a culture of excessive secrecy on the part of the Health Service Executive (HSE) management. The HSE has consistently failed to publish any of the reports into the deaths of children in its care. It only became apparent that there was a report in existence on Ms Fay's death when details were leaked to this newspaper last year.
>
> Even the most basic statistics regarding social work services are far too often hidden behind a veil of confidentiality. For example, an annual report into the adequacy of child and family services is heavily censored and omits virtually all criticism of child protection services.

While the location of care has moved from institutional settings into the community, the child care service in Ireland remains a minimalist response to the needs of deprived children. Health Service Executive (HSE) figures indicate that up to 188 children in care or in contact with Irish social services have died over the past decade (O' Brien, 2010a). Carl O'Brien (2010b) reported on a 'potential dereliction' of duty over the safety of foster children in parts of Dublin. These accumulated reports suggest that while children are being cared for in the community the quality of service offered by the Irish state continues to be a poor service for poor children. It is difficult to avoid the conclusion that there is a problem of incivility in Ireland, underpinned by weak civic bonds. Public morality continues to be predominantly defined within the medieval value system of the Catholic Church. Human rights in general and children's rights in particular have no place in this world view.

The second campaign

By the end of the 20th century, attention turned to exposing the abuses that had taken place in the industrial and reformatory school system in a campaign led by the media and the survivors' movement. The year 1999 proved to be a watershed. Mary Raftery produced her television documentary series, *States of Fear*, which was accompanied by her revelatory book, co-authored with Eoin O'Sullivan, entitled *Suffer the Little Children: The Inside Story of Ireland's Industrial Schools*. These two important events changed the public consciousness. There followed an apology from the then Taoiseach (prime minister), Mr Bertie Ahern, and the establishment of the Commission to Inquire into Child Abuse that, in 2009, produced the Ryan Report. It was the culmination of a half century of campaigning for children's rights by social reformers, rights activists, liberal intellectuals, social workers and survivors of child abuse. A key element in changing public opinion in relation to children's rights has been the role of the campaign group One in Four. Arnold (2009: 227) notes that 'the One in Four group became quite outspoken on behalf of the abused generally at this time and countered what it called an attempt to rewrite the history of sexual abuse'. Under the dynamic leadership of Colm O'Gorman, One in Four, began to transform Irish public consciousness regarding the significance of child abuse in Irish society. There were many other survivor groups who also became instrumental in unlocking their own narratives including: Irish Survivors of Child Abuse (Irish SOCA), SOCA (UK), The Irish Deaf Society, Right to Peace, Right to Place, Alliance Victim Support, Irish Survivors of Institutional Abuse International, the Aislinn Centre and the London Irish Women's Group (CICA, 2009: 1: 1.149). All of these organisations began to provide a survivors' perspective on the growing public scandal of institutional child abuse that challenged both the church to account for its actions and the state for a serious failure of regulation in human rights terms.

Survivors groups became a moral voice that could not be ignored. Truth was beginning to assert itself. Colm O'Gorman (2009: 119) in his autobiographical book, *Beyond Belief*, asserts:

> Abuse is only possible in a silent world. And just like the rest of society, my family was silent; there were certain words that were never spoken for fear of what consequences they might bring. Instead, we demanded the silencing of truths that would inevitably tear apart our idealistic view of ourselves. The truth demands action while secrets and lies allow us to avoid taking action, they allow us to continue to pretend that everything is fine, even when it is most definitely not.

The survivors' voice became the evidential basis of the Ryan Report, which was modelled on the post-apartheid Truth and Reconciliation Commission (TRC) that existed in South Africa between 1995 and 1998 (Keane, 2008: 693-5). It is the survivors' truth told with a compelling authenticity that cannot be denied that makes the Ryan Report one of the most important events in the social history of Irish children since the inception of the state. It put children's rights at the centre of public discourse and shamed both church and state. Child abuse has arguably become a metaphor for the failure of the Irish public sphere to modernise.

The testimony courageously provided by the survivors enables us to revisit their experience. Through their intense social suffering, we begin to gain access into a secretive world where a policy of persistent dehumanisation shaped their lives – a world of unrelenting medieval style terror. This process has begun to confront Irish civil society with the task of shaping a civic vocabulary that goes beyond outrage and results in policy responses that acknowledge the rights of children in public discourse and legal action. The Ryan Commission saw the value of a process of opening up the truth and democratising survivors' memories as a means to symbolically heal the wounds of the victims and hold the victimisers to public account. In this way it followed the South African TRC model.

The Ryan Report's anatomy of child abuse

Volume 3 of the Ryan Report (2009) provides statistical and verbatim analysis of survivors' evidence given by witnesses to the Confidential Committee regarding the nature and scale of child abuse in Irish institutional care up to 1989. There were 857 reports of child abuse, involving 474 males and 383 female survivors, given to the Confidential Committee. This evidence is corroborated by testimony from 493 survivors given to the Investigation Committee, summarised in Volume 4 of the Ryan Report (CICA, 2009: 4: 5.01-5.142). The mandate of the Confidential Committee was to hear the evidence 'of those survivors of childhood institutional abuse who wished to report their experiences in a confidential setting … to be conducted in an atmosphere that was informal and as sympathetic to, and understanding of, the witnesses as was possible in the circumstances' (CICA 2009: 1: 1.09). It exposes a catalogue of physical, emotional and sexual abuse in tandem with neglect that cannot be explained by unique historical or cultural circumstances. While most of the reported abuse occurred prior to the Kennedy Report (1970) which, as already noted, recommended the closure of the system, complaints continued up until 1989, the end-date for the gathering of statistical evidence. The clergy emerge as the primary agents of child abuse in both statistical and verbatim evidence, which would seem to be incontrovertible and could not be considered normal in any culture at any time. While the forms of child abuse within the reformatory and industrial school system encompassed physical, emotional, sexual abuse and neglect, the overarching form of abuse was physical.

Physical abuse

The Ryan Report (CICA, 2009: 3: 7.06) defines physical abuse as: 'The wilful, reckless or negligent infliction of physical injury on, or a failure to prevent such injury to, the child'. There were 474 reports of physical abuse, involving 26 reformatory and industrial schools, given in evidence to the Confidential Committee by 403 male witnesses (98%), some of whom had been admitted to more than one school (CICA, 2009: 3: 7.08). Similarly, the Confidential Committee received 383 reports of physical abuse from 374 female witnesses (99%) in 39 schools (3: 9.06). In total, calculating all reports from male and female witnesses there were 857 reports of physical abuse.

The Ryan Report (CICA, 2009: 3, 7.16) records a wide variety of forms of physical punishment from the male witness statements, including:

> punching, flogging, assault and bodily attacks, hitting with the hand, kicking, ear pulling, hair pulling, head shaving, beating on the soles of the feet, burning, scalding, stabbing,

severe beatings with or without clothes, being made to kneel and stand in fixed positions for lengthy periods, made to sleep outside overnight, being forced into cold or excessively hot baths and showers, hosed down with cold water before being beaten, beaten while hanging from hooks on the wall, being set upon by dogs, being restrained in order to be beaten, physical assaults by more than one person, and having objects thrown at them.

Females were also subjected to severe physical abuse in the industrial school system, in which they traditionally constituted the larger gender group. The survivors reported high levels of violence by staff, with 166 female witnesses testifying to being beaten with various objects, including wooden sticks, black thorn sticks, rulers, pointers, window poles, wooden spoons, chair legs, wooden crutches, hurling sticks, cricket bats, coat hangers, towel rollers and sally rods. In addition, 77 witnesses reported being beaten with bamboo canes and 99 with leather straps (CICA, 2009: 3: 9.14).

Neglect

The Ryan Report (3: 7.156) defined neglect as:

> ... failure to care for the child which results, or could reasonably be expected to result, in serious impairment of the physical and mental health or development of the child or serious adverse effects on his or her behaviour or welfare...'

367 male witnesses (89%) made 408 reports regarding their care and welfare in 22 schools. Similarly, 367 female witnesses (97%) made 374 reports of neglect. Neglect was frequently reported in combination with other forms of child abuse. In the case of male witnesses, 41% reported neglect in combination with physical, emotional and sexual abuse. Reports from female witnesses reveal 60% reported neglect in combination with physical and emotional abuse, with a further 33% reporting neglect in combination with physical, emotional and sexual abuse. Only one witness from each gender group reported neglect as the only form of abuse that they had experienced.

The Ryan Report categorised neglect under a series of headings: diet, hygiene, healthcare, education and a lack of supervision. There were 379 reports from male witnesses of inadequate food in 21 schools and

168 female witnesses (46%) complained of being constantly hungry or 'starving' (CICA, 2009: 3: 7.163 and 9.126). Male witnesses reported having to survive on a diet of 'unsweetened sludge' made up of bread dipped in dripping and shell cocoa. Female witnesses told a similar story of hunger: 'if you saw anybody eating anything you just went up and grabbed it, we were always hungry' (3: 9.127). Amongst the female witnesses, 22 reported eating grass, leaves and berries and 26 remembered lack of drinking water and having to drink water from the toilets (3: 9.132).

Emotional abuse

The Ryan Report defines emotional abuse as 'any other act or omission towards the child which results, or could reasonably result, in serious impairment of the physical or mental health or development of the child or serious adverse effects on his or her behaviour or welfare' (CICA, 2009: 3: 7.213 and 9.190).

It recorded survivors' testimony of emotional abuse with regards to: deprivation of family contact, personal identity, secure relationships, affection and approval, and a lack of protection. The Ryan Report observes:

> Witnesses reported a daily existence in the Schools that was dominated by fear, humiliation, loneliness, and the absence of affection. Fear was strongly associated with the daily threat of being physically and otherwise abused and seeing co-residents being abused. Constant apprehension about the next abuse to which they would be subjected was also a feature. (CICA, 2009: 3: 7.221)

The Confidential Committee heard 327 reports of emotional abuse from 293 male witnesses (71%) and 354 from female witnesses (94%) (3: 7.215 and 9.192). Amongst the male survivors, 194 described a lack of verbal and physical affection (3: 7.222).

Sexual abuse

The Ryan Report (3: 7.109) defines child sexual abuse as 'the use by a person for sexual arousal or sexual gratification of that person or another person'. The testimony it received from survivors included sexual abuse ranging from contact sexual abuse encompassing rape and associated physical violence to non-contact abuse such as enforced nakedness or voyeurism. Survivors understandably found it difficult to talk about their experiences of sexual abuse. 242 male witnesses (59%) made 253 reports of sexual abuse in 20 schools. There were 128 reports of sexual abuse from 127 female witnesses (34%) (3: 7.110 and 9.70).

The Confidential Committee compiled a list of categories of sexual abuse of both male and female children. Sexual abuse within the reformatory and industrial school system was clearly part and parcel of institutional life, with a disturbing lack of supervision and control. Sexual abuse was sometimes associated with grooming and inducements including treats such as sweets, soft drinks, comics and extra blankets. As one male survivor put it, 'on our birthday you got a bottle of orange but you would have to … you had to go up and sit on their lap' (CICA, 2009: 3: 7.130). But often child sexual abuse in industrial and reformatory schools was associated with violence and threats. Male witnesses identified 186 perpetrators of child sexual abuse by name of which 100 were also named as physical abusers (3: 7.137). Similarly, female survivors 'consistently reported that the sexual abuse occurred in an environment of fear and secrecy' (3: 9.84).

Contextually, the dominant use of physical abuse could be interpreted as the exploitation of the body as a site of punishment and domination in line with the prevalence of corporal punishment at the time. The evidence suggests corporal punishment was also a psychological weapon used to terrorise children in care. What we constantly need to bear in mind is that the survivors' narrative of institutional child abuse is experientially and morally on a par with survivors of penal regimes in totalitarian societies – there is a common thread of an absence of a human right to bodily integrity associated with democratic societies (Raftery and O' Sullivan, 1999; Arnold, 2009). Power was total and exercised without restraint. This disadvantaged child population had no protection and no rights. They were systematically dehumanised by their clerical custodians. The publication of the Ryan Report in 2009 unlocked this world of uncontrolled violence, where children were dehumanised on a mass scale in an atmosphere of terror and humiliation, ironically in the name of charity. Violence became the language of the control of these children, which Ferguson (2007: 13) argues were 'socially constructed as a grotesque other'. The state somehow remained morally blind to this macabre reality, supporting a child care policy that was driven by the banality of evil, in which human rights were simply dispensed with as irrelevant. The value of the Ryan Report is that it has provided a public forum in which these human rights violations could be ventilated and a civic vocabulary constructed to give context and meaning to child abuse within the context of institutional care.

There was a summary of the main findings of the Ryan Report on the British Broadcasting Corporation's (BBC) News Website on 20 May 2009:

- Physical and emotional abuse and neglect were features of the institutions.
- Sexual abuse occurred in many of them, particularly boys' institutions.
- Schools were run in a severe, regimented manner that imposed unreasonable and oppressive discipline on children and even on staff.
- Children were frequently hungry and food was inadequate, inedible and badly prepared in many schools.
- Many witnesses spoke of being constantly fearful or terrified, which impeded their emotional development and impacted on every aspect of their life in the institution.
- Prolonged, excessive beating with implements intended to cause maximum pain occurred with the knowledge of senior staff.
- There was constant criticism and verbal abuse and children were told they were worthless.
- Some children lost their sense of identity and kinship, which was never recovered.
- Absconders were severely beaten, at times publicly. Some had their heads shaved and were humiliated.
- Inspectors, on their occasional visits, rarely spoke to children in the institutions.

These facts confirmed Raftery and O'Sullivan's (1999: 11) conclusion that the industrial and reformatory schools had been based upon a myth of religious charity: 'the first and most pervasive myth was that the children within the system were objects of charity, cared for by the religious of Ireland when no one else would do so'. The Ryan Report exposed the charity myth by revealing a Kafkaesque world of abuse, neglect, enforced labour and sexual exploitation (see Chapter 8). Why was it allowed to exist for over 100 years?

The distinguished Irish writer and literary editor of *The Irish Times*, Fintan O'Toole, has sought to provide an answer to explain why the system of industrial and reformatory schools was not reformed much earlier. He argues that it continued for three reasons: 'power, sex and class'. According to O'Toole (2009a), the first force enabling the abuse of children was power: 'The perpetrators abused children because they could. They drew that power from the immense stature of the church, its ability to command deference and intimidate dissenters'. The second force, identified by O'Toole (2009b) is sex: 'There was a religious hatred of the body, expressed in an infinite variety of ways the Brothers found to hurt and violate the bodies of their charges. There was also a perverted sexuality that swung between an obsession with purity and the rooting out of *badness* on the one hand and obsessive sexual predation on the other'. In O'Toole's (2009b) analysis the third force behind the saga of institutional child abuse is class: 'This was a society in which the middle classes expressed their insecurity about their own status in a hysterical contempt for the poor. The function of industrial schools was to punish poverty'. In addition to these three factors, O'Toole (2009b) suggests a fourth force, which evokes the Darwinistic side of the Irish social mind:

> That violence was fuelled by a psychotic hatred of everything that did not conform to the model of the good, respectable Christian family. 'What are they', one Brother remembered being told by a superior, 'but illegitimate and pure dirt'. In Goldenbridge [Industrial School], girls were told they were 'filthy', 'dirty', and 'worse than the soldiers who crucified Christ'. Boys who were the sons of single mothers were told their mothers were 'slags' and 'old whores'. Children from working-class backgrounds were told their families were 'scum', 'tramps', and 'from the gutter'.

The connection with the foundling hospitals of the eighteenth century in terms of social attitudes was direct (see Chapter 8). The children in industrial schools, in the eyes of their fellow citizens, were also lesser beings. As one unnamed educational journalist from a national newspaper put it during the 1960s, the children in industrial and reformatory schools constituted 'the lesser breeds within the law', which was cited in the Ryan Report (CICA, 2009: 4: 3.109). The state's unwillingness to intervene and defend the human rights of the inmates of the Irish industrial and reformatory school system can ultimately only be explicable in these Darwinistic terms. Irish democracy was a dark democracy that rejected the weak and poor, visiting its contempt and moral Puritanism upon defenceless children. Fintan O'Toole (2009b) concludes: 'These warped relationships to power, sex and class were played out with nightmarish clarity in the institutions, but were woven into the broader society. They were the dark shadows of a Republic that had never really come into existence'.

Mary Raftery (2009a) asserts that the Ryan Report was 'devastating' in its critique: 'it is a monument to the shameful nature of Irish society throughout the most of the decades of the 20th century, and arguably even today'. While the Catholic clergy were the perpetrators of these human rights violations, at the very least they had the tacit support of both the Irish state and civil society. The abuse of children in Irish institutions was a 'known unknown'. There is certainly evidence that coming to grips with the truth about children in care continues to be constrained by systematic resistance. We will discuss tabloid media reaction to the publication of the Ryan Report later in the chapter in the context of popular reaction.

Moral monopoly and institutional child abuse

The President of Ireland, Michael D. Higgins, observed in reference to the historic abuse of children in Irish industrial and reformatory schools: 'There is evidence of institutional collusion that was deep, continuous and sinister in terms of its relations between church and state.[1] Tom Inglis (1998: 45), in his influential book *Moral Monopoly: the Catholic Church in Modern Irish State*, asserts the church's control of social services was crucial to the development of the church's moral monopoly. This was the basis of its social power. In *Suffer the Little Children*, Mary Raftery and Eoin O'Sullivan convincingly argue that government capitation payments (based on a fee per child) and the ruthless exploitation of child labour was at the core of an essentially commercialised system of institutional child care (Raftery and O'Sullivan, 1999). Moral monopoly, in their view, produced economic rewards for the Catholic Church. The book graphically describes brutal work regimes on adjoining farms where starving boys competed with the animals for food. Young girls looked after infants, made rosary beads and sewed priest vestments on empty stomachs. There was virtually no education and training in the industrial and reformatory school system, which was essentially a labour camp regime (Raftery and O'Sullivan, 1999: 155). Yet it was legitimated by a charity myth that represented the clergy as the benevolent carers of deprived children. Myth and reality were sharply at odds as Raftery and O'Sullivan (1999: 15) forcefully point out: 'the reality is that the Catholic Church and the state in partnership made certain choices, not so much out of ignorance but more for reasons of financial expediency. The institutional model for the processing of children into adulthood by religious orders was

---

[1] *Irish Examiner* 2 June 2014.

undoubtedly the cheapest option available'. For the state, there were clear financial gains.

One survivor described the system graphically: 'We always saw it as a prison, never a school. I used to call it Little Auschwitz' (Raftery and O'Sullivan, 1999: 46). Another survivor called Barney observed, in relation to Artane Industrial School, that 'the thing that reminds me of it is a film like *Schindler's List*. It really was like a concentration camp for children'. He concluded:

> Children are a country's most precious asset. But not in Ireland. WE were treated like we were unwanted, something to be hidden, to be ashamed of. There's so much shame, not just shame of a person who was raped, but shame of a nation that allowed it to happen. It made Ireland into the child molestation capital of the world. Shame on us. (Raftery and O'Sullivan, 1999: 274)

Within the reformatory and industrial school system, exploitation of child labour, corporal punishment and sexual abuse created regimes based on terror.

The role of the NSPCC/ISPCC: voluntary sector complicity?

Skehill (1999: 156) has estimated that there were 97 professionally trained social workers in Ireland prior to 1970. There was only one social worker involved in child care and three in family casework. Ferriter (2009: 228) notes 'those seeking to ask questions about the vulnerable inevitably found themselves stepping on the toes of the powerful Arch-bishop McQuaid [of Dublin]'. He was anxious to ensure complete control of social work. That meant that professional social work in the field of child care was effectively impossible prior to 1970.

In lieu of a statutory child care system, the voluntary sector – largely in the form of the National Society for the Prevention of Cruelty to Children (NSPCC), an Irish branch of which was founded in 1889 and which in 1956 changed its name to the Irish Society for the

Prevention of Cruelty to Children (ISPCC)[2] – provided a national child protection service. Between 1889 and 1955 the original Irish branch of the NSPCC was involved with 478,865 Irish children. After the ISPCC was established in 1956, it dealt with 2,500 cases per annum. It has been estimated that only 2% of cases resulted in removal from the parental home (Ferguson, 2007: 127). The ISPCC in its evidence to the Ryan Commission stated the figure for removal from the parental home had fallen to 1.3% in 1956 (CICA, 2009: 5: 4). This evidence suggests a proportionate and prudent policy was pursued by the society.

However, the Ryan Report came to more critical conclusions about the ISPCC's overall role. It also attributed a much higher level of responsibility for the institutionalisation of children to the Society. Instead of the 1% or 2% involvement in admissions to industrial schools acknowledged by the Society, the Ryan Report (CICA, 2009: 5: 5), put the figure at up to 37%. This estimate puts a very different complexion on the role of the ISPCC. It concluded 'the NSPCC/ISPCC played an important role in committing children to industrial schools. The extent of this involvement cannot be accurately ascertained because of a lack of documentation, but it can be stated it was significant' (5: 9). It is also notable that the public image of the Society was that of an agency that removed children from their parental homes. As the Ryan Report (5: 5) put it, 'the general public perception at the time was that the society was heavily involved in committing children to industrial schools, hence the apprehension in the minds of the public associated with the 'cruelty man'. In 1941, one prominent social activist, Frank Duff, accused the system of ISPCC inspectors and district court judges of 'shovelling children into industrial schools' (CICA, 2009).

The ISPCC vigorously rejected this image of being excessively zealous in placing children in industrial schools (CICA, 2009: 5: 6). These accusations of over-zealousness were also linked to allegations of 'bribery' or inducements offered to inspectors by industrial schools eager to augment their funding by increasing their numbers. The Ryan Report (CICA, 2009: 5: 9) did find some evidence to partly support this allegation; albeit, these payments could equally be interpreted as legitimate expenses. The Ryan Report concluded 'it is clear from documentation furnished by the Christian Brothers, that the NSPCC

2   The first Irish branch of the NSPCC was founded in Dublin in May 1889, with branches founded in Cork and Belfast in 1891. In 1956, the Irish Society for the Prevention of Cruelty to Children was founded as a successor to the National Society for the Prevention of Cruelty to Children, which had operated in Ireland from 1889 to 1956.

inspectors in the early 1950s were accustomed to receiving payment of expenses. This clearly was in contravention of the rules laid down in the *Inspectors' Directory'* (5: 9). In fairness to the ISPCC, the task it was required to undertake in a poverty stricken society was well beyond the remit of any voluntary sector organisation.

The role of civil society: public discourse and moral ambivalence

Manifestly, the key social institutions within Irish society – church, state and the voluntary sector – failed needy children. But what was the role of civil society? Social constructionists have sought to deconstruct the discursive basis of public responses to child abuse. Ferguson (2007: 130) asserts:

> I want to argue that children were treated harshly in the industrial schools *because* they were victims of cruelty. This is perhaps the most painful aspect and paradox of the entire history … In many respects the key to unravelling the meaning of child abuse and institutional care lies in understanding the concept of neglect and its link to sexual morality and the notion of moral danger.

There was within public discourse a profound moral ambivalence towards the 'child victim' (Smart, 1999). Both Ferguson (2007) and Smart (1999) relate the treatment of victims of child abuse to public morality and the control of sexuality, including the threat of physical, social and moral contagion. Ferguson (2007: 132) observes:

> The moral status of abused children was seen as dubious. Children were not worked with in terms of what they were – such as victims of abuse and neglect – but *what they were going to be*. They were seen as future threats to social order as much as victims. The child in danger would in time become the dangerous child. The challenge then was to catch these children early and channel them into an appropriate regime of moral rehabilitation. The whole point of the schools regime was to mould children into the kinds of good citizens that the Church and State wanted them to be. No abuse victim or child at risk of abuse was immune from this kind of treatment. Indeed, those children whom we might expect to be most in need of a different kind of

response – such as sexual abuse victims – were viewed as the most 'contaminated'.

Smart (1999: 403-4) asserts:

> The child victim became the moral leper who therefore merited the same sort of treatment as that meted out to criminals. The solution was seen as lying in the Industrial School where they could be contained and where they would not harm innocent children. In this discourse, the abuse of the child was recognised as harmful, but the victim of the abuse became a non-person as a consequence of the harm done to her … So although there was some understanding that abused children were 'damaged', it was nonetheless thought that they became evil or wicked and that they subsequently 'chose' an immoral course of behaviour. Those children who did persist in talking about their experiences, or who 'acted out' their abuse in any way, usually fell foul of this 'discursive trick' of renaming. That is to say, they moved from being innocent victims to being pariahs and 'lepers'.

Diarmaid Ferriter (2009: 227) in his archival study on court records, *Occasions of Sin: Sex and Society in Modern Ireland*, confirms the existence of moral ambivalence in public discourse in the period 1940–60, where sexual immorality could interchangeably mean juvenile prostitution or child sexual abuse: 'there also remained little public discussion of the sexual abuse of young girls which continued to occur on a regular basis, with devastating consequences for the victims who were often deemed, it seemed, to share the guilt'.

What emerges from the child abuse scandals in Ireland is an absence of civicness. While religious virtue was preached from the pulpit, civic virtue was absent in Ireland. This was due to the lack of an ethical civil society based upon the principles of civicness and civility.

Church, state and child abuse: the issue of responsibility

The official response to the public scandal of institutional child abuse has been slow and, at times, controversial. Arnold (2009: 89) critically observes 'from the Taoiseach down, the public picture that was presented was a meretricious one: that this was on behalf of the abused. It would take many years for truth to emerge, and even now the detail continues to be hotly argued.' A state historically dominated by the Catholic Church has had difficulty in facing its past. While the model officially adopted in 2000 was based on the post-apartheid South African Truth and Reconciliation Commission, in the form of the Commission to Inquire into Child Abuse (and the resulting Ryan Report), there has arguably been a lack of good faith from both state and church. These are essential ingredients in the process of disclosure. As we shall see later in this chapter, media reaction to a 'Secret Deal' between the state and the church, which indemnified the latter from the costs of compensation, have led to public cynicism about the state's willingness to hold the church accountable for the historic abuse of children in institutional care. This is perhaps not very surprising, since the state clearly shares responsibility for this historic abuse of children. The reality has been that since the inception of the Irish state in 1922, it has been, both in terms of constitutional theory and practice, a Catholic state (Powell, 1992). Within this constitutional configuration, politicians have arguably been supine in their subservience to the church. However, detraditionalisation has undermined the church's moral monopoly over Irish society. There are signs of potential change. The most powerful condemnation of the Catholic Church to date has come from the Taoiseach, Enda Kenny, elected in 2011. In an unprecedented speech on 20 July 2011, in response to the clerical abuse of children in the Diocese of Cloyne, Mr Kenny stated: 'the rape and torture of children were downplayed or "managed" to uphold instead the primacy of the institution, its power, standing and reputation'. He made it clear that he was not referring simply to historical issues but to contemporary reality, accusing the Catholic Church of 'dysfunction, disconnection [and] narcissism'.[3] Clearly, the elaborate mythology that underpinned Catholic power in Ireland had been exposed as an unsustainable belief system.

The revelations of the Ryan Report are so damning that some commentators have sought to question the validity of the report, and others its public reception and the balance of media reportage. Fr Tony Flannery, a Redemptionist priest, has edited a book, *Responding to the Ryan Report*, that critically interrogates the report. In the introduction to the book, Flannery (2009: 9–10) asserts:

> What was most needed was something that would broaden the debate and introduce the sorts of voices that I felt were largely absent. I believed that the issue was of such crucial

[3] *The Irish Times* 21 July 2011.

importance to the future of our society that all attempts at scapegoating had to be contested, and the focus brought back to the extent, the nature and possible solutions to the problem. So I decided that the best way to respond was to try to get a wide range of people, from different backgrounds and expertise, to address it for me.

The view that the Catholic clergy have been made 'scapegoats' for the failures of the industrial and reformatory school system is the core argument in *Responding to the Ryan Report*, initially in the introduction and then by several subsequent contributors. Fr Donal Dorr (Flannery, 2009: 112) asserts that he wishes 'to challenge the kind of scapegoating which has taken place, where the blame for the radical failures in the system has been loaded unfairly on just one segment of those who were responsible'. Another contributor, Dr Fainche Ryan (2009: 155), a theologian, similarly argues 'it is too easy to condemn and judge the past. To scapegoat or blame, comes easily to many of us. The religious are easy scapegoats. In Ireland by and large they are elderly, and somewhat lost'. The 'scapegoating' argument put forward by these contributors to *Responding to the Ryan Report* seeks to highlight the failures of state regulation. While there is considerable truth in this argument, the unpalatable reality is that most of the abuse was carried out by members of the clergy, which is clear from the statistical analysis of the Ryan Report. But it is clear that the Irish state also bears culpability. Some commentators argue that it was the agent of abuse through its failure to regulate. For example, Arnold (2009: 11) argues that the state was ultimately responsible: 'The state did know of them [abuses] and it did not act'. His argument is that the state provided a legal system and prison system for destitute Irish children that it failed to regulate. He also notes the key role of voluntary organisations in sustaining the system of industrial and reformatory schools, notably the ISPCC, which was (as already discussed) heavily criticised in the Ryan Report (Arnold 2009: 4). Clearly, the Irish state and some voluntary organisations were morally blind and share culpability with the church. Furthermore, the state almost completely failed to regulate the industrial and reformatory school system. This cannot be denied and contextualises the concerns of the clergy about scapegoating. The allocation of responsibility is clearly a very complex task involving church, state and civil society.

However, the fact that the Irish state lamentably failed in its duty of regulation does not absolve the Catholic Church from being the primary actor in the narrative of child abuse. The public perception of the Catholic Church is that it is morally ambivalent about child abuse. Public antipathy towards the Catholic Church has been fuelled by its apparent unwillingness to fully grapple with the two underlying principles that informed the approach of the Ryan Report – truth-telling and reparation.

The church's insistence of anonymity for the perpetrators of abuse (both living and dead) suggests to a sceptical public that it is still in denial about the enormity of the human rights violations for which it was directly responsible. Recent news reports that the Vatican regards the ordination of women priests as one of the greatest crimes in church law, morally equivalent to clerical child abuse, suggests a moral incapacity to understand the gravity of child abuse (Hooper and Siddique, 2010). This legacy of moral ambivalence has made it very difficult for the Catholic Church to address the issue of clerical child abuse. It consequently continues to fail to confront its past and the need for public atonement, even though Pope Francis has shown considerable leadership in this regard.

Furthermore, intense public anger has been caused by the alleged unwillingness of the Catholic Church to fully pay compensation to the victims. This is an essential step in the process of reconciliation and atonement for clerical child abuse. The church's view is that financial responsibility should be shared with the state. This is not an unreasonable position, given the state's clear culpability, but the critic's perception is that the church doesn't want to pay its fair share and is in league with the state against the interests of the abused. Arnold (2009: 147) asserts: 'It was the Church that was protected, and, in company with the state, is committed to the protection of the state as well. Meanwhile the abused will remain abused'.

The Irish state failed to regulate the industrial and reformatory school system and remained morally blind to the human rights violations perpetrated within them for most of the 20th century. The Ryan Report (CICA, 2009: 4: 7.03) has concluded 'the lessons of the past should be learned', adding:

> For the State, it is important to admit that abuse of children occurred because of failures of systems and policy, of management and administration, as well as of senior personnel who were concerned with Industrial and Reformatory Schools. This admission is, however, the beginning of a process. Further steps require internal departmental analysis and understanding of how these

failures came about so that steps can be taken to reduce the risk of repeating them.

The Congregations need to examine how their ideals became debased by systemic abuse. They must ask themselves how they came to tolerate breaches of their own rules and, when sexual and physical abuse was discovered, how they responded to it, and to those who perpetrated it. They must examine their attitude to neglect and emotional abuse and, more generally, how the interests of the institutions and the Congregations came to be placed ahead those of the children who were in their care.

An important aspect of this process of exploration, acceptance and understanding by the State and the Congregations is the acknowledgement of the fact that the system failed the children, not just that children were abused because occasional individual lapses occurred.

Tabloid media reaction to the publication of the Ryan Report in May 2009 focused on injustice and betrayal. The front page of the *Irish Daily Mail*[4] declared 'Truth – but no reconciliation. Six decades of ritual abuse covered up by church and state is finally laid bare but hundreds of abusers will never face justice'. The *Irish Daily Mirror*[5] proclaimed 'You evil monsters ... priests systematically raped and beat thousands of children during decades of abuse in institutions'. It further reported 'victims' fury as report fails to name the perverts'. The *Irish Daily Star*,[6] in similar declamatory language, stated on its front page 'Devil's Disciples ... but not one abuser named and shamed'. *The Irish Sun*[7] called the revelations a 'Holy disgrace,' adding a front page headline a few days later: 'Get the monsters'.[8]

Media anger soon turned to the issue of compensation of the survivors. The Residential Institutional Redress Act 2002 had established the Residential Institutions Redress Board, charged with providing compensation for the survivors of 123 institutions who had experienced abuse. Its establishment was accompanied by what was (as noted earlier) called 'The Secret Deal' that indemnified the Catholic Church for its involvement and cooperation in the redress scheme

4   *Irish Daily Mail* 21 May 2009'.
5   *Irish Daily Mirror* 21 May 2009'.
6   *Irish Daily Star* 21 May 2009'.
7   *The Irish Sun* 23 May 2009'.
8   *The Irish Sun* 26 May 2009.

(Arnold, 2009: 206). The terms of the agreement limited the church's liability to €128 million, despite estimates of the total cost of victim compensation exceeding €1 billion. The *Irish Daily Star*[9] called it a 'Raw deal'. The *Irish Daily Mail* demanded: 'Make the church pay'.[10] Four days later, The *Irish Daily Mail*[11] appealed directly to the church: 'In God's name pay up!' The *Irish Daily Mirror*[12] declared: 'Church should pay for its evil'. *The Irish Sun,*[13] with a headline 'Church abuse fury,' demanded 'Pay for your sins'. It answered its own headline the next day with a report stating child abuse victims had been ignored by the religious congregations under the headline: 'No, we won't pay for sixty years of abuse'. It noted that the Residential Institutions Redress Board had received 14,584 claims from survivors and processed 13,190 at an average pay-out of €63,320[14] and it predicted 'Orders' refusal [to pay compensation] is the death knell of the Church'. The *Irish Sun*[15] reported progress on the compensation of victims: 'Orders will pay more compensation'. The vexed issue of the relative responsibilities of church and state continues to be debated as Irish society comes to terms with the legacy of the Ryan Report and the survivors seek to reclaim their broken lives.

Conclusion

There is both a sense of circularity and progress in analysing the evolution of children's rights in Irish social policy. It is circular in the sense that social conservatives constantly seek to deny the past and frustrate change and social reform. On the other hand, there is a human rights strand in this narrative that has gradually gained momentum over the past half century as social reformers in civil society have pressed for change and disclosure. Ireland has not only modernised during this period, it has also internationalised by joining the United Nations (1955) and European Union (1973). Both of these developments have put pressure upon the state and civil society to adopt higher standards in the treatment of children and young people. Modernisation and internationalisation have also turned Ireland into a more secular society

9   *Irish Daily Star* 24 May 2009.
10 *Irish Daily Mail* 22 May 2009.
11 *Irish Daily Mail* 26 May 2009.
12 *Irish Daily Mirror* 25 May 2009.
13 *The Irish Sun* 22 May 2009.
14 *The Irish Sun* 23 May 2009.
15 *The Irish Sun* 30 May 2009.

in which a growing detraditionalisation has gradually undermined the social power of the Catholic Church and the mythology that supported its hegemony. We have noted the influence of pressure groups in civil society (eg, JCWSSW, Tuairim, CARE, Children First, ICCL and the Irish Association of Social Workers) in promoting the agenda of social reform and moral responsibility. Such liberalising campaigns were effective in their determination to vindicate children's rights, but much remains to be achieved.

Perhaps the most impressive development within Irish civil society in relation to children's rights has been the emergence of survivors groups. The power and authenticity of their narrative voice confronts Irish civil society with the reality of its moral ambivalence and human rights record in relation to children. Organisations like SOCA (Survivors of Child Abuse), One in Four, the Aislinn Centre and many others speak truth to power based upon survivor experience. Their courageous attempt to confront both church and state with their failures takes civil society into new and unexplored levels of consciousness in relation to the rights of the child. All the signs indicate that this is a difficult process of truth, revelation and reparation in reference to many damaged lives. In relation to social reform and children's rights much remains to be done, but moral literacy is growing despite a conservative grain of denial and resistance. The Ryan Report has not only exposed the culpability of the church but also the moral blindness of the Irish state over most of the 20th century, and the moral blindness of most of Irish civil society.

Irish industrial and reformatory schools were based upon a philosophy of dehumanisation that subjected the bodies and minds of their inmates to regimes of medieval violence, involving cruelty and in many instances torture. The Ryan Report (2009) is not simply a narrative of child abuse. Its revelations of human rights violations against children in institutional care belong to the same realm of violence and oppression as Soviet Gulags and Nazi concentration camps. In some respects, the issues are even more morally challenging. These human rights crimes were not committed by a totalitarian state, but by church organisations in a state that purported to be democratic. All of the victims were children. Most of the perpetrators were clergy. How do we make sense of these events? How do we deal with the social and moral issues? We have discussed the Catholic Church's difficulties with engaging in a process of atonement and reconciliation. The value of the Ryan Report (2009) is that it is an exercise in truth-telling, even if it is flawed by the anonymity of the accused. This was the compromise the Commission to Inquire into Child Abuse was prepared to make in order to provide the survivors with a forum to tell their truths, and Irish society with the opportunity to bear witness to that truth. The challenge for Irish society is to engage with the moral and social legacy of the Ryan Report. This legacy demonstrates a lack of civility among the clergy, who were responsible for the administration of the reformatory and industrial school system. But their moral ambivalence towards these victims of child poverty was shared by both the post-independence Irish state and civil society. There was a fear of what Smart (1999) has called 'moral contagion' in which the child victim is reconstructed as the 'evil or wicked' other. The consequences of this moral ambiguity was that the children placed within the reformatory and industrial school system were dehumanised and without the most basic rights to bodily integrity, food, education, health care and love.

While the Ryan Report (2009) primarily addresses historical child abuse in industrial and reformatory schools, there is evidence of continuing violations of human rights up to the present day. The Ryan Report (CICA, 2009: 4: 6.43) found evidence of child abuse in 161 other care institutions up to the year 2000. Judge Reilly's 2012 *Report on the Inspection of St Patrick's Institution*, a juvenile justice facility for the incarceration of young adults and children, concludes that human rights violations are an ongoing problem. These violations include bullying, intimidation and degradation. The Reilly Report (Reilly, 2012: 3.84) asserted that there was an undesirable culture' in St Patrick's, adding:

> To say that there is a culture in St. Patricks where the human rights of some prisoners are either ignored or violated is a serious statement. Individual instances where the rights of prisoners appear to have been ignored or violated, may not indicate a culture. However when the number of instances found by me ... are taken together the cumulative effect can only lead to the conclusion that there is a culture in St. Patricks which results in the human rights of prisoners (children and young adults) being either ignored or violated.

St Patrick's Institution was finally closed in 2013. But questions remain, about the civility of Irish systems of social care, the civicness of Irish civil society, and the role of the Irish state, as we shall see in Chapter 5.

FIVE

Child abuse, cultural disbelief and the patriarchal family

> We have become complacent, developing a new language around explaining why children have been damaged by the actions of adults rather than expressing any new ambition to reduce the occurrence of such events ... It is time that the authorities turn their minds to tackling the hard question and making decisions in principle about how child death inquiries should function. Decisions need to be made and agreements reached on a range of issues including: how information is to be shared and placed in the public domain; what is expected of State agencies in terms of their accountability to the public; the time frame for inquiries and the involvement of family members. (Emily Logan, Irish Ombudsman for Children, *Sunday Business Post*, 17 May 2009)

These observations from the Ombudsman for Children in Ireland crystallise the public frustration and fatigue concerning child abuse reports. The paradox is that while child abuse reports expose deep flaws in the system of child protection, it doesn't appear to improve – or does it? Are the tragedies that are investigated preventable? Do professionals, media and public hold shared understandings of who is responsible and what can be done to prevent child abuse? Is there a culture of disbelief about the social reality of child abuse? In this chapter, we seek answers from four Irish inquiries into child abuse by posing three simple questions: How did it happen? Why was such bad professional practice allowed to go on undetected and uncorrected? What can be done to improve the child protection system? The four public inquiries that we analyse are:

The Kelly Fitzgerald Report (1996)
The McColgan Report (West of Ireland Farmer case) (1998)
The Monageer Inquiry (2009)
The Roscommon Child Care Report (2010)

These four inquiries were among 29 child abuse inquiries and reviews carried out in Ireland between 1993 and 2012 and have been identified by Buckley and O'Nolan (2013: 50) as being among the most significant. Along with the landmark Kilkenny Incest Inquiry (1993) discussed in Chapter 2, these are considered as being the five core family inquiries in any analysis of Irish child abuse reports. Buckley and O'Nolan (2013: 25) view child abuse inquiries as a form of public catharsis and reassurance: 'the reassurance provided by inquiries is normally understood as a form of collective or public reassurance'. However, they also note that inquiries can heighten rather than allay public concern because they 'focus on events that cannot be guaranteed to never happen again' and may even 'undermine public confidence, if they point to major problems that are difficult and costly to address' (Buckley and O'Nolan, 2013: 25). The media clearly plays a critical role in interpreting child abuse inquiries to the public. There are two aspects to media reporting of child abuse inquiries: (1) looking back in time by clarifying the sequence of events and allocation of individual, agency and professional responsibility and (2) looking forward by making recommendations for policy reform and systems improvement.

The problem with the allocation of responsibility is that it can lead to a 'blame culture', in which social workers and other public officials (police, nurses, managers) are 'named and shamed' in the media (Munro, 2004). Media campaigns can turn into witch-hunts, in which public servants are personally held accountable for the inadequacies of public policy and sometimes lose their jobs. We will examine each of the four Irish inquiries sequentially and consider the media reaction to their conclusions and recommendations. In doing so, we will also seek to evaluate the media's contribution to making the public aware of child protection, and we will consider the need to change laws supporting the patriarchal family and invest in services so that child abuse can be prevented in the future. Such provision is a more positive side of the media's role in reporting on child abuse inquiries. It is also notable that several of these cases involved both the United Kingdom and Ireland, highlighting the challenge in managing child protection across national borders. Developmental gaps in child protection services are exposed by these inter-state cases, as well as the need for European protocols and oversight. Issues also arise in relation to children's rights and the policy deficits that contribute to children's vulnerability to abuse by adults.

The Kelly Fitzgerald Report (1996): a media crusade

The Kelly Fitzgerald case is an example of a crusading media intervention in a child protection case, forcing the publication of an inquiry report. A report in the *Irish Independent*[1] published extracts from this inquiry into the facts surrounding the death of Kelly Fitzgerald, and this led to a parliamentary debate about the failure to publish the report and the conclusions and recommendations contained within the findings. The inquiry had been initiated by the Western Health Board and completed five months earlier but withheld on legal advice. The Kelly Fitzgerald inquiry had been established on 2 May 1995 and reported on 14 November 1995. The short timescale suggests a very efficient approach to its task by the inquiry team.

Kelly Fitzgerald's parents were both born in England and were of Irish ethnic extraction. When Kelly was born, her mother was 17 years old. Her parents married in response to family pressure. At the time Kelly was born, her parents were living with the Traveller community at a location near London. Following the eviction of the Travellers from their halting site, the family moved in with her mother's parents in London which proved to be an unhappy experience. Kelly was born during this period, on 4 June 1977. Shortly afterwards, the family was housed by the local council. Kelly was a premature baby, weighing 5lbs 7ozs. On 29 September 1977, it was noted that the nearly four-month-old baby was underweight and she was referred to a general practitioner (GP). Her mother was thought to be diluting the feed excessively and advice was offered to rectify the problem. A subsequent appointment to monitor Kelly's progress four days later was not kept (Houses of the Oireachtas, 1996: 13).

On 23 October 1977, Kelly was admitted to the A&E department of St Thomas' Hospital, London. Kelly was suffering from weight loss and was described as emaciated and dehydrated to the extent that her survival was in doubt. X-rays showed that Kelly had two healed fractures. A Place of Safety Order was granted. There was uncertainty as to whether the alleged neglect was due to maternal ignorance or was deliberate. A case conference decided not to place Kelly on the 'at risk' register but recommended ongoing support from the social services as an 'urgent requirement'. There appears to have been no further social services involvement until 1988 when Kelly was referred to child guidance for behavioural problems. The Fitzgerald family was

---

[1] *Irish Independent* 7 March 1996 'Extracts from the Kelly Fitzgerald Report'.

now composed of six children; four girls and two boys (Houses of the Oireachtas, 1996: 14).

On 31 May 1989, Kelly was placed by Lambeth Social Services Department on the Social Services Child Protection At Risk Register because she was deemed to be at risk of 'emotional deprivation and abuse and at times suffers extreme mental cruelty from her parents'. Against the wishes of her parents, who (allegedly) would have preferred her to be 'punished' by being placed in a children's home, Kelly was sent to live with her grandparents. A case conference on 22 November 1989 noted that Kelly was flourishing in her grandparents' care but was allegedly ostracised by her parents. However, there were concerns about her younger sister, who was placed on the 'at risk' register under the heading 'Grave Concern' (Houses of the Oireachtas, 1996: 14-15).

At this time the Fitzgerald family moved to County Mayo in the West of Ireland and bought a small farm and house, reportedly with compensation from a road traffic accident. Kelly remained in London with her grandparents. In December 1990, Lambeth Social Services sent its child protection files to the Western Health Board in Ireland. The Western Health Board immediately began to monitor Kelly's sister's weight. In 1991 and 1992, Kelly spent her summer holidays in County Mayo. She subsequently contacted her parents requesting that she permanently join the family in Mayo. They assented and she joined them in September 1992. Within four months, Kelly was back in London at St Thomas' Hospital and she was terminally ill. Doctors at St Thomas' Hospital reportedly queried physical abuse and neglect. Kelly was 30 lbs lighter than her weight should have been and her protein levels were one-third of what would be expected (Houses of the Oireachtas, 1996: 117). Kelly died of septicaemia at St Thomas' Hospital on 4 February 1992, resulting from an infected wound. On 1 November 1994, her parents were sentenced to 18 months imprisonment by Castlebar Circuit Criminal Court after pleading guilty to a charge of wilful neglect (Houses of the Oireachtas, 1996: 118).

The report suggested that media reports involved an element of 'confusion' between Kelly and her younger sister, adding: 'Kelly's death, any child death where abuse and neglect are at least contributory factors, is a tragedy of most frightening and distressing dimensions' (124). The inquiry addressed itself to the question of whether Kelly's death was preventable. It identified at least 10 actions between December 1990 and January 1993 that might have prevented Kelly's death. However, it concluded that 'it has been recognised that any different approach or action by the health board would almost certainly have been met by a correspondingly different defensive reaction on the part of the family'.

The Kelly Fitzgerald Report identified three key features in the management of the case for particular criticism (Houses of the Oireachtas, 1996: 165):

1. The lack of a comprehensive health board assessment of the family and the degree of risk it represented to at least some of the children;
2. The ineffectiveness of the case conferences held on the family;
3. The arrangements in place to support and supervise frontline staff.

It concluded: 'we find that the intervention of the health board, in spite of the best efforts of individual staff, was naïve and ineffective when pitted against parents who represented a significant danger to at least two of the children'. On a slightly more optimistic note, the inquiry observed that these events had occurred before the publication of the Kilkenny Incest Investigation Report (1993), which had resulted in improvements in the practice and resourcing of social work.

In 2007, the *Irish Independent*,[2] in an article on the Kelly Fitzgerald family, noted that Kelly's 'pitiful death at the age of 15 ignited a blaze of headlines in 1993', but it dismissively concluded that 'nothing has changed to ensure that this same nightmare would not befall another child'. In 1993 the *Irish Independent*[3] had contributed to the incendiary media comment with its own heading 'Girl died after visit to parents: Burnt and Beaten teenager had a gangrenous wound, Inquest told'. However, it also took up a strong position against 'reactionary self-styled campaigners' dismissing their opposition to the insertion of children's rights into the Irish Constitution as a 'facile and pernicious' proposition.[4] The Kelly Fitzgerald case has continued to attract media attention in Ireland as a child protection parable despite the fact that most of her life was spent in the UK, where she eventually died. The moral of the parable is that family life can be dangerous for children. The media have been instrumental in exposing this unpalatable truth.

The McGolgan Report (1998): social work versus cultural disbelief

An inquiry was established in 1995 after a West of Ireland farmer was sentenced to 12 years imprisonment for serious child abuse offences against his children. The four children subsequently successfully sued

[2] *Irish Independent* 5 June 2007 'The door is open for repeat of torture'.

[3] *Irish Independent* 23 April 1993 'Girl died after visit to parents'.

[4] *Irish Independent* 5 June 2007.

the North Western Health Board and the family GP for a €1million settlement, following a 13 day High Court hearing. After his release (with remission) nine years later, the West of Ireland farmer moved to the UK. While there, he was prosecuted for child pornography offences and sentenced to 30 months imprisonment by Exeter court. The McGolgan Report was produced by a review group that was convened in 1995 and reported in 1998. It was suspended for over two years in order to enable the children's case for damages to be heard.

On the eve of the publication of the McGolgan Report, Don Lavery, writing in the *Irish Independent* in August 1998,[5] commented that 'the family are still traumatised by the brutality administered by their father from the mid-1970s to the early 1990s in a family home which was likened by psychiatrist Professor Ivor Browne as being akin to a Nazi concentration camp'. In a subsequent article in the *Irish Independent* (1 December 2012) Kevin Myers described the case as 'the worst sexual abuse of children, that an Irish court has ever heard', adding that the father exposed his daughter to a 'frenzy of violation' after mass. In 2010, the *Irish Daily Mail*[6] described the West of Ireland farmer as the 'Beast of Sligo'. Susan McKay (1998: 167) in a book about one of the children notes that newspaper front-page headlines on 22 February 1995 dubbed the West of Ireland farmer: 'Ireland's most evil Dad', 'Sex beast father', and 'Monster'.

The West of Ireland Farmer case constitutes a narrative of physical, sexual and emotional abuse of four of the six children in the household. It commenced in 1976. At the time, the three eldest children were aged seven, six and four years. The abuse continued until 1993. The family GP, social services and the gardaí (police) were aware of the physical abuse of children from 1979. In that year the mother had requested that one of her daughters be voluntarily admitted to care, but this did not happen. Subsequently, in 1992, a criminal case was initiated against the father for an alleged assault of one of the children but was adjourned and later struck out.

During 1983, the eldest child was taken into care at his own request when he refused to return home after school. While in care he alleged the sexual abuse of himself and his sister by his father. Nonetheless, he was permitted to make weekend visits home, and he left the children's home after six months. The full scale of the abuse was not made public until three of the children were adults. It is notable that there was no social services involvement with the family between 1984 and 1993,

[5] *Irish Independent* 31 August 1998 'Health Board Bungled Incest Case'.
[6] *Irish Daily Mail* 23 June 2010 'Beast of Sligo'.

despite the children being 'subjected to horrific abuse' (Buckley and O'Nolan, 2013: 53-4). The facts behind this troubling narrative suggest a system of child protection that was not fully engaged with the issues, a professional lack of understanding of child abuse, and a fundamental lack of legal protection for children at that time.

Buckley and O'Nolan (2013: 74) have addressed the weaknesses in the child protection system in the West of Ireland Farmer case as systemic:

> One of the main weaknesses identified in the West of Ireland Farmer case was a failure by different services to be alert to the possibility of child abuse and exchange information with colleagues. Many of the recommendations focused on clarification of roles and responsibilities, different aspects of information-sharing, the need for better quality recording and case conferences, and improved linkages between services. There was a distinct emphasis on the need for improved vigilance and regular review of situations where children were deemed to be at risk. It also advocated for out-of-hours services and services for adult survivors of abuse. The Report made recommendations specifically for support and services in respect of the case under inquiry, and its recommendations on training focused strongly on the need for an inter-agency dimension.

But there was also a cultural context to the West of Ireland Farmer case, revealing deeply traditional social attitudes that militated against state intervention by the health and social services and the police and the courts.

What clearly emerges from the West of Ireland Farmer case is a social worker positively seeking to promote statutory intervention. Kevin Myers, writing in the *Irish Independent* in December 2012,[7] refers to how 'the valiant efforts of one social worker to expose what was going on, came to nothing. Her report quivers with rage at what she found.' The social worker's report, dated 3 April 1984, is included as an appendix to the West of Ireland Farmer Case Report. It demonstrates a highly apposite judgement of the situation in which the social worker observes: 'It is my opinion that I am dealing with a very pathological family. The degree of abuse both physical and sexual is at an extraordinary level. The defensiveness and collusion in this family

---

[7]   *Irish Independent* December 2012 'The worst case of sexual abuse of children'.

is at an exceedingly high level. Abuse is the norm' (Bruton, 1998: 54). The social worker observes in relation to the West of Ireland Farmer: 'I have formed a professional opinion that he is an extremely sick man … I feel he has everyone terrorised and keeps control by terrorising. His personality disorder is such that he could not be considered a fit parent. His sexual activities regarding the children can only be described as criminal' (Bruton, 1998: 54).

What is particularly striking about the social worker's report is that despite her analysis, which argues that this is a very serious case of child abuse, she is not confident that a case conference would support her judgement that the children needed to be taken into care. The social worker argues 'serious controls are needed in this case' and concludes:

> I feel very strongly about my recommendations and while the case conference has the decision-making role and whatever decision is made at the conference will have to be implemented, I must state that I feel if my recommendations to take action in this case, which I feel is necessary to protect these children and prevent further damage are not taken my position as the social worker to the family will be untenable. In writing this report I am aware how strongly I feel about the case. I am also awake to the very slight possibility that I could be wrong in my estimation. Only time and subsequent events will determine that. My only answer to that criticism or possibility is that if I am making a mistake I am making it in the best interests of these children as I see it. (Bruton, 1998: 57)

Despite this trenchant professional social work analysis and prophetic warning, the child protection system failed to respond. Why? The McColgan Report (Bruton, 1998: 44) provides the answer:

> The review group is satisfied that a particular critical combination of factors occurred in April/May 1984 which indicate that the operational child protection system fell down. A focused insightful report prepared by the field social worker was not presented to a case conference as none was called by either the senior social worker or Director of Community Care and Medical Officer of Health.

The next case conference didn't happen for nearly a decade! There existed at the time a culture of disbelief in relation to the existence of child sexual abuse among members of the medical profession and within social services management. Disclosures of child sexual abuse were regarded with 'shock, horror and disbelief' (Bruton, 1998: 42). Furthermore, intervention within the family was legally problematic with social workers being exposed to constant intimidation (Bruton, 1998: 14, 21–22 and 33). The social worker had allegedly been met at the family home by an irate farmer 'brandishing a shovel and threatening to set his dogs on her if she didn't go away and leave his family alone' (McKay, 1998: 83).

The West of Ireland farmer was arguably allowed to abuse his children because the law was on his side in a culture that enshrined family rights in its 1937 Constitution as 'inalienable and imprescriptible'. It turned the children into prisoners within an abusive family, as the eldest daughter reported:

> We were prisoners in a tower with no door. The care workers, so called, knew we were in prison, but they didn't seem to care. They looked and then they looked away again. I was trying to make a door to let other people see in, and to let us out, but sometimes I felt like the Lady of Shallot. She was locked up in a tower and she could not even look out. She used to weave a tapestry all day, and she watched the world in a mirror. In the end, she sees the handsome knight in the mirror and she is tempted and she turns and looks. She leaves the tower and gets in a boat and floats down the river to Camelot. She is beautiful but she dies. (McKay, 1998: 109)

She clearly sees few escape routes from child abuse other than death.

A report in the *Irish Independent* in November 2011[8] concluded that while the physical abuse was overt the sexual abuse was covert. The family watched the West of Ireland farmer interrogate and beat his eldest son 'like a court' while 'educated people' failed to intervene. But, at a deeper level, it was not just a failure of professional expertise in this case; it was a cultural failure to acknowledge child abuse, particularly sexual abuse. It was also a moral failure in a deeply traditional Catholic culture, where the patriarchal family was regarded as sacrosanct and beyond the reach of the state by professionals, police and courts. The implementation of the Child Care Act 1991 has changed the legal framework for family intervention; changing the traditional cultural

---

[8] *Irish Independent* 24 November 2011 'McColgan family part of Irish social history'.

context will be more challenging, as is evident from more recent reports.

The Monageer Inquiry (2008): a case of familicide?

A familicide is a form of murder-suicide; a murder or mass killing within an immediate family. It is also called 'family annihilation'. The Monageer Inquiry into the Dunne family appears to be a classic example of a case of familicide. Ironically, the inquiry did not address the issue of familicide because it was not within their terms of reference (Brosnan, 2008: 8.26). Instead, the inquiry addressed itself to the circumstances of the deaths of the Dunne family, which was composed of two adults, Adrian and Ciara Dunne, and two young children, Lean (aged five) and Shania (aged three) and the role of police and social services in responding to the Dunne family tragedy. The facts of the case are clearly set out in the Monageer Inquiry Report:

> Adrian Dunne died by hanging on the weekend of 20th-23rd April 2007. His wife Ciara Dunne died by ligature strangulation. Lean and Shania died by smothering. It was clear from the evidence before the Inquiry that Adrian Dunne and Ciara Dunne were planning the deaths of the family. The Inquiry Team are satisfied from the profile that emerged of Adrian Dunne that he was the driving force behind the planning and execution of the deaths of Ciara Dunne and their two children, Lean and Shania. The Inquiry Team concluded that there was no third party involvement.
>
> The Inquiry Team did not discover any single definitive motive behind the deaths of the Dunne family. Instead, the Inquiry Team believe that several factors contributed to Adrian and Ciara Dunne's decision to end their lives and that of their children. Important factors were the death of Adrian Dunne's father on 9th April 2006 and the recent death of his brother James by hanging on 29th March 2007.
>
> The following factors may also have contributed to the decision to end their lives: Adrian Dunne's controlling and dominant influence within the family; Ciara Dunne's docile, childlike nature making her very compliant and subservient to her husband's wishes; Adrian Dunne's ability in isolating Ciara Dunne from her family; their mounting debts; the option of a move to Liverpool no longer seeming feasible

and the idealised notion of the family being together forever in heaven.

The time of death cannot be established with certainty, but, having considered all the evidence available, the Inquiry Team believe the most probable time of death of the two children and Ciara Dunne was on Saturday morning, the 21st April, 2007 before the 'suicide' text message was sent at 10.17 a.m. and that Adrian Dunne died soon afterwards.

The Inquiry Team believe that even if the Gardaí [police] or Social Services had called to the Dunne family home during the course of the weekend, it is likely that the tragedy would not have been averted given Adrian and Ciara Dunne's capacity to provide a plausible explanation for their bizarre funeral plans as had happened with the Clonroche Curate [local priest]. (Brosnan, 2008: 7.18-7.22)

What was most striking about the case was that the Dunne family organised their own funeral in advance, including provision for white coffins, wills and the type of clothing to be worn. Yet, while alerted by the local funeral director, the gardaí and social services failed to intervene on time to prevent the tragedy occurring at the family home in Monageer, County Wexford. Social services were alerted by the gardaí but had not visited because there was no out-of-hours/weekend service.

Adrian Dunne, the father, was blind. Ciara Dunne, the mother, was mildly intellectually disabled. Both children had bi-polar cataracts and were in receipt of medical and early child intervention support. The family had an annual income of €38,400 but were in debt. Neither parent was ever in full-time or part-time work. The Monageer Inquiry characterised the social context of the family as isolated:

The Inquiry Team, having heard evidence from family, friends and neighbours have come to the conclusion that Adrian Dunne was a complex character, very much the dominant partner in the relationship and exerted a very strong influence over Ciara Dunne. It appears that he isolated her from her family. Ciara Dunne appeared to have very little communication outside the home on her own initiative. In addition, the family appears to have been unusually isolate[d] from both wider family and friends. (Brosnan, 2008: 4.26)

The Dunnes moved home frequently, making it difficult for the health and social services to maintain contact (Brosnan, 2008: 7.3). While Adrian Dunne emerges as a manipulative and domineering personality, no definitive motive for the tragic event was established.

The media reception of the Monageer Inquiry Report was highly critical, which was in part attributable to the redacting of a substantial part of the report for 'legal reasons'. Raidió Teilifís Éireann (RTÉ) reported that the solicitor representing the Dunne family said in his opinion and in the opinion of the family the report was a 'whitewash'. The Minister for Children, Barry Andrews, 'said a number of aspects of the report had been censored due to legal advice but denied there was any question of a cover-up' (RTÉ news report, 13 May 2009).

In an article in the *Sunday Business Post* in May 2009,[9] the Ombudsman for Children, Emily Logan, took the government to task on its decision to redact key aspects of the Monageer Inquiry Report:

> The deletion of certain passages from the Monageer report has been attributed to legal concern raised regarding their content. The specific nature of those concerns has not, however, been clarified. The omission of such information is in itself questionable, given that there are means open to the Minister to publish the report in a manner that would address the most obvious bases upon which a legal challenge could be raised. But even if one accepted that such a redaction was necessary, it would still be essential to provide a detailed explanation setting out the nature of the information and specific concerns raised.

The Ombudsman for Children further noted:

> A matter that has provoked widespread criticism is the fact that seven of the 26 recommendations set out at the end of the report were blacked out. The deletion of these recommendations is qualitatively different from the deletion of the other material set out in the report. One of the stated aims of the report is to inform and improve practice and, presumably, the deleted recommendations relate to this objective. It is difficult to see how these recommendations relate to this objective. It is not sufficient that the public bodies in question are aware of them as to

[9]   *Sunday Business Post* 17 May 2009 'E. Logan Opinion Article'.

accept this would be tantamount to accepting that public accountability in implementing such recommendations is unimportant. Establishing who is responsible for carrying out the recommendations of the report and monitoring implementation are key considerations.

Emily Logan finished with a damning conclusion:

> The redaction of this report serves to undermine the difficult work of the Inquiry Team and more importantly lays bare a family in need, cruelly stripped of their dignity. The result of redaction is an unbalanced account of events with an over reporting of unnecessary and intimate details regarding the background and family life of the Dunne family.

On the issue of the privacy of the Dunne family, the Ombudsman for Children questioned the inquiry's inclusion of 'certain personal information'.[10]

There was no allocation of blame to any individual, but there was criticism of the public services. The gardaí were considered remiss in their poor communication with the Dunne family's relatives before and after the tragedy (Brosnan, 2008: 7.29 and 7.32). Furthermore, the Monageer Inquiry Report, in its recommendations, asserted 'where a member of An Garda Siochána [police] received a report … he/she should take immediate action to ensure the safety of the child' (Brosnan, 2008: 8.2). In evidence a senior police officer had told the Monageer Inquiry that he did not see social intervention as part of policing: 'we are not qualified to carry out risk assessment of people if they had mental problems or any other problems' (5.109). He added that it would have been inappropriate for a member of the force to use 'gombeen policing methods' to gain access to the Dunne household (5.110). It was evident that the police and the inquiry team had radically different views on the issue of police intervention in relation to children 'at risk' under Section 12 of the Child Care Act 1991, which permits police intervention.

The Monageer Inquiry Report (Brosnan, 2008: 7.47) noted with concern that 'while there were many services of the health board [now HSE] and other agencies working with the family, the Inquiry team did not identify any one person/key worker who had access to all

[10] *Sunday Business Post* 17 May 2009 'E. Logan Opinion Article'.

the information'. The identification of a key worker is a fundamental canon of good child protection practice.

The absence of an out-of-hours social work service was a key point of the inquiry's deliberations but it was not deemed to be responsible for the tragic deaths of the Dunne family. Nonetheless, it became central to media reporting of the tragedy and was the first recommendation of the inquiry: 'The provision of a national out of hour's social work service structured and resourced to ensure an appropriate response to all child protection and welfare concerns'.

The media response to the report (apart from concerns about the issue of whether it was a 'cover-up,' largely arising from the substantial degree of redaction) focused on the 'disjointed' nature of public services' responses to the Dunne tragedy. On 12 May 2009, the website Politics.ie posted this:

> Monageer Report: Father blamed, but services 'chaotic'
> 'It seems extraordinary that the purchase of coffins for the children of a man with a history of violent fantasy does not seem to have been taken as sufficient grounds to protect the children.'
> 'Not for the first time, the lack of weekend services seems to have contributed to unnecessary deaths.'

The *Herald* [11] adopted a more tabloid approach with the headline 'Dad sent a suicide text before killing his family', adding that the misspelled message told exactly what was going to happen: 'Ciara and Aidan are so very sorry. We nott going to Livepol. Instead we pick heaven. Please forgive.' The text referred to a change of plan to move the family to Liverpool and instead choose death as an escape from reality. The *Herald* report summarised for the public the key elements in the Monageer Inquiry Report in three succinct sentences:

> Even when the family went to an undertaker on the day before their deaths and planned their funeral down to the music, the clothes the girls would wear and the white coffins, the gardaí were slow to respond to the concerns raised by the undertaker.
> Social services put off contacting the family until the following Monday evening, three days later when gardaí

---

[11]   *Herald* 13 May 2009.

broke down the door and found the tragic murder–suicide scene.

Adrian Dunne's family have demanded the full publication of the report, large portions of which are blacked out for legal reasons.

While the imagery informing the *Herald*'s reportage is emotive, it does convey with powerful logic the core elements of the tragedy. The public could be in no doubt about the nature of the tragedy, including its bizarre background. The *Herald*, unlike the Monageer Inquiry Report, was prepared to allocate blame, which is clearly attributed to the police and social services in its reportage. Here we see a clear division between inquiry reports and media reports. The redaction of large parts of the Monageer Report raises questions about child abuse inquiries' capacity to tell the full truth in public. Media reports, on the other hand, feel less constrained in allocating blame. The issue of the Dunne family's privacy raises further concerns. Do child abuse inquiries need to reveal all of the personal details of a family's private life in their search for the truth? What emerges from the Monageer tragedy is the complexity of truth-telling in child abuse inquiries, and the media's fascination with the bizarre and its willingness to allocate blame – regardless of the conclusions of inquiry reports and official attempts to redact the truth.

The Roscommon Child Care Report (2010): the power of family rights

The Roscommon Child Care Report, published on 27 October 2010, detailed 'a litany of failures by the authorities to protect children' and outlined 'the way children in question were continually neglected' (RTÉ news report, 27 October 2010). The publication of the report followed permission from the High Court. The news programme also reported that the presiding judge at the hearing said 'it was impossible to convey in words [the children's] sense of anger, hurt, frustration, betrayal and fear and they were fearful of the publicity involved in the publication of the report. The Health Service Executive (HSE) issued an 'unreserved' apology to the children (HSE media statement, 27 October 2010). In a report on the trial, Carol Coulter wrote that 'Anonymous letters were received alleging neglect of the children, drunkenness, prostitution on the part of the mother and general lack of hygiene. The children's school also reported its concerns'.[12]

The Roscommon Child Care Inquiry bears a striking resemblance to the Sligo West of Ireland Farmer case in terms of a serious failure to intervene by the statutory authorities in a case of very serious child abuse. The 'A' family first became known to the Western Health Board (WHB) in 1989 after the birth of their first child. The WHB continued to be involved with the 'A' family until May 2005, when care orders were granted in relation to their six children. Early in the case, a public health nurse had been alerted by a concerned neighbour alleging excessive alcohol consumption by the parents – including feeding alcohol to the baby. In 1990, the public health nurse again called to the house to assist at the birth of a baby. The mother reportedly confided to her several days later that she had consumed eleven vodkas on the evening of the birth. During 1993 a further complaint was received alleging child neglect.

The 'A' family fell into arrears with rent and electricity. There is a record of a social worker providing assistance with rent arrears in 1994. The family were also supported by the Home Management Advisory Service during this period with the budgetary problems. The other service involved with the family up to 1996 was the Speech and Language Service, which addressed the children's development problems (Gibbons, 2010: 19-20).

In April 1996, a new social work case file was opened when Mrs 'A' sought help with rent arrears, which at this point had led to an eviction notice being issued to the family. There were now four children in the family and the public health records for the period note that the 'mother was advised re hygiene' (Gibbons, 2010: 21).

A social worker was allocated to the family in May 1996. She was in a part-time job-sharing role. Her initial assessment of the family home was that it was 'very stark, cold and bleak'. She also noted, following subsequent visits, that there were poor parenting skills and that the parents had an alcohol problem (Gibbons, 2010: 21). Clearly there were serious concerns being expressed by the social worker in relation to child neglect at this stage of social work intervention.

The WHB convened a case conference in November 1996. It was the first of twelve case conferences and reviews held between November 1996 and October 2004, when the children were finally taken into care. The first case conference was composed of WHB staff. There was no representation of either the family or the school (many of the twelve

---

[12] *The Irish Times* 10 February 2010.

case conferences were sparsely attended.) A care plan was devised based on increased supports for the family. Consideration was also given to seeking a supervision order but no application was made. In October 2000, following proposals for a shared-care plan, Mrs 'A' (with the assistance of a right-wing religious organisation) successfully sought an *ex parte* High Court order restraining the WHB from removing the children from their home, without a further High Court order. The WHB, which was not represented, was notified several days later. The senior social worker involved in the case at that time observed 'the High Court disabled us from acting, it disabled us from acting on our responsibilities under the Child Care Act' (Gibbons, 2010: 39). The right-wing organisation was reportedly a loose group of individuals led by Mina Bean Uí Chroibín.

The principle at stake in the High Court action initiated by Mrs 'A' was: 'I say that I and my husband as a married couple have inalienable and imprescriptible rights over our children and I ask this honourable court for an order entitling us to keep our children together' (Gibbons, 2010). Mrs 'A' was citing the constitutional right of the family, as guaranteed by the 1937 Constitution, which vested child citizenship in the family. The Roscommon Child Care Report (Gibbons, 2010: 43) concludes in reference to the High Court decision: 'The Inquiry team notes that from Autumn 2000, following the granting of the High Court order Mr and Mrs A were less co-operative with the WHB personnel and that the WHB staff were unsure how to proceed when new concerns arouse. This is evidenced by the hesitancy in following up a complaint without first seeking legal advice that the six children are left in the care of a thirteen year old child'. Family rights had triumphed over children's rights (which at the time were effectively absent from the Constitution). The consequences for the children were very damaging. The political pressure on the WHB continued with a letter being sent to the Minister for Children requesting that she intervene 'to stop [the WHB] from persecuting the family' (Gibbons, 2010: 49). It was further suggested that the WHB withdraw from the case for six months to 'allow the children forget the threat of removal' (51). The children in the 'A' family were the victims of a profound constitutional ambiguity about their rights.

The WHB, following a case conference on 19 September 2000, decided that the interests of the children would be best served by taking them into care (Gibbons, 2010: 47). In the event, the WHB applied to the District Court for a supervision order for the six children but following a series of court adjournments the case was struck out in March 2002 at the request of the WHB on the basis that voluntary cooperation was preferable to a care order. In the summer of 2004, at his own request, the eldest child was admitted to care and in October 2004 his five siblings were placed in care following the granting of an emergency care order. It was an irony that following adult failure to protect the children it was a child who finally had to act to defend his siblings.

In September 2004, one of the children made allegations against her father of physical and sexual assault. On 5 March 2010, Mr 'A' was sentenced to 14 years imprisonment after he had been convicted on 47 counts of rape and sexual assault. Mrs 'A' was sentenced to seven years imprisonment in 2008 after she was convicted of incest, ill treatment of her children, and their neglect.

The Roscommon Child Care Report (Gibbons, 2010: 69) included that 'all the workers which provided services to the family were well-intentioned and concerned for the family's welfare … Despite the good intentions of the staff involved there was a failure to identify the extent and severity of the neglect and abuse suffered by each of these children from the time of their birth until their admission to care in 2004'. This was a very serious indictment; the Roscommon Report put the causes down to 'a number of interrelated factors,' including a failure to listen to 'the voice of the child', 'local rationality' (meaning a traditionalist preference for family support over child protection), ineffective and faulty decision-making and management processes, an inability to learn from previous case reviews and inadequate opportunities for continuing professional development.

The Roscommon Child Care Report (Gibbons, 2010: 81) noted that the case 'had attracted huge public interest and media comment. It emphasised the importance of protecting children from media reportage that may have a detrimental effect and the child's right to anonymity. The nature of the case and convictions of both parents in the courts of sexual abuse, neglect and ill treatment fed media publicity. There was a sense of fatigue and frustration with the failures of the child protection system. What the Roscommon Child Care Report did crystallise was the constitutional vulnerability of children in Ireland. A shadowy right-wing group had been able to frustrate the child protection services. A constitutional referendum followed the publication of the Roscommon Child Care Report. It was an important step along the road to giving children a voice in their own lives.

In response to the publication of the Roscommon Child Care Report in 2010, University College Cork (UCC) held a conference on child protection at which some of the key social work actors in the case spoke. The proceedings were reported in the *Irish Examiner*[13] in 2011 by Catherine Shanahan in an article entitled 'The Blame Game'. It contained very serious criticism that the focus and approach taken by the Roscommon Child Care Inquiry was overly focused on individuals (allocating blame) and record-keeping, with too little attention, in the view of some of the speakers, being concentrated on systems failure, which served to decontextualise the analysis. In the article, one social worker involved in the case observed, in relation to the approach taken by the inquiry, 'it wasn't a partnership. It was more an interrogation than a conversation, it was quite adversarial in a lot of ways. The lack of support set the tone … the corporate support wasn't there'. She concluded, 'many of those who worked with the family were crucified', adding 'we were vilified … We had hoped the report would show the context in which we worked, the lack of resources we worked with, our huge efforts, for years, to improve the services in Roscommon, but that wasn't recognised'. The social worker told the conference she had learned about the report's publication when her sister texted her that it was on the internet. Another social worker from Roscommon told the conference that she was 'nearly afraid' to admit she was a social worker. Yet there was an acceptance that the inquiry had been 'worth it' because it put child protection 'on the map' and lessons were learnt.[14]

These lessons learnt from the Roscommon Child Care Report exposed a system of child protection that was inadequate to the task. While individuals were blamed for their inadequacies, a chaotic service is clearly visible in the backdrop to the report. It was poorly organised, managed and resourced. At a deeper cultural level there was a resistance to state intervention to protect children in a violent family. The role of a political fringe group, dedicated to upholding traditional values, was an important influence on the case. The lack of constitutional rights at the time that would have afforded the children care and protection is perhaps the most serious indictment of the state in this case. The website Political World (28 November 2010) summarised the core of the Roscommon failure: 'the inquiry team said the voices of the six children were not heard in this case over the years'. That was the root of the problem.

[13]   *Irish Examiner* 26 November 2011.
[14]   *Irish Examiner* 26 November 2011 'The Blame Game'.

Child abuse reports and monitory democracy

Ursula Kilkelly (2012: 8), in a commentary on the overall impact of these child protection reports, has stated:

> Ireland's modern history is littered with high profile stories about the physical, sexual and emotional abuse of children. National inquiries have played an important role in telling the stories of children abused and neglected and they represent an important vindication of the rights of individual children. The inquiries have also identified the failure of the authorities to protect children from harm and made recommendations as to how this can be improved. Although each inquiry had varying terms of reference, scope and status, together they address a wide range of issues of both specific and general significance to the issue of child protection. Focus is clearly placed on how child protection practice can be improved but many of the inquiries also comment on the legal framework and make recommendations for the reform of various aspects of child protection law and policy.

In her analysis, Kilkelly (2012) identifies three core issues arising from the reports.

(1) Mandatory reporting of child abuse

First, Kilkelly (2012: 18) observes that while 'it is clear from many child abuse inquiries that failure to report suspicions, complaints or allegations of abuse to the authorities has been a major barrier to the protection of children from harm … the argument for making this legally mandatory – is not as straightforward as might appear'. The reports reveal systematic difficulties ranging from public apathy and indifference to ineffectiveness on the part of the state to intervene. The problems also appear to be cultural, as well as legal and policy-related. There is a problem of deference to the church, suspicion of the state and the unwillingness to report on neighbours (*informing* – an Irish taboo) that makes mandatory reporting counter-cultural. The 'sacredness' of the family in Ireland also makes it difficult to vindicate the rights of the child. The Roscommon Child Care case politicised this issue of family rights, rendering state intervention ineffective.

(2) Accountability, inspections and complaints procedures

The second issue that Kilkelly (2012: 18-19) raises relates to evidence from the child abuse inquiries regarding a lack of accountability within the personal social services. The Ryan Report (CICA, 2009) exposed a system of institutional child care largely beyond the control of the state, where abuse was allowed to occur on the systematic scale. In 2007, the Social Services Inspectorate was absorbed into the Health Information and Quality Authority (HIQA), which has the necessary statutory power to inspect and close child facilities. However, there remains considerable concern regarding the treatment of children in care and the lack of adequate aftercare services. The *Report of the Independent Child Death Review Group* (ICDRG) (Shannon and Gibbons, 2012) investigated the deaths of 196 children between 2000 and 2010 and recorded the following causes of death:

i. Children in Care: 36 deaths
   - 19 deaths from natural causes
   - 17 deaths from non-natural causes
ii. Children and Young People in Aftercare: 32 deaths
   - 5 deaths from natural causes
   - 27 deaths from non-natural causes
iii. Children and Young People known to HSE: 128 deaths
   - 60 deaths from natural causes
   - 68 deaths from non-natural causes

Out of a total of 196 child deaths the report revealed 112 were from non-natural causes, four-fifths of which were of teenagers over the age of 14 years. The ICDRG Report cites risk-taking behaviours in some of the cases as the cause of death, notably drug-taking. Some of these children committed suicide. Others were unlawfully killed. While the report found 'elements of good practice' in some cases, it concludes that there was significant evidence of 'sporadic and inconsistent' social work support and intervention. The suggestion from the ICDRG Report is that better social work practice might have avoided some of these tragedies. It recommended 18 steps towards the improvement of social work practice, including regular case reviews, professional supervision and the keeping of proper records. The establishment of the Child and Family Agency in 2014 is a further development, which removes the personal social services from the Health Service Executive (HSE). It is hoped that the Department of Children and Youth Affairs and the Child and Family Agency will bring higher standards to child protection services. Unlike the UK 'Baby P' case, there has been comparatively little media targeting of social workers' ineffectiveness to date, albeit the Roscommon Report (Gibbons, 2010) did attract negative media coverage, particularly in the tabloids.

(3) Constitutional reform

Third, Kilkelly (2012: 19-21) raises the issue of constitutional reform. The Socialist Democratic Programme (1919), as already noted in Chapter 4, had singled out children's rights in the new Irish state as a political and social priority:

> It shall be the first duty of the Government of the Republic to make provision for the physical, mental and spiritual well-being of the children, to secure that no child shall suffer hunger or cold from lack of food, clothing, or shelter, but that all shall be provided with the means and facilities requisite for their proper education and training as Citizens of a Free and Gaelic Ireland.

The Democratic Programme aspired to establish a more equal and humane society in post-colonial Ireland. It was stillborn. The new Irish state became both sociologically (due to the partitioning of Ireland) and constitutionally Catholic. The 1937 Constitution enshrined Catholic values in the basic law. The 'inalienable and imprescriptible' rights of the family (Article 42) became the touchstone of the social policy, within the Constitution.

The Kilkenny Report (McGuinness, 1993) and the Roscommon Child Care Report (Gibbons, 2010) had advocated the case for constitutional reform. Its final realisation in 2012 potentially opens open a new chapter in children's rights in Ireland. However, moving beyond the rhetoric of constitutional reform will be a major challenge during the years ahead. The importance of this constitutional recognition of children's rights is a victory for what John Keane (2008: xxvii) calls 'monitory democracy', by which he means that civil society through the mass media has harnessed 'power-monitoring and power-controlling devices' to deepen political debate. In relation to children's rights, child abuse inquiries have focused public attention on this issue. Mass media reports have become the vehicle for transmitting the analysis and recommendations of child abuse reports into the public sphere. In earlier chapters of this book, we have analysed this key media–society interface. It brings together core sociological debates about the meaning and definition of childhood in postmodern society. While child abuse inquiries focus on the experiences of children in abuse cases, the media turns this experience into public discourse. The resulting debates have the power to transform public perspectives regarding the rights of children in the age of the internet. But, as we shall see, there the complexity begins. Are children in need of more protection or should they be liberated from adult power? That is the most fundamental question about childhood and children's rights.

Conclusion

So what have child abuse inquiries achieved? Have lurid tabloid headlines proved a serious distraction from the real issues? Does the media engender fatigue and frustration in the public mind? Does the public want to confront the social reality of child abuse? Is there a culture of disbelief? Are there deeper cultural forces at work in the 'local rationality' as the Roscommon Child Care Report suggested? In a cultural sense, all of these reports are about scandal because they bring into public view the darker secrets of traditional patriarchal family life. They tell us that the much idealised family can fail with traumatic consequences for the children, whose lives may be destroyed. Patriarchal power produces asymmetric power in the family that undermines the role of women and children. The child abuse reports also expose the failings of the child protection system and the tendency of government (in its widest sense) to resist and redact the information for legal and other reasons, which may or may not be justifiable. In a sense, child abuse enquiries are about the revelation of 'known unknowns 'and sometimes 'unseeing' officials, who may not want to hear the child's voice. Cultural constraint is always a key factor in child protection decision-making. Rationalities collide. The child is abused or dies. A scandal is made. A life is destroyed. All four of the child abuse reports cast light on Ireland's child protection services as under-resourced and poorly organised. The establishment of the Child and Family Agency in 2014 may fundamentally change the quality of child protection in Ireland. If the Child and Family Agency is to succeed, it will need to tackle a deeply embedded cultural resistance to family intervention. Perhaps the most significant lessons to learn from these four child abuse inquiries is that family life can be violent and the state has responsibility to protect children from abuse.

PART 2
The context

SIX

Rethinking children's rights

The most recent phase of childhood – let us call it the age of the child citizen – is one in which the principle that children are capable of living within civil societies, and that they are honorary citizens, serves as both a rallying point for many organisations, networks and groups, and as the focus of conduct and policymaking in the fields of government, law and civil society. Although the emancipation of children as full citizens is bitterly contested – there is plenty of resistance from government administrators, paediatricians, social workers, nurses, day care centre employees, school teachers and child therapists – there are also many indications that the release of children from bondage, into civil society and its political and legal entitlements, is now under way. The old dogmas of quarantine and welfare regulation are crumbling; it is as if civil societies and governments have decided that they cannot live with the incivility that they formerly inflicted on children. The consequence is not only that the dualism between children and civil society becomes blurred in many people's minds; the power-ridden division between child and adult becomes questionable, and is publicly questioned, with politically unsettling effects. (John Keane, 2008: 16)

Professor Keane is widely regarded as one of the foremost authorities writing about civil society in the world. His argument that it is time to consider the emancipation of children from 'age-patriarchy' – involving an imbalance of power, control and resources between adults and children – therefore takes on a powerful resonance. John Keane's argument also finds support among scholars working in the field of childhood studies. Chris Jenks (2005: 37) asserts that childhood is defined in terms of its 'contingency' (ie, power relationships between adult–child, parent–child, teacher–child and so on). David Buckingham (2000: 4) observes 'the sacred garden of childhood has increasingly been violated; and yet children themselves seem ever more reluctant to remain confined within it'. John Holt (1974: 27), in a sardonic comment on the garden metaphor that represents childhood as Eden, comments: 'some children experience childhood in just that way. I do not want to destroy their garden or kick them out of it. If they like it, by all means let them stay in it. But, I believe most young people, at earlier and earlier ages, begin to experience childhood not as a garden but as a prison'. Clearly, childhood is undergoing significant change in contemporary civil society. But what does it mean? It means that traditional conceptions of childhood as a conferred status, in which children are culturally and socially represented as dependent, ignorant, immature and emotionally volatile, is being contested in the changing social reality of postmodernity (Alderson, 2008: 4). This chapter explores the impact of these changes on the rights of the child.

The print media and the invention of childhood

It is now generally accepted that childhood was invented in the modern world. Philippe Aries (1973: 123) in his monumental study *Centuries of Childhood* (first published in 1960) argued 'in medieval society the idea of childhood did not exist'. Aries (1973) contended that childhood was 'discovered' in modernity. His study was to transform cultural understandings of childhood. In a subtle and skilful historical and sociological analysis, Aries argues that children made a quick transition to adulthood in medieval society (if they survived that long) once they were physically capable of doing so, essentially from the age of seven years onwards, or even as early as two years of age. Children were dressed as adults and participated in adult social life without any regard to their particular physical or emotional needs. Representations of children in art, studied by Aries, presented them as miniature adults. There was virtually a complete lack of public consciousness of childhood. Lloyd deMause (1976), in a subsequent book entitled *History of Childhood*, validated Aries thesis. Both Aries and de Mause transformed public understanding of childhood by arguing that it was socially constructed and by implication was not a fixed identity in society. They viewed childhood as a transitory stage during which the child is socialised into adulthood.

In this reconstituted moral and social reality, child development became a major focus for modern society interested in understanding how young people's minds and characters are formed. Enlightenment humanists, such as John Locke (1632–1704) and Jean Jacques Rousseau (1712–78) took a much more positive view of childhood than religious thinkers. Locke, writing in the late 17th century, viewed the child as a 'tabula rasa' (blank slate), whose personal development was determined by the child's social experience and education. Neil Postman (1994: 59-60) links Locke's blank slate to a metaphor of a developing text: 'indeed, the *tabula rasa* sees the child as an inadequately written book, advancing towards maturity as the pages are filled'. John Keane concludes that the simile of the discovery of childhood is somewhat misplaced. Childhood was, according to Keane (2008: 4), invented by moralists, lawyers, priests, men of property and philanthropists 'who felt the ground of certainty shaking under their feet, who sensed that the abandonment of old patterns of authority and the push for self-government required the definition and special treatment of young people, to shape their earliest emotional experiences so that they could be prepared for the shock of adult citizenship'.

Mass education emerged in a new cultural context. The invention of the public printing press created mass literacy and a political public. It transformed the world. Postman (1994: 20) argues that the printing press 'created a new symbolic world that required in its turn a new conception of adulthood. The new adulthood, by definition, excluded children. And as children were expelled from the adult world it became necessary to find another world for them to inhabit. That world came to be known as childhood'. Thus childhood was invented.

Buckingham (2000: 33) observes that 'The history of childhood is ultimately a history of representations'. Children's history largely remains 'hidden from history'. Occasionally, we get glimpses from survivors narratives contained in reports into institutional child abuse and neglect, such as the Irish Ryan Report (CICA, 2009), the Dutch Deetman Report (2011) and the UK Waterhouse Report (2000). Historically, the representation of childhood has been idealised in postromantic fantasies of childhood (Buckingham, 2000: 35). The dystopian images contained within the Ryan, Waterhouse and Deetman Reports confound these images. This dystopian imagery is not new.

The child-saving movements in the late 19th century presented a powerful, dystopian version of childhood, influenced by Charles Dickens's social novels (Kampmark, 2012: 2). Feminists also contributed to this politicisation of childhood. A patriarchy thesis that attributed child abuse to male dominance – supported by violence within the family – raised fundamental issues about the governance of the domestic sphere (Jenks, 2005: 100). These divergent representations of childhood by adults set the social policy agenda. Problematically, children were excluded from shaping their own narrative or influencing policy. This reflected a wider exclusion from participation in the dominant realms of the adult civil society. Yet young people have constantly invented and reinvented their own world from which adults are in turn excluded.

It's called 'youth culture'. Youth civil society is usually presented as subversive, anomic and threatening (Cohen, 1973). Keane (2008: 7) concludes: 'so the invention of children and childhood went hand in hand with new strategies of control that on the surface of things had little to do with the norms and institutions of civil society'.

Youth[1] are regarded – and regard themselves – in very different ways in different historical contexts and in different cultures. The meaning of 'youth' is not a fixed parameter but is in constant negotiation between different social actors and institutions, between generations as well as in young people's intimate relationships with families and friends. Public discourse, institutional policies, everyday practices and, last but not least, academic study of 'childhood' and 'youth' are permanently re-defining what 'childhood' and 'youth' mean in different contexts. These interpretations and understandings are not always homogeneous and quite often are in stark contrast from each other (Powell et al, 2012b). Many of the commonly accepted definitions of 'childhood' and 'youth' have also developed out of 'adults' preoccupations and panics – at least over certain groups of children and young people, and by certain groups of adults (Griffin, 1993). As Buckingham (2000: 7) puts it, 'Childhood is thus a shifting relational term whose meaning is defined primarily through its opposition to another shifting term adulthood'. He questions the fate of childhood in the 21st century and speculates whether the impact of the electronic media will abolish the distinction between adulthood and childhood or widen the generational gap further. In a world where children are no longer protected (or excluded) from the adult world of violence, commercialism and politics arguably new strategies are required in order to protect their rights as citizens and as consumers. This poses a fundamental question: 'should children be protected from the adult world or emancipated to adult status?' (Buckingham, 2000). John Holt (1974: 90) observes: 'we underestimate so much and so continually the competence and drive for competence in the young'.

Child liberationists and child protectionists: two models

John Keane (2008: 2) has posed two seminal questions regarding child citizenship: Can children become full members of civil society? Do they have the capacity to enjoy its rights of association and property, legal protection and citizens' power to vote for representatives of their

---

[1]   The terms 'children' and 'youth' will be used interchangeably as referring to people of less than 18 years.

choice in free and fair elections? There are two principal schools of thought regarding children's rights: (1) a child liberationist or self-determinationist model; and (2) a child protectionist or nurturance model. It is important to note that the UN Convention on the Rights of the Child 1989 (UNCRC) incorporates elements from both models as aspects of human rights thinking in relation to children's rights. However, the models do represent two very divergent ways of approaching children's rights, as active and passive rights. Child liberationists want to equalise children's rights with adult's rights (active citizenship). On the other hand, child protectionists want to shield children from adult exploitation (passive citizenship). The issues are further complicated, as Article 12 of the UNCRC asserts the child's right to participation in civil society in accordance with the age and maturity of the child (see later in this chapter).

The sociological contribution of the child liberationists reflects the growing influence of cultural politics that can be dated back to the 1960s youth movement. Children and young people can be social actors in their own right. James and James (2008: 11) comment that 'the concept of agency draws attention to children's subjectivities as independent social actors within the social, moral, political and economic constraints of society ... the fact that children's agency is not generally acknowledged by the adult world is something that not only contributes to children's minority social status but also shapes children's subjectivities and therefore helps reproduce their relative powerlessness'. They end their discussion of the child's social agency by posing a question 'are they [children] outside the cultural politics of any society or can the things that children do, either as individuals or as a group, have an impact upon society, instigating processes of social transformation, as well as social and cultural reproduction?'

In order to answer this question we need to consider childhood as a social structural space within civil society. The existence of childhood as a universal social phenomenon across time and space is open to contestation. While the existence of the social space called 'childhood' may be universal, it is shaped by prevailing practices (James and James, 2008: 23). In medieval culture, as already stated, childhood was almost socially invisible. Occasionally, events, such as the Children's Crusade in 1212, brought children into the historical foreground. But the children's crusade was an exceptional event in the medieval world, where the pace of social change was glacial. Nonetheless, Gary Dickson (2010), in his remarkable study of the children's crusade as a medieval youth movement, explores a link between medieval history and modern 'mythistory' (mythic history). He cites Agatha Christie's novel *Passenger to Frankfurt* (first published in 1970) in which she evokes the children's crusade to denounce 1960s youth culture as 'misguided, pathetic and wide-eyed' (Dickson, 2010: 2). As Dickson (2010: 1–3) puts it, Agatha Christie, possibly unintentionally, translates a medieval tale into a pop art /photo-fit image of the hopelessness of the quest for social agency by children and young people. Her historical metaphor suggests that children have no place as social actors in an adult world. This 'knowing their place' in the social structure has come to be questioned by child liberationists.

Americans John Holt and Richard Farson pioneered the movement towards children's liberation. This movement drew on the emancipatory ethos of the 1960s' liberalism. John Holt's (1974: 25–6) *Escape from Childhood* provocatively asserts:

> In short, by the institution of childhood I mean all those attitudes and feelings, and also customs and laws, that put a great gulf or barrier between the young and their elders; that make it difficult or impossible for young people to make contact with the larger society around them, and, even more, to play any kind of active, responsible or useful part within it; that lock the young into eighteen years or more of subservience and dependency, and make them, as I said before, a mixture of expensive nuisance, fragile treasure, slave and super-pet.

Farson's (1974: 27) *Birthrights* states explicitly:

> The issue of self-determination is at the heart of children's liberation. It is, in fact, the only issue, a definition of the entire concept. The acceptance of the child's right to self-determination is fundamental to all rights to which children are entitled.

In essence, the child liberationists are arguing that children are entitled to full self-determination in the governance of their own lives, including:

- the right to choose their place of residence and own property;
- the right to travel;
- political rights (ie, the right to vote and participate in elections);

- economic rights (ie, the right to work and be financially independent);
- the right to choose one's education;
- legal rights (ie, be legally responsible and entitled to justice and fair treatment by the courts). (Farson, 1974; Holt, 1974)

Child liberationists acknowledge that children already have human rights to care and protection but argue that their incapacity and vulnerability necessitates that they be accorded the same legal status as adults (Archard, 1993: 47). The liberationist position is, however, deeply problematic. Behaviour is inevitably governed by age. Competence to make decisions is dependent on rationality. While in medieval society childhood ended at the age of seven years, which is still regarded as the age of reason by the Catholic Church, few would regard seven-year-olds as fit to exercise full citizenship rights. Perhaps the most problematic issue in the child liberationists' argument is the culturally sensitive matter of child sexuality. In the UK, a *Daily Mail* campaign has linked the National Council for Civil Liberties (NCCL) to the Paedophile Information Exchange (PIE) during the 1970s.[2] However tenuous the alleged link, it underlines a fundamental shift in social attitudes since the 1970s. There were pressure groups (including the North American Man/Boy Love Association (NAMBLA) and PIE that campaigned for the decriminalisation of the law in relation to intergenerational sex. In France in 2003, there was a scandal when it was suggested that some public intellectuals had during the 1960s and 1970s supported attempts to decriminalise the law in relation to paedophilia (Kitzinger, 2004: 35). Similarly, Fleischauer and Hollersen, in an article in Spiegel Online, claimed 'Germany's left has its own tales of abuse. One of the goals of the German 1968 Movement was the sexual liberation of children. For some this meant overcoming all sexual inhibitions, creating a climate in which even paedophilia was considered progressive' (Fleischauer and Hollersen, 2010).

On the culturally sensitive issue of children and sexuality, both Holt and Farson are circumspect. Farson (1974: 129-53) advocates free access to birth control information and devices as well as liberation from sex-role stereotyping. Clearly, in relation to teenagers these are now widely accepted positions. Holt (1974: 270-6), while criticising 'dead letter' laws, accepts that parents and guardians have both rights and responsibilities to protect children from sexual exploitation. This

---

[2]   *Mail Online* 25 February 2014.

acknowledgement of children's rights to protection in this vital area suggests that the child liberationists acknowledge that there are limits to child freedom. Age does, after all, matter! Why? Because ontologically, epistemologically and temporarily childhood is defined in opposition to adulthood – a world from which children are excluded. This binary distinction between adults and children underpins age normativity ['ought-ness'] within which childhood is both socially and culturally constructed. Unlike some other binary oppositions, such as gender and ethnicity (which have experienced deconstruction and emancipation within the postmodern world), childhood remains within a protected and dependent identity status (Jenks, 2005: 2-3). It makes the child liberationist perspective seem fantastical, even dangerous, because it is counterintuitive in terms of childhood normativity. The child liberationists are viewed as challenging the signifying discourses that encode the ascribed meaning of childhood within our contemporary civilisation, which rejects the possibility of equating adult and children's rights (Kitzinger, 2004: 35).

Child liberationists are not insensitive to these normative challenges. Buckingham (2000: 196) insightfully comments: 'in practice, however, even the most 'extreme' advocates of children's liberation tend to draw the line somewhere'. Archard (1993: 67-8) acknowledges that 'the child liberationists overstate their case when they represent all childhood incapacity as mere conventional, enforced dependency … Thinking of all children as incapable is credible when the contrast is between a helpless infant and an able-bodied adult. It is less so when it is a teenager who stands next to the adult. A 16-year-old is not just an innocent incompetent in the way a 16-month-old is.' Few would disagree. Archard (1993: 68) concludes that 'the modern presumption of children's incompetence is self-confirming'. He suggests the contribution of the child liberationists is their advocacy for greater rights to self-determination for children, who he argues have been deskilled by the adult world (Archard, 1993). Buckingham (2000: 197) concurs 'children may be more competent than they are typically credited with being, but the fact remains that they acquire this competence gradually'. The problem with the child liberationist perspective has been its tendency to regard children as a homogeneous group, which has 'stretched the credibility of most observers' (Buckingham, 2000: 196). There is a plurality of childhoods. But child liberationists do highlight that there are major issues that need to be addressed by the adult world in relation to children's rights and the need for greater self-determination and participation in the adult world. That is a very important and valuable contribution to the debate about children's rights.

There are also differences within the child liberationist camp. It is not a monolithic position. Radical child liberationists want to give full rights of autonomy to children over five years. Moderate child liberationists want to limit its application to children over 12 years of age (Lipson and Vallentyne, 1992: 2). The child liberationist perspective is consequently quite diverse. Initially, the child liberationists had little impact on social policy. Since the UNCRC 1989 there has been renewed interest in children's rights to participate. Interpretations of what a right to participate means vary from narrow legalism (ie, participation in care/legal proceedings) to debates about lowering the age of consent and extending the right to vote to young people between 15 and 18 years. Children's rights to participate is likely to pose a major policy issue during the 21st century, challenging 20th-century western consensus on children's rights as a right to care and protection. Keane (2008: 16) has sharpened the debate by arguing that we live in 'the age of the child citizen'. However, the public debate is largely focused on the child's right to care and protection.

Archard (1993: 51-7) calls this 'the caretaker thesis'. The principles of care and protection underpin 'the caretaker thesis' as the basis of the child protectionist model. The Welfare State acts in accordance with the principle of *parens patriae*, which makes the state the higher or ultimate parent – a parent beyond the parent. The protectionist model replaced the traditionalist model of family governance that reposed authority in the parents. From the 1875 Mary Ellen Wilson case in New York, child protection became the overarching principle that governed children's welfare. The guiding philosophy behind the child protection model is that the carer (be it family or state) has a duty to act in 'the best interests of the child'. It represents a growing universalisation of concern for children, which is endorsed by the UN Convention on the Rights of the Child, 1989. Sharon Pinkney (2000: 112) argues that children are in reality 'welfare subjects' within the discourse of care and protection. She asserts that 'social policies reflect the forms of representation and normative assumptions about the family and consequently children'. Within this discursive framework, issues of 'need' and 'risk' are framed. The UNCRC challenges the status of the child as 'welfare subject'.

Panter-Brick and Smith (2000: 11) have questioned the idea that the best interests of the child should be a hegemonically determined 'proper childhood', arguing that it leaves 'little room for negotiation and reconciliation of plural childhoods' and assumes 'against the evidence that children are passive and dependent'. In reality, the construction of abused or neglected children solely as passive victims denies the reality that they are often active survivors. This is a fundamental weakness in the child protectionist model and highlights the need for children's perspectives on their lived experience.

Child protection is founded on a shifting intellectual and moral paradigm of child abuse (as noted in Chapter 1). In the 19th century it was viewed as a social problem; a problem that included the exploitation of child labour ('white slavery'), cruelty and neglect (the 1875 New York Mary Ellen Wilson case) and the use of corporal punishment in disciplining young people. The discovery of X-rays led to the recognition of 'the battered child syndrome' during the 1960s, and a psychological perspective emerged during the 1980s and 1990s in terms of child sexual abuse. As we have entered the 21st century, public safety has become a dominant paradigm, shaped by growing media concerns about the abuse of adult–child relations in institutions (for example, the Irish Ryan Report in 2009; the Dutch Deetman Report in 2011 and the Waterhouse Report in the UK in 2000), the private sphere and on the internet. In terms of violence towards children, we are witnessing a similar public concern as has applied towards domestic violence towards women. Essentially, children are being afforded parity of rights to protection in the legal system. Arguably, this is placing children's human rights to bodily integrity and safety on the same basis as adults (Costin et al, 1996: 10). However, it isn't that simple.

The child protection model in media debates has become increasingly open to media criticism following a growing crisis of trust in both the family, religion and the state, as evidenced in child abuse reports. The concerns that child abuse inquiries raise about adult authority challenge the denial of a right to autonomy comparable to an adult citizen. This concern is compounded by reports of parents' and professionals' inability to respect or encourage expressions of a child's concerns or the right to participate in the determination of her/his welfare. Instead, children are relegated to the status of a 'welfare subject' (Pinkney, 2000). If we take one of the most recent examples of a failure of child protection services – the Baby P case in the UK in 2007 – it is clear that effective care and protection is an essential right in civilised society (see Chapter 4). But the state sometimes fails to vindicate this right, due to incompetence or disinterest.

Libertarian critics of the child protection model have suggested that the debate is 'polarised', arguing that 'the child is a pawn', the focal point in how social relations are structured within civil society. What the child thinks or does becomes less important that the broader considerations that attach to what the child *might* think or do. Child abuse, according to critics of social intervention, is '*constructed* and *moulded*' (Kampmark, 2012: vii). The argument is that child abuse is the product of 'altruistic' adults, who have turned 'child-centeredness' into 'an official orthodoxy' (Kampmark, 2012: 5-6). This, it has been argued, has led to the creation of 'child protection industries,' a 'culture of fear' and public scapegoating. Kampmark (2012: 97) declares: 'child protection has become the metaphor of a society, which must, overall, be protected by the censor'. This libertarian critique of child protection suggests 'the child' has become 'sacred' in postmodern society, making crimes against children particularly heinous, while feeding a media frenzy of hysteria. In support of his contention, Kampmark (2012: 44-6) cites celebrities, such as Roman Polanski and Michael Jackson, who were accused of child sex abuse in a process of trial by media and prurient public speculation. He also cites media treatment of child abduction, such as the Madeline McCann case, as examples of media exploitation of private tragedies (2012: 37-40). Clearly, Kampmark is making a valid point about media manipulation of public opinion and the sensationalising of child tragedies, but it does not detract from the need to protect vulnerable children. This is the basic flaw in the child liberationist case. Kampmark has not addressed this fundamental weakness in the libertarian argument regarding children's rights to adult equality (ie, their age and maturity). His critique of social work education as leading to 'an intellectually blinkered professional life' based on 'fashionable stereotypes and shibboleths' suggests that Kampmark's position is somewhat polemical. However, Kampmark does concede that social workers have to confront exceptional complexity in their professional practice. Manifestly, the public debate about children's rights is complex. It is not reducible to one polar position – nor should it be, given children's vulnerability.

To return to Buckingham's question regarding how we choose between the liberationist and protectionist positions, in practice it would seem to be something of a false choice. Children do depend on adults for their biological needs, care and protection. Maturity is a real issue in terms of making rational choices, which the division between 'moderate' and 'radical' child liberationists reveals. The construction of 'adult power' as a monolith, imposed on unwilling children, is clearly a caricature of adult–child relations (Buckingham, 2000: 15). Children do need to be protected from abuse in the adult world. Child protection laws and social services, including social workers, are an essential part of this reality. Child liberationists in many respects reflect the Romanticism of Rousseau's *Emile* (1762), which was publicly burned, even though it was later rehabilitated as an educational model in revolutionary France. But child liberationists also raise a profound issue regarding the child's voice within civil society and in terms of governance of their own lives. This is very important. The extensive use of corporal punishment until recent years reminds us of the abuses of adult authority through the physical subjugation of children over many centuries. Corporal punishment became a metaphor for the abuse of adult power over children. The Ryan Report (CICA, 2009) in Ireland, the Waterhouse Report (2000) in the UK and the Deetman Report (2011) in the Netherlands remind us of the repressive use of authority within care institutions in recent history. The emergence of child protection arose directly in response to adult abuse of children.

However, the consequences of the paternalism inherent in child protection practice raise its own issues for civil society. Buckingham (2000: 15-16) comments:

> Nevertheless, I would argue that the dominant construction of children as pre-social individuals effectively prevents any consideration of them as social beings, or indeed as citizens. Defining in terms of their exclusion from adult society, and in terms of their inability or unwillingness to display what we define as 'adult' characteristics, actively produces the kinds of consciousness and behaviour which some adults find so problematic. The differences which are observed to exist between adults and children justify the segregation of children; but this segregation then gives rise to behaviour that justifies the perception of difference in the first place.

This issue of the construction of children as 'welfare subjects' goes to the core of the concerns raised by child liberationists. The denial of a voice to children in the public sphere and its supporting corollary that children are not competent to participate in the decision-making processes of society will be a core social policy debate during the 21st century. Already, moral conservatives are taking up their position – defending traditional values.

The 'death of childhood' thesis

The advent of the electronic media has led to the 'death of childhood' thesis. Some commentators argue that the electronic media has robbed children of their innocence and created a parallel cyberspace for children from which adults are excluded. This has undermined the social institution of childhood leading to the 'death of childhood' thesis (Postman, 1994; Meyrowitz, 1985; Steinberg and Kincher, 1997). What unites these studies is the belief that childhood has been culturally undermined and the electronic media are responsible for its disappearance.

In his book *The Disappearance of Childhood* (1994), Neil Postman has argued apocalyptically that the age of the electronic media has 'disappeared' childhood. He asserts: 'it is clear if we turn over to children a vast store of powerful adult material childhood cannot survive. By definition adulthood means mysteries solved and secrets uncovered. If from the start the children know the mysteries and the secrets, how shall we tell them apart from anyone else?' (Postman, 1994: 88). What Postman is suggesting is that childhood is being destroyed by sex and violence in the electronic media. Others echo this pessimistic analysis of modern media influences on childhood. Joshua Meyrowitz's book, *No Sense of Place: The Impact of the Electronic Media on Social Behaviour* (1985), contends that childhood and adulthood are becoming merged. Meyrowitz asserts that the electronic media takes us 'backstage', revealing facts that contradict dominant social myths and ideals of childhood. In essence, the electronic media exposes the 'secret of secrecy', undermining adult paternalism in social relations with children. In this communicative revolution the meanings and boundaries of child–adult relations within society become blurred in a process of cultural deconstruction. Essentialist views of childhood have been challenged.

Buckingham (2000: 73), in a penetrating analysis of 'the death of childhood' thesis, argues that its proponents may have oversimplified the argument. He asserts that while the boundaries between adulthood and childhood have 'indeed become blurred; yet in several respects, they have all been reinforced and extended'. Buckingham suggests 'children's leisure time has become more curricularized and more consumer oriented, and the difference between the two is not always easy to identify. On this account, childhood – or at least young people's period of dependency on adults – is being extended rather than curtailed. Children it would seem, no longer want to be children; and hence we must try even harder to encourage them to remain so' (2000: 75). On the positive side, Buckingham concludes that in the postmodern world 'one can identify a process of *individuation*, a kind of extension of the rights of citizenship to children. In this sense, children could be seen as one of a number of social groups (such as women, ethnic minorities, or the disabled) which were previously excluded from the exercise of power, and are now given access to it' (Buckingham, 2000:

75). Viewed from this perspective, we are not witnessing the death of childhood in postmodernity but its reconstruction in the age of the electronic media. However, adult authority and childhood innocence are not victims of this reconstruction, as conservative moralists fear. What we may be witnessing is a greater recognition of children as people coupled with more subtle and sophisticated understanding of the child's world and adult–child power relations (Hendrick, 1997: 57).

However, there are very real policy tensions, as Allison James et al (2008: 85) have pointed out: 'although rights to protection and participation are enshrined by the UNCRC as key children's rights, in contemporary English society these are becoming increasingly incompatible, as calls for child 'protection' – by adults on children's behalf – begin to work as forms of restraint on children's active social participation and to constrain their potential as citizens'. They argue that 'contemporary representations of childhood are actively repositioning children as both irresponsible and vulnerable, a representation that lessens their opportunities for active citizenship' (James et al, 2008: 85). They set the issue of childhood representation within a context of classification and boundary setting that makes children's citizenship problematic; James et al observe: 'to confer children with equal citizenship rights would be to breach the boundaries that separate children from adults, the boundaries that help constitute their difference' (2008: 86). They conclude: 'on account of being a child, of being different from adults, children cannot participate as equal citizens and it is through the thin red line of protection that takes place as both care and control that this difference is both justified and sustained and children's dependency on adults confirmed' (James et al, 2008: 87). What does this insightful comment tell us about children's futures?

The futurity of childhood: 'citizenship from below'?

The futurity of childhood is seminal to unlocking western adults' construction of childhood as a temporal space in the child's journey towards adulthood. James and James (2008: 63) observe: 'although components of the experience of childhood and the parameters that define its historical, cultural, political and social constitution vary considerably, childhood is universally seen as an apprenticeship for adulthood.' Futurity also implies that the child's journey has a terminus called 'adulthood'. This is the point of a child's liberation for which they are being prepared. Western society is deeply invested in its own future through the 'interpretive reproduction' of children as the next generation – the future of western civilisation (James and James, 2008:

64). The construction of childhood as temporal space/journey and the child as an apprentice/learner adult clearly implies subordination to adult dominance over children. Futurity raises fundamental questions about the existential experience of being a child. Manfred Liebel (2008: 37) considers these questions in a reflective comment on the paradoxes of citizenship:

> One constant topic in writings on children's rights is the fact that children and young people have a profound feeling of impotence and exclusion, and the question arises what this means for the view of children as subjects or actors which is a central element of the childhood studies of today. Are children degraded to the status of objects by exclusion, marginalization and the withholding of political rights, or is the feeling of impotence and exclusion precisely an indication of the fact that children do regard themselves as subjects, which prevents them from resigning themselves to being reduced to the status of objects? In other words, can one imagine that children could effectively influence political life, or at least attempt to do so, despite their feeling of impotence and inadequate political rights?

In considering the relationship between futurity and agency in terms of child citizenship, Liebel introduces the concept of child 'citizenship from below', based on two African examples. First, Liebel cites a Children's Charter devised by children from South African Townships in 1992 that proclaims:

> All children have the right to be protected against political violence and violence in townships, and to find a 'safe place', and they have a right to institutions to which they may turn for assistance and protection from violence.
>
> - Children have the right to say "no" to violence […] and […] to found youth groups to protect them from abuse.
> - All children have the right to demand health and medical care, without obtaining permission from their parents or mentors.
> - All teachers should be qualified and should treat children with patience, respect and dignity. All teachers should be trained and prepared to guarantee that they protect the children's rights.

- All children who do not have a family should be given a proper and clear place in the community in which live, where they are accommodated and receive food and clothing.
- All children have the right to protection from slavery and from obligations to work inherited as a duty from their parents or relatives.
- All children have the right to participate in governing the country, and particular attention should be paid to negotiations with children on their rights and their situation. (Liebel, 2008: 39-40).

In the light of events in Gaza during 2014, during which many innocent children under the protection of the United Nations became the targets of a military operation and were injured and killed, the African Children's Charter takes on a powerful resonance.

Second, Liebel (2008: 40-1) cites a '12 Rights' manifesto developed by the African Movement of Working Children and Youth in 1994, which states these rights as:

- The right to be taught a trade: Organize ourselves so that we can take part in our own training schemes, and those set up by the government or others. Get sponsors for this training, work for the realization to training even for those that work during the day.
- The right not to have to migrate (to stay in our villages): We, the working children, work a lot in the cities and earn very little. We are not respected, we are exploited and we are afflicted by many sicknesses for which we get no treatment. We want to remain in our villages to develop the activities that allow us to be responsible for our own future. To do this, we must organize ourselves in our villages.
- The right to security when working: To work without being harassed by the authorities and people in general (not to be man-handled, to be trusted).
- The right to access to equitable legal aid (in case of trouble): Children never win against employers, authorities and those who have the money even though everyone is supposed to be equal in the eyes of the law. We demand this equality and the possibility to be given aid to establish the truth if we are not satisfied with the official version.
- The right to play: There should be both recreation time and space available to children, house workers should be allowed to watch

the television. We should be allowed to play with our friends on Saturdays and Sundays.
- The right to be listened to: Respect us and pay attention to what we say. Adults and authorities should consult us when making decisions that affect us.
- The right to light and appropriate work (adapted to our ages and abilities): When we take up the work, we negotiate the type of work which is appropriate to our age, but this agreement is never respected. There are no fixed hours, we start early and finish late. We ask that we not be given hours of work and tasks that you would not ask your own children to do.
- The right to respect: Recognize our jobs, our contribution to the economy. Recognize that we are human beings, children and full actors in the development of our country.
- The right to rest when sick: We should be given rest when we are sick to allow us to fight the illness and recover.
- The right to health care: We should be able to take care of ourselves if we do not have enough money to get professional help. We should have access to cheaper health services, just like school-children do.
- The right to learn to read and write: To learn how to read and write in French or Portuguese …and then in our own languages. Lend support to the training schools that we create in our neighbourhoods.
- The right to self-expression and to form organization: To assemble, unite, speak as one and defend our group interests. Speak without gags, to say what we think, to be listened to and to give our opinion. We have to believe in what we are doing, believe that our strength lies in our unity, organize ourselves and set up legally recognized associations.

What is clear from this cross-cultural comparison is that there are plural experiences of childhood globally. The politicisation of children in developing societies is evident in terms of child/youth movements seeking to articulate an egalitarian agenda of rights – 'citizenship from below' (Liebel, 2012). It is in marked contrast to the libertarian perspective of Holt and Farson, which focuses on individual rights rather than social justice. The United Nations has sought to promote an inclusive global agenda of children's rights within a human rights discourse. This is both an empowering and disempowering approach in the sense that it treats children and the child citizen as different from the adult citizen.

The exclusion of the child's voice from society holds back the process of democratisation. Thomas Hammarberg, UN Advisor on Human

Rights, argues that children will almost always have an intellectual interpretation of their circumstances and how they can be improved or changed – often more incisive and interesting than that of adults, who put themselves forward to speak on their behalf.[3] He adds, in relation to the exclusion of the child's voice, 'but much more importantly it is leaving a critical voice out of the picture on lots of issues and it is delaying the development of democracy'. Hammarberg concludes, 'I know that children and young people have perspectives adults just cannot have on things like schools and how they function, discipline, what problems are'. Why, asks Holland (2014), are adults so resistant to hearing children's voices? Is it because they think that children are unable to speak for themselves, or that they shouldn't be allowed to speak for themselves, or that they are just too difficult to talk to? Or do adults fear the power of the child's voice? There is a profound issue of social justice at stake here, and it goes to the core of the children's rights debate.

Childhood, rights and participation

Arguably, the adult world needs to rethink and reform attitudes towards children's participation in the governance of their own lives in accordance with their emotional and cognitive capacities. The timelessness of this issue has been highlighted by Elisabeth Young-Bruehl's book, *Childism: Confronting Prejudice Against Children*, published in 2012. Young-Bruehl argues that prejudice against children shares common features with other forms of prejudice based upon gender, ethnicity, sexuality, and so on, which have historically subordinated many social groups within the population.

The United Nations has played the defining role in determining children's rights in the post-war world. It produced two seminal documents. First, the Declaration on the Rights of the Child, published in 1959. Second, the UNCRC 1989. The latter is primarily concerned with the implementation of the former. The Preamble to the Convention on the Rights of the Child (1989) asserts that children are entitled to 'special care and assistance' and that 'the best interests of the child' should be the principles informing social policy and law reform. As already noted, the big questions are around who decides what is in 'the best interest of the child,' and whether the child is given a voice in determining their own future. These questions require urgent and meaningful answers.

[3]   *The Irish Times* 25 April 2014.

The signatory nations to the UNCRC (all nations except the United States and Somalia) committed themselves to developing policy based upon 'the 3 Ps' (ie, provision, protection and participation). The stated objectives contained within the 1989 Convention were the elimination of child poverty, the provision of children with the means for preschool development, including education, health care, shelter and social security, as well as protection from abuse and neglect. More radically, UN Convention Article 12 envisages young people's participation in governance of their own lives, in accordance with their emotional and cognitive ability. Young-Bruehl (2012: 11) comments that 'the promise of the third P, participation, is truly revolutionary'. She concludes: 'it has provoked enormous counter-revolutionary opposition, especially from adults who believe children belong to their families, governments, religious institutions or corporations that act as proxies for families or governments (Young-Bruehl, 2012: 11). However, the UNCRC is based on developing specific rights for children, not the rights associated with adult citizenship (James and James, 2008: 110). Sharon Pinkney (2000: 121) insightfully comments that 'the big idea of participation itself is problematized in that it has come to mean everything and nothing'.

Rights as an abstraction do not provide a magic solution to child abuse. The interpretation and application of rights bring them into contact with the child's social reality. The 3 Ps in practice need to address child poverty, protection of children from adult abuse, and give children a real voice in their own lives; the latter means more power in the decision-making processes in their lives that affect schooling, leisure, problem-solving and family governance. One of the most striking features of the families in the four child abuse cases analysed in Chapter 5 was their patriarchal structures. There was no evidence of family participation. Instead of Giddens' (1998) 'democratic family', there was tyranny. Similarly, tyranny describes the examples of institutional child abuse outlined in Chapter 4. Rights go to the core of defining child citizenship. Without rights, children have no protection against abuse, and there is no social justice for children.

The implication of the UNCRC 1989 for social justice is quite fundamental. In setting down the three principles of provision, protection and participation, the UN has substantially reimagined the nature, meaning and extent of child citizenship. It invites policy-makers to reimagine child–adult power relations within civil society by giving children and young people a voice in shaping their own narrative. Young-Bruehl (2012) contends this is a revolutionary proposal. It sets out to deconstruct adult–child power relations in the conditions of postmodernity. She is suggesting that for the first time children may be offered a role in governance of their own lives. But implementation will be crucial if Article 12 is to move beyond rhetoric. Arguably, many of the child tragedies of the 20th century could have been avoided if children and young people were allowed to participate in the polity.

The UNCRC 1989 establishes as a guiding principle age appropriate participation within civil society by according young people a right to express their views on matters affecting them (Article 12). However, there is considerable debate about the implementation of the child participatory principle. Critics argue that young people lack the emotional and cognitive capacities needed to make rational choices and therefore cannot legitimately participate. Supporters of child participation counter this argument by asserting when young people are allowed to express their views it enhances their sense of self-respect and personal development (Johnny, 2006: 23). These supporters point to the reality that in the core areas of social policy, young peoples' lives are vitally impacted upon in terms of the 3 Ps: provision, protection and participation (Young-Bruehl, 2012). However, there is a fundamental contradiction at the core of social policy. While adults may genuinely strive to act in 'the best interests of the child', it is easy to overlook the impacts of social policy on young people's lives because of their exclusion from decision-making processes. Intentionality and service delivery may not be in harmony unless young people are invited to participate in the process by being included in civil society. Youth parliaments, youth local assemblies, school councils, student unions all represent attempts to institutionalise youth participation, but these initiatives still exclude children and young people from the adult world and are open to accusations of tokenism. Pinkney (2000: 124) observes 'it is not enough simply to state that children may attend decision-making meetings about themselves; the changes required to facilitate children's representation would require wider reaching changes than these'.

The concept of child participation in civil society is consequently both complex and contested. Roger Hart, a sociologist with UNICEF, has developed an eight-point ladder of child participation from non-participative interactions to full participation:

1 manipulation
2 decoration
3 tokenism
4 youth assisted but informed
5 youth consulted and informed
6 adult initiated, shared decisions with children

7 child initiated and directed
8 child initiated, shared decisions with adults

(Hart, 1992: 8)

Hart's ladder of opportunity demonstrates a spectrum of participation, with the first three steps representing adult abuse of their power over children. It highlights how children's lack of power is used to subordinate them in civil society. But Hart also identifies the basic principles for child participation, which centres on the issue of inclusion in decision-making. He skilfully juxtaposes good practice versus bad practice. However, it is important to acknowledge that a child's age and maturity are inevitable considerations in the decision-making process. Allison James et al (2008: 87) suggest that the imperative of including children within civil society requires 'a new model of citizenship that can acknowledge and accommodate the difference between a child and an adult, rather than make it the basis for discrimination and exclusion. In the case of children such a model would be focused primarily on children's participation as active social and civil citizens'.

Checkoway (2011: 342) reminds us that the 'most active participants are not representative of the general populations'. He concludes that 'differential levels of participation are normal in society' (Checkoway, 2011: 342). These observations remind us that participation is influenced by a variety of variables that include age, social class, ethnicity, access to education, disability, and so on. It also highlights the reality that established forms of child participation, such as youth parliaments, school councils and unions, reflect only one dimension of this phenomenon. Those who choose not to engage in these fora may be involved in other types of youth participative activities, which they regard as appropriate to their age, gender and interests (eg, sports, youth clubs, youth cafes and so on). These youth should, therefore, not be automatically regarded as 'disengaged from democracy' or 'disinterested in participation' or excluded from civil society. Democracy is essential in the interior life of the family. Children need to be part of family governance. They all need to be encouraged to be active citizens in civil and political society. That is what the child's voice is about. The media needs to understand and address this reality. Social workers need to recognise the centrality of the child's voice in decision-making, as citizens rather than 'welfare subjects'.

Conclusion

In this chapter we have sought to sketch out the key themes that are informing the debate about children's rights in postmodern society.

There is a pervasive sense of pessimism that the 'Garden of Eden' children once occupied may have turned into a children's prison. The electronic media is perceived as corrupting children and turning them against adult authority. In order to make sense of the debate about 'the death of childhood', we have examined the conflicting philosophical approaches promoted by child liberationists and child protectionists. In the postmodern world, dominated by the electronic media, children's emancipation would appear to be advancing in the face of adult resistance. However, the child liberationist position is problematic. While childhood may be socially constructed, it is impossible to deny its biological reality. Children need to be protected from adult exploitation. Arguably, this objective can best be achieved by giving them a voice in the governance of their own lives. The social position of children is suffused with paradoxes. What is certain is that childhood is not fixed in time. What is also clear is that children's position within civil society is fluid and changing. However, the complexity of this change is influenced by the interplay between the child's maturity and their capacity for decision-making as much as it is influenced by adult and professional resistance to change. The UNCRC 1989 has probably struck the right balance in terms of framing child citizenship within the 3 Ps: care and protection, provision and participation, but the challenge of interpretation and implementation is considerable, with implications for child participation within civil society needing further policy elaboration. The debate that John Keane has urged about 'age-patriarchy' is both necessary and timely. It is also important that we look beyond the northern hemisphere in our search for models of children's rights. Africa is a continent where children have spoken with clarity about what they want as rights. We need to be able to reflect on this diversity in the debate about children's rights if we are to find responses that genuinely support children's rights. John Keane's assertion of the idea of child citizenship offers a fundamental challenge to all adults engaged with children (which is basically all adults) to be more reflective and inclusive. Child protection is not an adequate response (however vital it is) to the challenge posed by children's rights. Children need to be empowered in our society. That is likely to be the shape of the 21st-century narrative of childhood in which children finally find their voice. But it can only happen with adult support and a willingness to reconceptualise childhood within the welfare state so that children become 'child citizens' rather than 'welfare subjects'.

SEVEN

Child culture and risk society

NARRATOR: In the frozen land of Naydore, they were
forced to eat Robin's minstrels. And there was much
rejoicing. (*Monty Python and the Holy Grail*, 1975)

In the script of *Monty Python and the Holy Grail* (1975), fantasy and the
surreal combine in an extraordinary comic satire. The film starts with
King Arthur of the Britons recruiting knights to join him at Camelot.
Arthur is joined by the wise Sir Bedemir and other 'illustrious' names
follow, including: Sir Launcelot the Brave; Sir Galahad the Pure; and
'Sir Robin the Not-quite-so-brave-as-Sir-Launcelot who had nearly
fought the Dragon of Agnor, who nearly stood up to the Chicken of
Bristol'. They are knights without horses and servants bang coconuts
to imitate the sound of horses' hooves. Instead of going to Camelot
they embark on a journey in search of the Holy Grail. The film
satirises events in history, such as witch trials, the Black Death and, as
noted earlier in this book, cannibalism. It highlights the dark side of
story-telling as a conveyor of truth-telling. There is normally a moral
in every tale.

Monty Python and the Holy Grail (1975) evokes Jonathan Swift's
Gulliver's Travels (1725) in its satirical approach, narrative form (a
journey) and in its shared audience of adults and children. Both
highlight the permeable nature of meaning-making in the narrative
form of a tale, where the moral is open to interpretation based upon
the age and rational powers of the implied reader/viewer (Rose, 1984).
This raises the questions: 'Do adults and children occupy the same
cognitive world of shared meanings or do adults culturally construct
(and arguably) control the imaginary lives of children?', 'Do fairy
tales contain culturally encoded messages?' and 'What is the meaning
behind these messages?'. That is primarily what this chapter is about.
We will seek to explore how media forms culturally construct the
child's reality, often paradoxically through the agency of adult fantasy.
As Jack Zipes (2012: ix) puts it: 'fairy tales continue to pervade, if
not to invade our lives throughout the world'. Their primary cultural
target is children's imaginations. This chapter also explores the advent
of the electronic media, which has arguably, given the child imaginative

agency (Buckingham, 2000). The chapter poses two further questions. 'Is the emergence of child agency on the internet deconstructing childhood? and 'Is this a positive or negative development?'

The constructed child?

The landscape of childhood is arguably largely mapped in cultural communication. Whether it is literature, film or the internet, it is virtually always the product of the adult imagination. This, in one sense, removes childhood from the reality of the child's lived experience and locates it somewhere within the adult human imaginary (Rose, 1984: 1). The media constitutes and creates a make-believe world, inhabited by characters that extend from the benign to the monstrous. Roald Dahl's (1916–90) *BFG* (Big Friendly Giant), published in 1982, represents the good adult culture as opposed to the bad giants that populate children's literature where size and fear are equated. The fairy tale provides the quintessential literary and cinematic form. The *BFG* was produced in both of these art forms. The computer game provides a new format that continues to exploit the fantastical imaginary, albeit with an element of interactivity.

J.M. Barrie's (1860–1937) play *Peter Pan*, first performed in 1904, attributes the origins of the fairies to the first child: 'when the first baby laughed for the first time, the laugh broke into a thousand pieces and they all went skipping about, and that was the beginning of the fairies' (cited in Rose, 1984: 98). In folk mythology, fairies belong to an imaginary world of supernatural beings that are often invisible. This imaginary world is also occupied by witches, sorcerers, ogres, giants, hobgoblins and other fantastic beings. Fairies can be good and beautiful but also have a capacity to play 'spiteful' tricks and cast 'wicked' spells as part of their repertoire of magical skills. There is a moral ambiguity about the exercise of their magical powers. Fairies are often represented as 'little people'. They cast a long shadow over the cultural construction of childhood.

Haruki Murakami's recent novel *1Q84*, published during 2011, demonstrates the enduring influence of magical realism over the fictional narrative. In an interview about the book and the meaning of the magical presence of 'the Little People', Murakami observed: 'the Little People came suddenly. I don't know who they are. I don't know what it means. I was a prisoner of the story [*1Q84*]. I had no choice. That is my work' (Murakami, quoted in Baxter, 2011: 25). *1Q84* is a postmodern fable (a story with a moral) about the invisibility and unaccountability of power. The 'Little People' became the 'unsignified signifiers' probing behind the mirror of power (Baxter, 2011: 25). The counterpoint with George Orwell's 'Big Brother' in his novel *1984* is striking. Power is elusive, arbitrary and omnipresent in our cultural world, which may be illusional since it is socially constructed. The fairy tale is a highly constructed narrative that enables the child to imagine the world in a mythical form. It is probably as old as civilisation itself and is universal. The origins of the fairy tale are in oral culture. Unlike the fable it has no moral per se but it does shape the moral imagination. In an assessment of the power of fairy tale in shaping consciousness, Zipes (2012: 11) asserts, 'the fairy tales we have come to revere as classical are not ageless, universal and beautiful in and of themselves, and they are not the best therapy in the world for children. They are historical prescriptions internalised, potent, explosive and we acknowledge the power they hold over our lives by mystifying them.'

J.R.R. Tolkien's first novel *The Hobbit* (1935) brought 'little people' in the form of the amiable hobbit, Bilbo Baggins, into the modern child imaginary. His monumental literary achievement, *Lord of the Rings* (1955), is populated by hobbits as major characters, including Frodo Baggins, Samwise Gamgee, Peregrine Took and Meriadoc Brandybuck, as well as many minor hobbit characters. There followed film versions: *The Lord of the Rings* (2001), *The Two Towers* (2002) and *The Return of the King* (2003). Tolkien's fairy tales, written in the wake of the near triumph of fascism, celebrate the contestation of good over evil – absolute evil – albeit from a highly conservative perspective (Zipes, 2012).

In the English-speaking world, the translation of the Grimm Brothers' fairy tales in 1823 and Hans Christian Andersen's *Snow White*, *The Ugly Duckling* and *The Little Match Girl* between 1835 and 1872 brought the fairy tale into being as a major literary genre. Lewis Carroll's *Alice's Adventures in Wonderland* (1865) locates the fairy tale in the world of the fantastic. One summer's day on a river bank, seven-year-old Alice falls down a rabbit hole and enters a world populated by a strange assortment of fantastical characters: the Cheshire Cat; the Mad Hatter; the March Hare and the King and Queen of Hearts. In the end Alice loses her temper – the dream ends and the magic spell is broken.

What does the fairy tale tell us about the adult world's perceptions of childhood and the cultural construction of the child's subjectivity? It tells us that adults view children as pre-rational and pre-social beings, subject to emotional tantrums and inhabiting a fantasy world close to nature. The animistic world of the fairy tale, populated by supernatural beings with strange and unpredictable powers, becomes the mirror image of the child's purported imaginary world. This in turn shapes the child's subjectivity. It also reflects the child's social exclusion from the adult world. In many ways, the fairy tale is a metaphor, which constructs childhood in a space that is imaginary rather than real. J.K. Rowling's seven Harry Potter fantasy novels capture this imaginary childhood. For children, this cultural construction has major social consequences. They are consigned to the *imaginary* real, while adults occupy the *real* real. The life of the child follows a trajectory from infancy, though childhood, to youth in a series of developmental stages before entering the 'reality' of the adult world. The underpinning cultural assumption is that childhood is a narrative progress from the pre-rational to the rational world. The fairies symbolise the imaginary nature of childhood in which the fairy (a word derived from Latin meaning *fate*) is cast in the role of fictional narrator of the child's ontology. The contrasting beauty of the 'fairy queen' and the horror of the 'giant ogre' demarcate the polar points in the child's imaginary narrative through the transition from childhood to adult status. Submerged in this imaginary world is the child's subjectivity – arguably, the metaphors in the fairy tale shape the child's consciousness of the world and the role of 'the Little People' within it as its 'unsignified signifiers'. But there the complexity begins.

Jack Zipes (2012: 11) in his classic study *Fairy Tales and the Art of Subversion* locates the fairy tale in its cultural and historical context:

> My concern is largely with the fairy-tale discourse as a dynamic part of the historical civilising process, with each symbolic act viewed as an intervention in socialization in the public sphere. To have a fairy tale published is like a symbolic public announcement, an intercession on behalf of oneself, of children, of civilization. It is a historical statement. History is conceived of here not as chronology but rather as absence and rupture – in need of a text. The symbolic act of writing a fairy tale or producing a fairy tale as play or film is problematized by asking questions that link fairy tales to society and our political unconscious. How and why did certain authors try to influence children or adult images of children through the fairy tale? How did these authors react to the prescribed fairy-tale discourse and intervene to alter it according to their needs and social tendencies?

In his analysis of fairy tales, Zipes argues that they constituted a discourse on civilisation, capable of being utilised to shape or destabilise children's attitudes and behaviour within our culture. Fairy tales originate in the oral tradition of folk culture. The print media gives birth to the literary form of fairy tales.

Jack Zipes (2012: 29) argues that the emergence of the literary fairy tale began in late-17th-century France as a distinct genre, aimed at children and serving 'to provide models of behaviour for the rearing and schooling of upper class children'. While Charles Perrault is regarded as its founder, women were the main authors of this genre of literary fairy tales (Zipes, 2012: 31). The link with the promotion of cultural tastes and manners – *civilité* – was explored in the metaphorical form of the fairy tale. Zipes (2012: 33) concludes that French fairy tales 'have become part and parcel of the general civilizing process in the West. There is a distinct line … to the Walt Disney cinematic fairy tale of the culture industry'. Of course, there is an earlier genre of the fairy tale in the oral tradition of folk culture. The advent of the print media begins the process of its translation into literary form.

During the 19th century, we witness the bourgeoisification (consciously and unconsciously) of the fairy tale in Germany at the hands of the Brothers Grimm. The Grimms' tales are arguably aimed at the socialisation of the emerging middle class in Germany. Zipes (2012: 69) concludes that 'the pattern of most of the Grimms' fairy tales involves a struggle for power, survival and autonomy … For a child growing up in a capitalist society in the 19th and 20th centuries, the socialisation process carried out by the pattern and norms in the Grimms' fairy tales functioned and still functions to make such a society more acceptable to the child'. In essence, Grimms' fairy tales are an unconscious appeal to the authoritarian imaginary of class domination and patriarchy. Their mission of promoting a culturally essentialist view of the world based upon the Protestant ethic and the spirit of capitalism, as the basis of child socialisation, was complemented by Hans Christian Andersen. The publication of Hans Christian Andersen's literary fairy tales between 1835 and 1874 enshrined bourgeois values within the literary canon of fairy tales (Zipes, 2012: 79).

The dark side of the fairy tale: the symbolic construction of child abuse

While the Grimms' fairy tales dominated the imagination of children in Germany and the Anglo-Saxon world, they were far from culturally innocent. In the aftermath of World War Two, Grimms' fairy tales were denounced for their 'cruelty, violence, and atrocity, fear and hatred of the outsider, and virulent anti-Semitism' (Tatar, 2003: xx). Fairy tales became culturally linked to the Holocaust.

In fact, the Grimms' fairy tales exist in many versions and were subjected to censorship by Wilhelm Grimm to meet the fastidious tastes of the German middle class. The stories are nonetheless dominated by sex and violence in the form of child abuse. Maria Tatar, in her multi-faceted study *The Hard Facts of the Grimms' Fairy Tales*, originally published in 1987, argued that murder, mutilation, cannibalism, infanticide and incest formed the darker side of classic fairy tales. In this remarkable book Maria Tatar speculates on why children are so engaged with fairy tales that focus on child abandonment (Hansel and Gretel; Snow White), murder and cannibalism (Snow White; The Robber Bridegroom; The Juniper Tree; Bluebeard), rape and incest (Little Red Riding Hood; Thousand Furs), child abuse and neglect (Cinderella; Hansel and Gretel).

Tatar (2003: 82), drawing on J.R.R. Tolkien, suggests an answer: 'the study of fairy tales tells us something about the way in which the mind draws on the double movement of language between literal meaning and figurative expression to fashion stories that dramatize psychological realities'. She argues that 'the symbolic codes woven into fairy tales are relatively easy to decipher ... Kings and queens as a rule represent parents; a prince or princess signifies the self. A deep, impenetrable forest symbolises the dark, hidden depths of the soul. A body of water is often associated with the process of birth; think of the countless tales in which the foundlings float down the river to predictable rescue by humble folks' (Tatar, 2003: 80). Witches often appear in the narrative form of the cruel stepmother who destroys the family (Tatar, 2003: 140-8).

Ultimately, Maria Tatar argues that the Grimms' fairy tales, while imbued with horror, are symbolically cautionary tales that warn against 'childish disobedience, curiosity and naughtiness' and legitimate adult power on the basis of superior wisdom. Tatar (2003: 192) asserts:

> ... these stories preach straightforward lessons about the virtues of telling the truth, suppressing curiosity, and practicing obedience. They seem consciously designed to impart specific lessons framed by adults for children. As cautionary tales, they demonstrate how children with undesirable traits – deceitfulness, curiosity, insolence – come to a bad end. Power is invested solely in adults, who use their superior strength and intelligence to teach children a lesson. These stories, with their single-minded focus on the transgression/punishment pattern, their unique power relationships, their explicit morals, and their implicit call

for conformity are the most horrifying stories in the Grimms' collection. By inverting the power structure and the underlying pattern of classic fairy tales, they are likely to instil fear rather than confidence in the children who hear them and read them.

For example, in the tale of Little Red Riding Hood, she disobeys her mother's instructions and wanders off into the wood collecting flowers, leading to her dangerous encounter with the wolf. The clear moral in the tale is that children should obey parental authority. Similarly, Snow White ignores adult advice and is poisoned by a witch. Tatar (2003: 192) concludes:

> Whether ferocity and violence take a tragic turn or lead to comic antics, the description of their effects exercises a powerful hold on the imagination of children. Adults also have not been immune to the charm of the fairy tale's horrors and the folk tale's cruelties. Few people look to fairy tales for models of humane, civilized behavior. The stories have taken hold for a far more important reason: the hard facts of fairy-tale life offer exaggerated visions of the grimmer realities and fantasies that touch and shape the lives of every child and adult.

The celebrated child psychiatrist, Bruno Bettleheim (1903–90), analysed fairy tales more benignly in his celebrated study, *The Uses of Enchantment* (1976). In this book, Bettleheim considers the dark side of fairy tales, as exemplified by the Grimms' treatment of child abandonment, abuse and neglect, murder, rape, cannibalism, incest and so forth, as enabling children to address their deepest fears in remote, symbolic terms. He believed that fairy tales facilitate children's emotional growth and development. Fairy tales, while not culturally innocent, were anthropologically important in child development.

Fairy tales and children's liberation

As the 19th century progressed, the cultural authoritarianism of the European fairy tale began to be challenged in the English-speaking world by writers, such as George MacDonald, Oscar Wilde and L. Frank Baum. These writers began the process of subverting the fairy tale at a point when it was gaining cultural acceptance in nurseries, schools and libraries in Europe and America, due to the energetic efforts of publishers to create a market of child consumers (Zipes, 2012: 107). George MacDonald (1824–1905) and Oscar Wilde (1854–1900), while emerging from very different social backgrounds in Scotland and Ireland, shared a common Christian socialist view of the world. MacDonald rejected the authoritarian imagination of the Brothers Grimm and sought to write fairy tales that liberated the child's mind. His fairy tales *The Light Princess* (1864) and *Little Daylight* (1867) parodied more conventional forms, such as *Sleeping Beauty* and *Rapunzel*. Similarly, Oscar Wilde's fairy tale *The Happy Prince* (1888) parodies the hypocritical values of the contemporary English bourgeois and their imperialist tastes and manners.

L. Frank Baum (1856–1919) sought to Americanise the fairy tale. He was less consciously political than MacDonald or Wilde but they share a common utopian view of the world that rejects bourgeois manners and tastes. Baum's utopia is paradoxically governed by a princess called Ozima, but Oz is not a class-based society. In the *Wonderful Wizard of Oz* (1901), Baum rejects the conventional American (capitalist) dream and replaces it with his own dream: 'somewhere over the rainbow, way up high, there's a land that I heard of, once in a lullaby', as the lyric to the 1939 MGM film version presents it.

The contribution of these utopian writers to the literary canon of the fairy tale was immense. They view the fairy tale as both potentially subversive and transformative. As the distinguished African writer Chinua Achebe (1930–2013) observes: 'imaginative literature … does not enslave, it liberates the mind of man. Its truth is not like the canons of orthodoxy or the irrationality of prejudice and superstition. It begins as an adventure in self-discovery and ends in wisdom and humane conscience'.[1] Achebe, who grew up in the colonial world of Nigeria, understood the oppressive nature of cultural domination by European imperial powers. He also understood the liberating potential of literature to interrogate and subvert cultural narratives designed to shape and constrain the moral imagination of humanity. Writers of children's fairy tales, such as George MacDonald, Oscar Wilde and L. Frank Baum, share this transformative vision of the world, based upon hope in humanity and the belief that the civilising process, as defined by Norbert Elias (1939), would lead to a more just and humane world.

The 20th century witnessed a change in the metanarrative of the fairy tale in a world increasingly shaped by consumer society with its celebrity Hollywood culture. Jack Zipes (2012: 169) observes that the

---

[1]   *The Guardian* 22 March 2013, 'Chinua Achebe obituary'.

ground-breaking work of writers, such as George MacDonald, Oscar Wilde and L. Frank Baum, opened up the genre to a more utopian and subversive fairy tale discourse, in which 'hope for liberating changes in social relations and political structures was conveyed through symbolic acts of writers who criticised abusive treatment of children and the repressive methods of social pedagogy'.

Sigmund Freud (1856–1939) became the interpreter of the 20th-century mind. He interpreted civilisation and society in his works *Totem and Taboo* (1913), *Group Psychology and the Ego* (1922), *The Future of Illusion* (1927), *Civilisation and its Discontents* (1930) and *Moses and Monotheism* (1937). In these works, Freud investigated the origins of morality, religion, social institutions and political authority. Freud explored the relationship between the conscious and consciousness. He was preoccupied with the influence of the primitive and archaic on modern culture (Wollheim, 1971: 219). Freud, the interpreter of dreams, links reality and fantasy in the human mind. In mapping the mind, Freud opens up the child's cognitive world, which the fairy tale seeks to connect with through the use of metaphor in its civilising mission. In this reconstructed cultural vision of humanity, new emancipatory fairy tales emerge with changed gender and social class themes; we witness 'the liberating potential of the fantastic', as Zipes puts it (2012: 168-90). Bruno Bettleheim (1976), in his study *The Uses of Enchantment*, views the fairy tale as 'fortifying' the child personality and resolving the Oedipal complex. But the change in the metanarrative of the 20th-century fairy tale was primarily in its artistic form. Film became the revolutionary new medium for the fairy tale. Zipes (2012: 194) comments: 'the next great revolution in the institutionalization of the genre was brought about by the technological development of the film, for the images now imposed themselves on the text and formed their own text in violation of print but also with the help of the print culture'. Walt Disney emerged as the master of this new genre of the fairy tale.

The Disneyfication of childhood

Walt Disney (1901–67) was an American producer (of animated cartoon films), entrepreneur and inspiration for Disneyland – a fantasy world that exists in the form of magical theme parks in both America (Florida and California) and Europe (France). After studying art and dabbling in advertising, Disney established his own Hollywood Studio in 1923, making animated classic cartoons. Between 1928 and 1937, Disney invented classic cartoon animated figures (including Mickey Mouse,

Pluto, Goofy and Donald Duck) that were to become universally known. In 1937 he adapted the Brothers Grimm fairy tale *Snow White and the Seven Dwarfs* into a full-length movie cartoon with worldwide success. He went on to create brilliant film adaptations of popular fairy tales, including *Pinocchio* (1940), *Cinderella* (1949), *Alice in Wonderland* (1951) and *Peter Pan* (1952).

Through animation Disney sought to replace the literary and oral canon of fairy tale by using film technology to make audiences awestruck and to celebrate the magical talents of the animator as demigod – a status Disney cultivated for himself (Zipes, 2012). But Disney was also a great populariser of the fairy tale, even if he culturally appropriates the genre, depriving the audience of their own unique imaginary experience. In his quest to take ownership of the fairy tale, Disney may have destroyed it as an imaginary form of cultural discovery. Zipes (2012: 198) views Walt Disney as being driven by a political mission to manipulate the audience:

> It is through the artful use of images that one can sway audiences and gain their favour. Animation is trickery – trick films – for still images are made to seem as if they move through automatization. As long as one controls the images (and machines) one can reign supreme, just as the hero is safe as long as he is disguised. The pictures conceal the controls and machinery. They deprive the audience of viewing the production and manipulation, and in the end, audiences can no longer envision a fairy tale for themselves, as they can when they read it. The pictures now deprive the audience of visualising their own characters, roles, and desires. At the same time, Disney offsets the deprivation with the pleasure of scopophilia and inundates the viewer with delightful images, humorous figures, and erotic signs. In general, the animator, Disney, projects the enjoyable fairy tale of his life through his own images, and he realizes through animated stills his basic oedipal dream that he was to play out time and time again in most of his fairy-tale films. It is the repetition of Disney's infantile anal quest to cleanse the world – the core of American mythology – that enabled him to strike a chord with American viewers from the 1920s to the present. However, instead of celebrating infantile curiosity, the child in us, Disney began insisting on taming if not instrumentalizing the imagination to serve the forces of law and order.

Nonetheless, Disney's films reflected the popular preoccupations of the times. For example, *The Big Bad Wolf* (1934) has been widely interpreted as representing the Great Depression and the pigs in the movie symbolised 'the little people' who stood up to the wolf (Zipes, 2012: 200).

Yet, despite his artistic triumph, Zipes (2012: 200-01) concludes that Walt Disney was a conservative 'cleanliness fetishist', who promoted conformity and order, advising the public against risk-taking, indulging in curiosity or challenging power structures; 'know your place in the order of things' and 'don't wander far from home'. *Snow White and the Seven Dwarfs* epitomised Disney's world view and his debt to Hans Christian Andersen, not just artistically but philosophically. Disney built a vast business empire through the commercialisation of the fairy tale but also achieved extraordinary artistic feats through his unique films. Disneyland, which dates from the 1960s in California, sought to translate the animated world of the cinema into a spatial reality, which children could visit and where they could become active participants in their own cultural fantasies. The child visitor is enveloped in a fantastical world that merges the past with the future. It is a utopia – but a utopia with a message that ideologically celebrates the globalisation of American cultural tastes and manners. This, in the view of the Disney Corporation, is both our real and metaphorical world – the *imaginary* real and the *real* real have become one. The project of Disneyfying childhood is complete. Or is it?

The imagined child

Jans Qvortrup et al (2011: 1), in their introduction to *The Palgrave Handbook of Childhood Studies*, have observed:

> ...one of the roots of childhood studies is the critique of the adult ideological viewpoint. Childhood studies can only move beyond this viewpoint when they make a distinction between children and childhood and ask: how is the child possible? This question can be answered not with an alternative image of the child, but through the analysis of the social conditions for making children observable.

Maria Luddy and James Smith (2009: 6) have written that 'the study of children and childhood, and concepts associated with these words, is only beginning'. They argue that 'much of the significant work on the history of childhood concerns itself really with the ways adults perceive and understand children, and traditional studies stress the cultural construction of childhood. Adults attach symbolic and psychological meanings to the figure of the 'imagined child' (Luddy and Smith, 2009: 76). In their analysis, Luddy and Smith detect a fundamental cultural and social ambiguity towards children and young people that simultaneously views the child as innocent and in need of protection, and at the same time dangerous and threatening, which led to mass institutionalisation in reformatories, industrial schools, orphanages and so on. There is a chasm between adult conceptualisations of childhood and the *real* lived experience of children (Luddy and Smith, 2009).

Child citizenship, consumer culture and media giants

Children and young people have become a major focus for advertisers in the media over the past half century. They are constantly targeted by television and commercially-based sites on the internet. YouTube, Google, Facebook and suchlike are the media giants that populate our children's lives. The social consequences are significant and raise important policy issues. Buckingham (2000: 148) comments: 'the convergence of media and the rise of integrated marketing have led to a situation in which all media texts could effectively be seen as advertisements for other media texts. And yet, the steady commercialisation of media aimed at children is also contributing to a widening gap between the 'information rich' and the 'information poor', in which viewers who are restricted to free-to-air broadcast channels and who do not have access to new technologies are significantly disadvantaged. This inequality of media access raises questions about consumption and citizenship in the lives of young people and how they participate in society. It reminds us that there are plural childhoods, mediated by class, ethnicity, gender and so on. Powell et al (2012b), in a recent study of youth in Ireland, noted that the symbolic and material treatment of youth in Irish society in general, and in the institutions of the church, state and civil society more particularly, reflect broad social and cultural shifts. In a historical context, it may seem that young people's autonomy and freedom to choose has increased significantly as the Irish welfare state has developed. However, Powell et al concluded that increasing choices available to young people in terms of biographical choices, lifestyles and consumption do not necessarily imply more freedom. Young people's ability to negotiate their lives in a market society depends on multiple factors, such as economic, social and cultural capital, which remains unequally distributed. Similarly, societal anxieties about young people in the form of moral panics about youth culture and behaviour remain as valid in public and policy discourses today as ever before, perpetuating deficit constructions of young people.

It is important to acknowledge that childhood is not a monolithic status. There are in reality plural childhoods defined by class, gender, ethnicity and geography, as well as disability, sexuality and religious influences. James and James (2008: 38) have commented in reference to the relationship between structure and agency in the cultural politics of childhood:

> In short, what are the precise ways in which social, economic, legal and political systems position children in any given society and culture, and what are children's and adult's responses to that positioning? The concept of the cultural politics of childhood seeks to provide a framework within which such questions can be considered by drawing attention to the dynamic, interrelated and intergenerational processes through which childhood is socially constructed. It also seeks to acknowledge the significance of the actions not only of adults but of children themselves in the social construction of childhood and their potential as agents of social change.

They conclude that, despite the plurality of childhoods, there are universal dimensions to the childhood experience in terms of (1) childhood being 'a particular biological phase in the life course of all members of society' and (2) the existential reality that 'eventually all children leave their childhood behind them' (James and James, 2008: 39).

In many respects, childhood is the product of the adult imaginary. The social construction of childhood is determined by adult modes of recognition and signification in our social world. In this regard the childhood–adulthood power relationship intersects with other bipolarised power relationships, such as male–female, black–white, able-bodied–disabled. Citizenship is constrained by social norms and cultural codes. In the age of the internet, childhood increasingly challenges these social norms and cultural codes that sequester it in the 'Garden of Childhood'.

Trolls, social media and online abuse

A number of teenage suicides in Britain and Ireland have led to a major media concern about the issue of cyberbullying. *The Observer* published a report based on NSPCC research that claimed one in five children have been victims of cyberbullying on social media sites over the past year.[2] The report further stated that 10% of 11–16-year-olds had been 'targeted daily by internet trolls'. Threats, which include rape and violence, feature in this abuse. But there is also a worrying dimension of psychological denigration and destabilisation. Trolls are people who post controversial, inflammatory and abusive messages online. The latter can be serious, prompting youth suicides in very extreme cases. This has led to media fascination with the internet troll and cyberbullying. The *Daily Mail* sensationally reported: 'Being a victim of internet trolls is now British children's biggest fear'.[3] In 2013, *The Irish Sun* launched a campaign to have 'cyber trolls brought to book', calling them 'vile bullies'.[4]

Geoffrey Shannon (2013: 90), the Irish Special Rapporteur on Child Protection, observes that cyberbullying in a social networking or blogging context can include a number of features:

- posting harsh messages or threats on a social network profile or blog that belongs either to the victim or the perpetrator;
- uploading manipulated images or other images taken without the victim's knowledge or consent;
- using the personal information disclosed by the victim against them in a different and damaging context;
- using the public forum to damage the victim's reputation;
- setting up a profile page or blog posing as the victim and posting provocative messages or humiliating posts.

The issue of e-society among what is often called the 'internet generation' has generated a public debate about the risks of online communication. Age and children's awareness are clearly important considerations.

The UK Byron Report (2008: 44) has analysed the age impacts on children's behaviour and the associated anxiety on the part of both children and parents arising out of internet usage (see Table 7.1).

[2]   *The Observer* 11 August 2013.
[3]   *Daily Mail* 5 February 2013.
[4]   *The Irish Sun* 13 January 2013.

Children are clearly sensitive to the appropriateness of what they are viewing and parental concerns. Age, taste and usage are interconnected. There are also a diversity of internet forums.

Table 7.1: Age impacts on behaviour, and anxiety

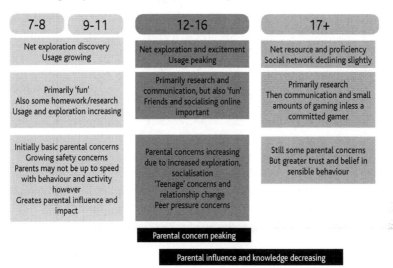

Source: Byron Report (2008: 44).

The internet provides virtual communication in the form of online forums, chatrooms and bulletin boards, some of which are text-based (Byron Report, 2008: 57). This is the arena in which cyberbullying occurs, often out of sight of adults. It is important to put cyberbullying in context. Parents regard offline bullying as a more serious problem (Byron Report, 2008: 55). *The State of the Nation's Children Report* (Department of Children and Youth Affairs, 2013: 59-62) recorded that in 2010, 24.3% of Irish children aged 10–17 reported they were bullied at school. Traveller children, immigrant children and children with a disability and/or chronic illness were particular targets. Boys and younger children were more likely to be bullied. Across 39 European countries, the average percentage of bullying at school was 29.2%. Reported incidents rates ranged from 11% in Italy to 54% in Lithuania. The UK rates were: England 27.6%; Wales 28.2% and Scotland 23.6%. It is notable that there has been relatively little media interest in the 'othering' of cultural minorities as a result of bullying at school, probably because this anti-social behaviour reflects tabloid media biases against immigrants and minorities.

Geoffrey Shannon (2013: 101-4) has raised the problem of homophobic bullying in schools as an issue for public concern. He found that rates of bullying were much higher among the lesbian, gay, bisexual and transgender (LGBT) population: 50% experienced verbal homophobic or transphobic bullying; 40% were verbally threatened by fellow students; 25% were physically threatened by their peers and 34% heard homophobic comments from their teachers (Shannon, 2013: 101). Based on research conducted by the civil society group Supporting LGBT Lives, Shannon records:

- 27% of LGBT people have self-harmed;
- 50% of LGBT people under 25 have seriously thought about ending their lives;
- 20% of LGBT people under 25 have attempted suicide.

Shannon (2013: 104) recommends in his Sixth Report that 'homophobic and transphobic bullying in schools should be considered a child protection issue'. He is particularly concerned about cyberbullying.

The UK Byron Report (2008) examined the impact of new technology on children. In relation to bullying, the Byron Report observed 'the nature of bullying changes when online, making it anonymous and potentially more damaging' (2008: 55). The Byron Report also notes that 'teenagers push normative boundaries and take risks as part of identity formation' (2008: 54). This is evident in online communication, where there are qualitative differences in the way people behave, particularly under the cloak of anonymity. There are harmful sites, such as pro-suicide, pro-anorexia and pro-Nazi (Byron Report, 2008: 56-7). Commercial organisations also track children's online behaviour, with a view to exploiting their spending power, using pop-up adverts, trading in their personal information and utilising pornographic imagery (Byron Report, 2008: 57).

The sale of video games is perhaps one of the most potent examples of the commercialisation of the internet. These are serious public concerns about the impact of video games on children. The Byron Report comments that 'the majority of concerns raised about risks to children and young people from video games centre primarily on two areas: content, especially violent material, and excessive use,' and the health impacts of playing video games 'ranging from repetitive strain injury to lack of exercise contributing to obesity' (2008: 17). But, as the report points out, the risks posed by video gaming can be controlled by 'a balanced media diet and range of play and other activities' coupled with parental supervision (2008: 17). Video games are only one manifestation of the risks posed to children by the internet.

Risks and benefits of the internet for children

The Byron Report has explored the risks that the internet poses for children (see Table 7.2.). It is clear that the risks are many and varied.

Table 7.2 Risks posed for children by social media

	Commercial	Aggressive	Sexual	Values
Content (child as recipient)	Adverts Spam Sponsorship Personal info	Violent/hateful content	Pornographic or unwelcome sexual content	Bias Racist Misleading info or advice
Contact (child as participant)	Tracking Harvesting personal info	Being bullied, harassed or stalked	Meeting strangers Being groomed	Self-harm Unwelcome persuasions
Conduct (child as actor)	Illegal downloading Hacking Gambling Financial scams Terrorism	Bullying or harassing another	Creating and uploading inappropriate material	Providing misleading info/ advice

Source: Byron Report (2008: 16)

However, the risks posed by social media are offset by its significant benefits to young people – 'having the world at your fingertips is amazing' (Byron Report, 2008: 43). In an analysis of the benefits of the internet, the Byron Report cites four key benefits: education and learning; participation and civic engagement; creativity; and identity and social connection (pp 61-2). It views the internet as empowering for children:

> Some of the key benefits of social networking sites are: being able to meet people with the same interests and find 'like-minded' communities, the ability to discuss sensitive issues anonymously in potentially supportive environments; and being able to overcome the disadvantages of some face-to-face environments in which there are unequal power relationships (for example, times when children's knowledge or opinion may not be respected). (Byron Report, 2008: 61)

In many respects, digitalisation has had a transformative impact on children's lives. Media comment has tended to focus on the risks. This has given rise to media-led moral panics about online abuse. While there are clearly serious issues at stake that raise child protection challenges, notably cyberbullying, there are also opportunities for children to find 'a voice' among their peers through virtual communication. For some children that is a very positive benefit, especially if they are experiencing social isolation.

Political displacement and media campaigns

Jacqueline Rose (1984) has explored the relationship between the commercialisation and sexualisation of childhood in Victorian society. In her study, *The Case of Peter Pan or the Impossibility of Children's Fiction*, in relation to the production of J.M. Barrie's Peter Pan as pantomime, Rose (1984: 98-9) observes:

> The voyeurism of this, the investment in the image, is surely unmistakable – the link between sexuality and the child re-emerging here with reference to *Peter Pan* and (or rather *as*) pantomime. What *Peter Pan* gives us better than pantomime, more than pantomime (perhaps this is the essential difference) is the right to look at the child. On stage, Peter Pan is of course, both child and woman. The transvestism is not new, and it goes beyond the traditional role of the principal boy … For this strange focus on a child always innocent and yet sexualised by the very focussing on of attention, could also be seen in late Victorian England in such an apparently different context from the stage as the campaign for the sexual protection of children, which has been one of the drives leading to the Criminal Law Amendment Act of 1885.

The 'discovering' of child prostitution in the late 19th century, precipitated by the popular journalist and keeper of the Victorian public conscience, W.T. Stead, led to a moral panic in the media. Rose (1984: 98-9) notes 'the child prostitute was seen both as a symptom and a cause of social decay (symbol of moral degeneracy of the time and a potential source of venereal disease) … But the campaign – the scandal it revealed – can in itself be seen as an act of political displacement, in so far as the focus on morality served to close off the more difficult questions about social inequality and poverty of which child prostitution was itself a sign.' She concludes that:

> ...the child prostitute became an emblem of social conscience which saw in the repairing of her moral and sexual innocence a corrective to fundamental problems of social inequality which would not otherwise be amenable to such highly personalised, caring and nurturing forms of redress. This child – object of social legislation – was at once (and this is the key) totally sexualised and totally innocent. The call for attention, the felt need and anxiety, all centred on the seeming paradox of a sexuality which would only be seen at the very moment it was blotted out. (Rose, 1984: 99)

David Buckingham (2011), in his important book, *The Material Child*, has sought to address the moral rhetoric and media 'claims-making' by 'moral entrepreneurs' about the commercialisation of childhood in contemporary society. He poses the question: Should we view children as the victims of manipulative marketing campaigns or as competent participants in consumer culture? Buckingham offers a more measured assessment which challenges 'claims–makers' on the right and left of the political spectrum, arguing:

> ... studying children's consumption means not only looking at advertising and marketing, but also at the many other ways in which commercial forces and market relations affect children's environment and their social and cultural experiences. It is not only about toys or clothes or food, but also about media, about leisure and about education. Ultimately, it is not just about objects and commodities, but also about social meanings and pleasures. (Buckingham, 2011: 2)

In a provocative critique of the cultural role of 'claims-makers', Buckingham (2011: 7) notes that 'key claims makers' (campaigners, politicians, experts, media commentators), through the mobilisation of public rhetoric and the harnessing of spectacular events, define social problems and create moral panics. He cites child abuse as the classic example of the social construction of risk in childhood discourse. Buckingham argues from a social constructionist perspective that 'framing' is a vital metaphor in terms of meaning-making in relation to the explication of social problems – '*diagnostic* frames, which specify the nature, meaning and cause of the problem; *motivational* ones, which explain why people should care about it; and *prognostic* ones, which identify what needs to be done' (2011: 22). In Buckingham's assessment, the 'commercialization' of childhood as vulnerable and innocent is clearly a major social concern in terms of exploitation. However, he argues, if a child empowerment perspective is adopted then the picture changes. A key aim of his book is to 'reframe the problem of the child consumer' (p 23). He rejects the 'toxic childhood syndrome' (pp 14-17). Instead, Buckingham offers the image of 'media savvy kids' in the age of 'kid power' (p 19). He acknowledges that the choice is based on a paradox between 'conservative/traditional' arguments that seek to protect children from exploitation and the marketeers' claims that they are embracing children's choice, power and self-expression. There is little by way of middle-ground between these polarised views of commercialisation of childhood.

Online pornography and media power

In 2013, the British Prime Minister, David Cameron, announced plans to control online pornography, which he claimed is 'corroding childhood'.[5] In future, British recipients of the internet will have to opt in for access to online pornography. The print media, advertising and mobile phones are not included in this initiative. Furthermore, it does very little to alter the commercialisation and sexualisation of childhood in the mass media.

The initiative was the product of an anti-pornography campaign by the *Daily Mail* newspaper. The *Daily Mail* sought to warn the public about the dangers of pornography, in terms of its impacts on children. The success of the *Daily Mail*'s campaign in changing policy on online access to pornography has received considerable media coverage. David Cameron, in response to the *Daily Mail*'s campaign, is quoted as saying 'nothing matters more than keeping our children safe', describing current access to online pornography as 'a silent attack on innocence' (cited in Greenslade, 2012). Yet these restrictions do not prevent the exploitation of images of young people's bodies in the print media. It would seem that pornography is in the eye of the media beholder. *The Guardian*, in a sardonic comment, observed that 'the *Daily Mail*'s preening claim to have "won" the battle against internet pornography had an appropriate sidebar beside it online,

5   *The Guardian* 23 July 2013.

showing multiple celebrities wearing teeny bikinis and flaunting their curves. Such is the contradiction of David Cameron's "war on porn on the web".[6]

Conclusion

In this chapter, we examined the cultural landscape of childhood through the prism of both the print and visual media. The existence of a particular genre of child literature (in the form of fantasy exemplified by fairy tales, the identification with 'little people' and magical forms) culturally separates the child's imaginary world from the real world of adult life. Yet the fundamental contradiction is that the 'imagining' is done by adults for children. It suggests that adults control the imaginary life of the child by monopolising the child's access to meaning-making. Childhood is constructed. The emergence of the electronic media, notably in the form of the internet, has challenged this monopoly over the construction of meaning in the child's world. This development has given rise to a literature lamenting the loss of childhood innocence. The argument is that children are being cast out of 'the Garden of Childhood' (Eden) into the real world of adulthood. What is clear is that the cultural phenomena of J.R.R. Tolkien's hobbits and J.K. Rowling's Harry Potter indicate that children's appetite for the imaginary world of fantasy remains undiminished. However, there are real issues arising from the advent of the internet, which has opened up a new cultural space for children. A major media debate has developed around online abuse, particularly the phenomenon of cyberbullying. However, it is important to acknowledge that cyberbullying is only one form of bullying, which is prevalent in all European countries. Media campaigns can lead to political displacement. Issues can be decontextualised. What is clear is that adult–child power relations can be exploitive. We need to take children's rights seriously.

---

[6] *The Guardian* 23 July 2013.

EIGHT

Angelmakers: the hidden history of child abuse

> I know I have vexed the Superior a good many times
> because I did not punish the boys severely enough for his
> taste. He told me hundreds of times never to spare them.
> I will give you his own words in brackets. What are they
> but "illegitimates and pure dirt"? (The Ryan Report
> [CICA, 2009: 1: 8.65])

The evidence cited in this quotation is from 'the Disciplinarian' at the notorious Letterfrack Industrial School, which also served as a 'Junior Reformatory'. Located in the West of Ireland, Letterfrack is a classic example of the 'othering' of deprived children, in which the blame for child abuse is displaced on to the victim whose guilt arises from their stigma as 'poor'. It is also, of course, an example of power dynamics, and a moral metaphor for the Irish Industrial and Reformatory School system. Michel Foucault (1967, 1980) exposed the power dynamics of 'othering' as a mechanism for legitimating abuse against 'problem' groups in the population by placing them outside the scope of normality and acceptability. Their stigmatised identity, arising from their marginal social status, leads to their social exclusion and victimisation. In this chapter we seek to contextualise the Ryan Report (2009) within a historical framework. We will argue that the power dynamics of child abuse involves a process of 'othering', by which a group of deprived children become discursively classified as 'not one of us' and, therefore, the object of exclusion, violence and discrimination. This cultural process involves the invocation of power relationships that utilise domination and subordination through 'technologies of power', including shame, secrecy, isolation and fear (Cullen, 2012). 'Othering' follows the classic lines of discrimination: class, gender, ethnicity, disability, sexuality and age. It places 'us' above 'them'. In relation to children, age is of pivotal importance since it legitimates adult power over children's lives, including the formation of identity, concept of self and social and economic opportunities.

This power of definition is, therefore, formative in terms of shaping the child's life experience and chances as a person. Discrimination springs from such forces (Rismyhr Engelund, 2012). When these power dynamics become pathological, abuse occurs in families, institutions, peer groups and communities. That is why the citizenship rights of children are of such importance in defining adult–child power relations within civil society. In this context, social class is the key determinant of the child's stigmatised social status. We have already noted that childhood is the product of modernity. For many children the transformation of their social identity evolved slowly, in some cases with disastrous consequences.

Poverty, 'parental indifference' and child abandonment

Philippe Aries (1973) argued that 'parental indifference' towards infants was a feature of traditional societies that were characterised by rampant poverty. In Aries' analysis the invention of childhood begins among the aristocracy during the 16th and 17th century. However, he argued that this transformation in the social 'identity' of childhood did not occur among the 'popular classes' until the last quarter of the 18th century and in some communities even later. Aries (1973: 24) concludes 'in the course of the seventeenth century a change took place by which the old usage was maintained in the more dependent classes of society, while a different usage appeared in the middle class, where the word 'child' was restricted to its modern meaning'.

The importance of 'parental indifference' in shaping public attitudes towards children and childhood is of great importance. Shorter (1975: 196-8) asserts that 'parental indifference' continued among the 'popular classes' into the 19th century, as is evidenced in practices such as swaddling (ie, binding of infants' bodies for purposes of control of movement). The child's life was conditioned by 'parental indifference' to emotion in the form of brutal physical chastisements and the similarly brutal everyday existential experience of a life in poverty. Shorter (1975: 171-2) observes 'it was not so much a question of brutality, child beating, and the like. Although physical violence certainly abounded in large city and small village, it persisted into our own day and in any case is not a good indicator of affection. Children were brutalised by the daily routines of life as much as the savage outbursts of parental rage'. Poverty and hardship dominated the lives of ordinary people – the toiling masses of society. With the invention of childhood we witness a fundamental change in public sentiment towards children. Swaddling disappears as a social practice (Shorter, 1975: 196). Indifference to high infant mortality rates ceased, despite time lags in peripheral regions (Shorter, 1975: 195). The invention of childhood is intimately connected with the rise of the nuclear family, which represented 'a privileged emotional climate' (Shorter, 1975: 204). For children born outside the nuclear family or whose family experienced decomposition (especially due to poverty), the existential reality of life was very different from the idealised nuclear family. These children frequently found themselves institutionalised, brutalised and abandoned to their fate. Their fate was often to die alone and abandoned. 'Parental indifference' was replaced by societal indifference and neglect. These children were called 'foundlings'. They were often the products of the sexual revolution that occurred during the 18th century. Shorter (1975: 89) records 'an enormous rise in illegitimacy and pre-marital pregnancy' between 1750 and 1850.

In the context of the 18th-century sexual revolution, illegitimacy became a major social problem leading to infanticide and child abandonment. However, between one-tenth and a quarter of abandoned children were older and legitimate (Shorter, 1975: 175). The methods employed in infanticide included strangling, smothering (often by overlaying in bed) and poisoning. However, abandonment was a common practice, leaving the child to its fate. Urban abandonment, which was particularly common in the 18th century, involved abandoning the child on the streets, as refuse to be collected, or on church steps. Historical examples of abandoned children include: Oedipus, Romulus and Remus, as well as Moses in the Bible. Foundling children were depicted in the contemporary literature, such as Henry Fielding's *Tom Jones* and Charles Dickens' 'Artful Dodger' and Mark Twain's *Huckleberry Finn*. Boswell (1998: 48) estimates between 10% and 40% of children were abandoned in Europe. Shorter (1975: 175) calculates that 33,000 children in France alone were abandoned during the 19th century, which he attributes primarily to poverty but also to parental indifference.

The foundling hospital, which dates from the 14th century in Europe, provided an institutionalised response whereby unwanted children could be abandoned without fear of prosecution (Boswell, 1998). While forms of infanticide, such as overlaying, provide a convenient legal fiction for infanticide (a capital crime during the 18th century), child abandonment obviated the need for such deception regarding the unwanted child's disposal. The foundling hospital ensured anonymity (using a swivel or revolving basket to anonymously deposit the child) and kept the child's abandonment a secret. However, there was little difference between infanticide and abandonment in terms of the child's fate. Shorter (1975: 175) concludes that 'abandonment was tantamount to infanticide.'

Angelmakers and abandoned children

The 2005 documentary film *The Angelmakers* tells the story of the Hungarian village of Nagyrév where the local midwife or 'wise woman', Fazekas, was accused of organising mass poisonings. The film is set in the shadow of First World War and covers the period from 1914 up until 1929, when the crime was finally exposed. Fazekas had a reputation as a local illegal abortionist, but was constantly acquitted by sympathetic courts. However, when a group of women from Nagyrév poisoned unwanted husbands who had returned from the war, the issue was transformed into a major media story of a murder epidemic. Domestic violence, arranged marriages, alcoholism and disability are all factors in this strange and disturbing narrative that continues to resonate in the popular imagination (Bodó, 2003). It also emerges that children were included in this murder epidemic – often the product of illegitimate unions.

The word 'angelmaker' has, in fact, a much older provenance. Its origins are in classical civilisation and medieval Europe. Angelmakers were wet nurses hired ostensibly to provide care in the community. Kertzer and White (1994), in a study of Catholic Europe in the 19th century, note the high numbers of abandoned children and the use of foundling hospitals to confine this 'problem population'. However, they also note that 'far from serving to save the lives of the unfortunates left to their mercies critics argued, the foundling hospital served, in effect, to kill them. 'Slaughter-houses', 'tombs', 'legal infanticide', and other such epithets were hurled at the foundling homes' (Kertzer and White, 1994: 452). Their study focuses primarily on Italy,[1] where child abandonment had been an issue since the middle ages due to early urbanisation. For example, the *gettatelli* (abandoned children) were cared for in the hospital of Santa Maria della Scala in Siena, which dates from the early Middle Ages. Similarly, by 1400 Florence had introduced laws to protect abandoned children and institutions for their care (Najemy, 2008: 225).

In France, the angelmaker also appears as the *faiseuse d'anges* carrying children over long distances to and from foundling hospitals. Many children perished – up to 90% (Lis and Soly, 1979: 188). Whether the angelmakers were akin to witches or simply poor women, ignorant of child welfare, is uncertain. What is certain is that in 'mythistory' (mythic history) the angelmaker possesses the characteristics and powers of witchcraft. She carries off children to an almost certain fate – death!

---

[1]   Kertzer and White also make reference to France, Spain, Portugal and Ireland.

Murder is her art. The *Hôpital des Enfants Trouvés*, established in Paris in 1670, was at the centre of the provision of care for abandoned children in France, with nearly one-third of its children coming from the provinces (Lis and Soly, 1979: 187). Those who survived the journey faced almost certain death in Paris, where 90% of the child inmates of the foundling hospital died (Lis and Soly, 1979: 188).

In Protestant England, the London Foundling Hospital was founded in 1741 by a philanthropic sea captain called Thomas Coram. Its mortality rate was also very high at 68%. Many of the children were sent from local workhouses and suffered a similar fate during their transportation as their European counterparts. An investigation commissioned by Parliament concluded that only 7% of abandoned children in English institutions survived. This followed Hanway's Act (1757), which sought to limit the period of children's institutionalisation to weeks. John Hanway, an astute businessman and philanthropist, founded the Marine Society, which employed 31,000 youths in naval service between 1756 and 1815 (Lis and Soly, 1979: 188).

Profound questions arise. Why were so many abandoned children allowed to die? Were these deaths due to deficiencies in the foundling hospital system? Were the widely demonised angelmakers the culprits? Or was it social ostracisation of illegitimacy that led to the 'othering' of foundling children as 'syphilitic children'? In reality, all of these factors contributed to their extraordinarily high mortality rates. But the 'othering' of them as 'syphilitic children' was probably the key factor in shaping this tragic narrative, as we shall demonstrate (in the following sections of this chapter) by making a detailed examination of the treatment of Irish foundlings. We will argue that abandoned children were 'othered' because they were widely perceived as the carriers of syphilis – due to their illegitimate birth status. This led abandoned children to be socially constructed as the products of prostitution and the carriers of venereal disease. Their parent's genes were 'bad', so the children must be congenitally bad – 'moral dirt' (Ferguson, 2007). They were the seeds of the social tragedy that led to the Ryan Report in 2009.

The great confinement

The English Poor Law Act (1601) was not extended to Ireland until 1838 and then only in the deterrent form of indoor workhouse relief. A contemporary physician, Dr Phelan (1835: 9) claimed that 'the medical charities are in fact the poor law of Ireland, always, when well managed, and as far as their sphere of action and the extent of their funds admit, conferring vast benefits on the sick poor'. The emergence of medical charities represented a response to population growth and urbanisation in Europe during the 18th century. The population of Ireland rose sharply during the 18th century and peaked at 8.5 million in 1845 before the Great Famine (1845–51) reversed the trend.

It was in the context of an economic commitment to demographic growth that health emerged as a major public concern. The French social theorist, Michel Foucault, concluded that this 18th-century European preoccupation with health gave rise to a number of developments, which he characterised in terms of an emergent public consciousness of the importance of hygiene and an official interest in the causes and extent of disease. As Foucault (1980: 176) put it, 'a medico-administrative knowledge begins to develop concerning society, its health and sickness, its conditions of life, housing and habits, which serves as the basic core for the social economy and sociology of the nineteenth century'. There is evidence of a dawning awareness of health and hygiene in early modern Ireland. One commentator observed 'wash and be clean, dig and be rich' (Brooke, 1759: 165). Dr Rogers (1734: 36-7) advised the population of Cork to clean up the city if they wanted to be healthy. Poverty was particularly associated with disease. Dr Kearney (1813: 2930) a Dublin physician, concluded that 'where such poverty prevails disease with all its concomitant horrors must follow in its train; and the hand of sickness is sure to press most heavily on those whom want and hardships and privations have already bowed to the earth'. Foucault (1979) in *History of Sexuality* explores how discourses and norms shape human consciousness and power relationships. He calls this process 'governmentality', which he associates with modernity.

As the arteries of government spread outward to encompass the regulation of the health of the population, medical knowledge emerged as the instrument of the transformation of the power of the state – biopower. Foucault has observed that the new climate of awareness of hygiene and disease led to the entry of the temporal powers into the previously religious domain of sexuality. As Foucault (1980: 171) puts it, 'the new noso-politics inscribes the specific questions of the sickness of the poor within the general problem of the health of the general population, and makes the shift from the narrow context of charitable aid to the general problem of medical police, imposing its constraints and dispensing its services.' The development of embryonic health services represented an attempt to interpose the state's authority into the regulation of the urban environment. Foucault (1980: 175) commented that 'the city with its principal spatial variables appears as a medicalisable object.' Segregative control became a key instrument of public health policy identifying 'problem' population groups and sequestering them in institutions away from the public. This was known in Europe as 'The Great Confinement'.

Foucault (1967: 58) has asserted that in early modern society the community acquired an ethical power of segregation, which permitted it to eject, as into another world, all forms of 'uselessness'. The impotent poor, which included syphilitic and orphan children, the sick, aged, and infirm as well as the disabled, were excluded from the community through a policy of institutional confinement. The social significance of confinement has been identified by Foucault. He asserted, in reference to the recipients of this form of institutional charity, 'between him and society an implicit system of obligation was established: he had the right to be fed, but he must accept the physical and moral constraint of confinement' (Foucault, 1967: 48).

The interdependent themes of segregation and confinement have been taken up by subsequent social control theorists. Doerner (1981: 163) has referred to 'the European wave of the sequestration of the poor'. Scull (1979: 27) has observed in this context 'pressures developed to differentiate and institutionalize the deviant population'. Furthermore he has asserted that 'clearly the adoption of an institutional response to all sorts of problem populations greatly increased the pressures to elaborate the distinctions amongst the deviant and dependent' (Scull, 1979: 41). Foucault (1991) in his study *Discipline and Punish* argues that institutionalisation became an essential part of the growth of a disciplinary society.

Chronologically, the first group to be segregated and confined on a large scale in early modern Irish society was 'syphilitic' orphan children, or 'foundling children' as they were more discreetly referred to by contemporaries. These children were one of the most overt examples of the 'problem population' of social outcasts, since they were by definition unwanted. They were normally the products of illegitimate births and were associated with the growth of the urban problem of prostitution. According to McDowell (1979: 26), prostitution was widespread in 18th-century Irish society. Apart from being a threat to the social fabric, prostitution spawned a series of other risks, which equally challenged the maintenance of public order. To the 18th-century Irish mind probably the most serious of these risks was venereal disease. Syphilis was the principal venereal infection. Endemic syphilis became prevalent in 17th and 18th-century Ireland. Both diseases were believed to be spread by social and sexual contact and were thought to be especially common among children living in poor and unhygienic conditions (Morton, 1972: 26-27). In this process the Foucauldian themes of the control of sexuality and the growth of a disciplinary society become linked.

The decision to outlaw infanticide (a common means of disposing of unwanted children) in 1707 led to the establishment of three foundling hospitals in Ireland located in Dublin, Cork and Galway. European society, as already noted, dealt with the problem of the unwanted child through the institutional solution of the foundling hospital. The latent purpose of the foundling hospital was bluntly characterised by Malthus (1878: 157) as follows:

> Considering the extraordinary mortality which occurs in these institutions … if a person wished to check population and were not solicitous about the means he could not propose a more effectual measure than the establishment of a sufficient number of foundling hospitals unlimited as to their reception of children.

Malthus's revealing remark encapsulated the outcast status of the foundling children and draws attention to their high mortality rates in the order of 80% (or even 90%) across Europe. For the foundling, child segregation and confinement usually involved death, which provided a permanent solution to the threat that contemporaries believed these children posed to the health of the population. Foundling children in 18th century Ireland were viewed as the syphilitic products of prostitution. They were popularly referred to as 'whore's brats' or 'whores gets' (Robins, 1980: 50).

Child deaths, public inquiries and popular prejudice

The mortality figures for the Dublin Foundling Hospital, which opened in 1730 as a national facility, were remarkably high even by the standards of the time. Ireland had a relatively high infant mortality rate, which Mokyr (1983: 37) has calculated to have been approximately 12% in 1838. In the first seven years following the opening of the Dublin Foundling Hospital, 3,235 children died out of 4,025 admitted representing a mortality rate of 80%. This level of mortality was to remain broadly consistent throughout the history of the Dublin Foundling Hospital with minor fluctuations. During the period 1737–43, the mortality rate fell slightly to 75% (Robins, 1980: 17). Between 1750 and 1759 the mortality rate rose to 89% (Robins, 1980: 22). Figures for the period 1756–71 indicate that the mortality rate fell again to 70% (25). During the period 1781-1790, out of 19,368 children admitted to the Dublin Foundling Hospital some 10,428 died. However, 6,526 were 'struck off' leaving only 2,414 definitely alive (*Journal of the Irish House of Commons*, 1791: XIV: ccci). Between 1796 and 1826, 41,524 children perished representing a mortality rate of approximately 80%. Many of these children died in the care of 'angelmakers' – 25,859 out of 49,260 (Third Report of the Commissioners of Irish Education Enquiry, 1826-1827: xiii, 5).

How can these consistently high mortality rates be explained? Several contemporary observers pointed to the presence of venereal disease. A physician employed at the Foundling Hospital remarked to a committee of inquiry into its conduct in 1758 'that the children were in a bad state of health when they came into the house: disorders mostly venereal' (*Journal of the Irish House of Commons*, 1758: VI: xcvi). The English social reformer John Howard reported to the Irish Parliament in 1788 on his visit to the Dublin Hospital, declaring that there was 'too little attention to cleanliness' and that 'most of the children (were) bad with a cutaneous [skin] disorder' (*Journal of the Irish House of Commons*, 1788, XII: dcccxlv). Howard's observations suggest that scurvy, rather than syphilis, was the cause of ill health. Scurvy is a disease caused by a Vitamin C deficiency. It is the product of poor diet and causes skin lesions, lethargy and ultimately death. Official reports produced by the officers of the Dublin Foundling Hospital tend to cite venereal disease as the major cause of death within the institution. For example, James Shaughnissy, the apothecary, declared that of the 4,204 children who died within the nursery at the Foundling Hospital between 1781 and 1789, 3,470 were suffering from venereal disease. (*Journal of Irish House of Commons*, 1791: XIV: ccci).

This perception of the presence of venereal disease encouraged public apathy towards the children's fate. Robins (1980: 123) has observed in reference to Lady Arable Denny's notable philanthropic involvement with the Foundling Hospital that it was almost unique, asserting 'it is remarkable that, with the exception of Sir John Blaquiere over 30 years later, she appears to have been the only prominent citizen sufficiently moved by the revelations of successive parliamentary investigations to make a sustained effort to make it a better place'. While Blaquiere's commitment to reform is undeniable, his attitude toward the suffering of children reflected the hypocrisy of the age in which attitudes towards destitute children were shaped by a system of social genetics that sought to 'cleanse' the population.

The Westmoreland Lock Hospital for the treatment of venereal diseases opened in Townsend Street, Dublin, later in 1792 and treated

2,000 patients in its first year (McDowell, 1979: 26). A parliamentary report in 1798 noted in reference to the Dublin Foundling Hospital 'that the proportion of children tainted with venereal disease ... was less than one to eleven of the number admitted' (*Journal of the Irish House of Commons*, 1798: XVII: 2: iv). This dramatic improvement in the rates of venereally infected children admitted to the Dublin Foundling Hospital suggests that the Lock Hospital was proving effective. However, the association between the Foundling Hospital and venereal disease remained. The Governor of the Lock Hospital publicly declared that many of the patients were former inmates of the Foundling Hospital (Robins, 1980: 51). It is clear that this youth population had been labelled 'syphilitic' and were ostracised into adulthood.

Disease was not the only cause of death. Those children who survived long enough to be fostered out to wet nurses or 'angelmakers' (prior to being returned to the hospital at the age of six to train and work) were often neglected and frequently died. The Blaquiere Inquiry in 1792 reckoned that the number of deaths of children fostered in the country during the previous year was 1,838 (*Journal of the Irish House of Commons*, 1792: XV: ccvii). Out of the 41,524 child mortalities associated with the Dublin Foundling Hospital between 1796 and 1826, 26,181 died while they were being fostered in the country compared with 15,343 in the institution (Third Report of the Commissioners of Irish Education Enquiry, 1826-1827: xiii, 5). The overall mortality rate is exceptional. The distinguished social anthropologist Margaret Mead has offered an explanation, suggesting that institutions for foundling children were 'only a prolonged, ritualized method of disposing of the infant for whom nobody wished to care' (Kadushin, 1980: 36). The Foundling Hospital was merged into the Poor Law system after 1838 and was ultimately replaced by the reformatory and industrial school system.

The high mortality rate is the most dramatic indicator of the level of child neglect in the Dublin Foundling Hospital. There is a considerable body of evidence that suggests that those who survived did not experience an appreciably better fate. Child abuse was rampant. Punishment was harsh; boys were publically whipped or placed in the dungeon or 'dark room' and tied to a log. A parliamentary inquiry in 1758 reported that several older boys who had attempted to draw the governors' attention to their dietary deficiencies were placed in the stocks and given 20 lashes for their audacity. One of these boys was disabled. He had his leg amputated due to infection contracted while in the hospital. Girls were also liable to be subjects of corporal punishment (Wodsworth, 1876: 28). In addition they were victims of sexual exploitation. The most notable case is that of Margaret Hayden. In 1744 she alleged that she had been used in an 'indecent manner' by the Treasurer of the Foundling Hospital, Joseph Purcell. Her case was discussed by the governors who did not at that time find sufficient grounds to relieve Mr Purcell of his duties. It is interesting to note that 14 years later he was discharged as the result of 'many instances of misbehaviour' (Wodsworth, 1876: 29). The children were poorly nourished, being fed mainly on a diet of 'ponada' (ie, bread and water pap with some milk). In 1801, the matron gave evidence to the effect that this food did not suffice to sustain life. Again in 1801, the governors petitioned the government, concerning the diet among other matters (Wodsworth, 1876).

A major factor in explaining the high mortality rate, apart from the general climate of neglect already outlined, was the grossly unsatisfactory standard of care – the invariable treatment for sick children being an elixir known as 'the composing bottle'. Visits from the designated surgeon, physician and apothecary seem to have been very rare occurrences. Figures prepared by the apothecary, James Shaughnissy, indicated that out of 5,216 children admitted to the infirmary of the Dublin Foundling Hospital between 1791 and 1796 only three survived, the other 5,213 perished (Wodsworth, 1876: 38). These extraordinary figures illustrate clearly the scale of the failure of the medical officers to meet the needs of the hospital's sick children. There is little need to expand on the facts in Shaughnissy's remarkable return, which was intended to be a cover-up! The figures clearly indicate that admission to the infirmary almost certainly meant death. In fact, it appears that children admitted to the infirmary went through a process of being 'stripped to die' (ie, their clothes were taken away for use by other children) (Wodsworth, 1876: 42). These dramatic revelations led to an enquiry into the management of the establishment by a committee of the Irish Houses of Commons in 1797. The committee concluded that the medical officers were the main cause of the high mortality rate, asserting that they had been negligent in their duties. Dr. William Harvey, the physician, was accused of never visiting the hospital. The committee asserted that Mr Philip Woodroofe, the surgeon, was deficient in his duties because he failed to visit daily and only treated surgical cases. James Shaughnissy, the apothecary, who resided in the hospital, visited the infirmary less than once a quarter and sometimes less than once a year, it was claimed. The committee recommended that they all be removed from their posts. It was also noted that the system of carrying nurses (angelmakers) was a major contributory factor to the mortality rate because the children were 'much abused' on the journey and often arrived at the hospital in a condition 'too shocking to relate'.

Outside Dublin, the foundling hospitals in Cork and Galway were local in character and little is known about them. In contrast to its Dublin counterpart, the Cork Foundling Hospital, which opened in 1747, was largely ignored in public enquiries. The first major inquiry into the operation of the Cork Foundling Hospital was carried out by the Whately Commission in the 1830s. Statistics concerning admissions and disposals between 1820 and 1833 suggest that mortality rates were somewhat lower in the Cork Foundling Hospital than its Dublin counterpart. Of the 3,247 children admitted during this period, 2,018 died, 516 were apprenticed, and 177 claimed – a mortality rate of 62% (*First Report of the Whately Commission*, 1836: Appendix C: Part 1: 32).

A connection between syphilis and the high mortality rate in the Cork Foundling Hospital was advanced by a contemporary. Dr Bullen, surgeon of the Cork North Infirmary, observed that syphilitically infected foundlings rarely survived. He was also critical of the Foundling Hospital as an institution. He claimed that foundling children who were sent out to nurse in the country spread the disease among the labouring classes. Dr Bullen concluded that the foundling child's chances of survival would be optimised if the child was nurtured by its mother (*First Report of the Whately Commission*, 1836: Appendix C: Part 1: 36). Another witness, described as a 'gentleman', put the case against the Cork Foundling Hospital rather more provocatively. He inquired: 'and what claim have the offspring of prostitutes to be better fed, clad, and educated than those of the lowest, independent labourer? and further, to be apprenticed with a large fee to respectable trades, with a reward held out to induce them to good conduct during their apprenticeship? – what claim can they have to be better provided for than the poor house children? If it be therefore considered necessary, in order to prevent infanticide, to have a place for receiving foundlings let it be made a branch of the poorhouse' (*First Report of the Whately Commission*, 1836: Appendix C: Part 1: XXX: 32). The Whately Commission shared this view and advanced several other arguments against the Cork Foundling Hospital:

> We have seen that the existence of such an institution has caused the substitution of infants through the medium of the parish nurses, whose interest, consequently, is, that the real foundling should die, in order to make room for an imposed child. We have also seen that the system pursued has caused the carrying of syphilis into the families of the

peasantry; and finally, there can be no doubt, from what has been stated, that the inhabitants of Cork are taxed to support many illegitimate or other children not the offspring of women belonging to the city (*First Report of the Whately Commission*, 1836: Appendix C: Part 1: 36-37).

These observations highlight the scale of hostility in Irish civil society towards foundling children. It also exposes the profound social hypocrisy of the age.

Swift's 'modest proposal': addressing social hypocrisy

Michael Mann (2005: 21), in a critique of the dominant liberal vision of civil society, originally advocated by Alexis de Tocqueville (1805–59) and subsequently developed by Robert Putnam (1993, 2000), describes this benign view as 'naïve'. The treatment of the foundling children by Irish charity was cruel and inhuman. Jonathan Swift (1667–1745), in a satire of social attitudes towards foundling children in eighteenth century Ireland, wrote his essay *A Modest Proposal* (1729) in which he addressed the wretched condition of Ireland as experienced by its pauper children. The essay is subtitled 'For Preventing the Children of Poor People from Being a Burthen to Their Parents or Country and for Making Them Beneficial to the Publick'. Swift (1965: 480-1) with surrealistic irony declared:

> I have been assured by a very knowing American of my acquaintance in London, that a young healthy child well nursed is at a year old a most delicious, nourishing, and wholesome food, whether stewed, roasted, baked, or boiled; and I make no doubt that it will equally serve in a fricassee or a ragout. I do therefore humbly offer it to public consideration that of the hundred and twenty thousand children already computed, twenty thousand may be reserved for breed, whereof only one-fourth part to be males; which is more than we allow to sheep, black cattle or swine ... The remaining hundred thousand may, at a year old, be offered in the sale to the persons of quality and fortune through the kingdom; always advising the mother to let them suck plentifully in the last month, so as to render them plump and fat for a good table. A child will make two dishes at an entertainment for friends; and when the family dines alone, the fore or hind quarter will make

a reasonable dish, and seasoned with a little pepper or salt will be very good boiled on the fourth day, especially in winter ... As to our city of Dublin shambles [ie, slaughter houses or meat markets] may be appointed for this purpose in the most convenient parts of it, and butchers we may be assured will not be wanting; although I rather recommend buying the children alive, and dressing them hot from the knife, as we do roasting pigs.

The sheer horror of *A Modest Proposal* is not simply the proposed slaughtering of innocent children and selling them at butcher shops as baby meat. What is equally disturbing in Swift's parody is the cold, calculating reason of the narrator, who reduces children to a commercial commodity. In this Swiftian world, civil society is exposed as deeply hypocritical in its attitudes towards children of the poor. As Dean of St. Patrick's Cathedral, Dublin, Swift was a witness to the grim reality around him, in which civil society colluded in the deaths of large numbers of children through public neglect. *A Modest Proposal* confronts Irish civil society with its response to children in need, which was defined by the principles of human genetics, selection and breeding that conspired to allow unwanted children to die.

An examination of debates within the 18th-century Irish Parliament and of endless public enquiries expose a world of institutionalised abuse, neglect and cruelty. Yet, despite many pious resolutions, nothing was done. The explanation of this failure to effect a regime change lies in public attitudes towards foundling children, which were shaped by social genetics. A contemporary described the Cork Foundling Hospital as 'the gathering place for all the bastards in the South of Ireland' (Robins, 1980: 57). The association between sexuality and sin condemned these children to death in most cases and to a life of intense hardship for the few survivors. After the establishment of the Irish Poor Law system in 1838, the Irish foundling hospitals were gradually phased out and replaced by a system of industrial and reformatory schools. There were already ominous signs of sectarianism that were likely to undermine the emerging responsibility of the state in Ireland for the care of children in the community (Robins, 1980: 58-9). The religious sphere was ready to assert its social power over the public sphere, shaping Irish civil society in its image. But there were early critics, most notably Swift, who exposed the underlying rationale of social policy in early modern Ireland (ie, social genetics, which sought to 'cleanse' the population of unwanted children). Swift's parody of

Irish civil society in the 18th century points to genocide – a word that did not exist in his day.

Children, famine and the poor law state

The Irish Poor Law, established in 1838, was a system of workhouse-based relief that catered for 1% of the population when up to 30% needed relief (Powell, 1992: 86). At a time of famine, it was a symbolic gesture towards the Irish poor from a government whose ideological loyalties were linked to laissez-faire free market capitalism. The tragedy that unfolded during the Great Famine (1845–51) bears cruel testimony to the inadequacies and unsustainability of the Poor Law. During the Great Famine, approximately one million Irish people perished and a further million emigrated, mainly to North America. Levene (2005: 257-8) describes this public policy failure as 'genocide', suggesting a hidden agenda. The Poor Law was a system of social repression that reduced recipients of relief to the status of paupers – that is to say, people without rights (Powell, 1992). Some young people responded with rebellion, openly occupying workhouses and rioting against cruel beatings (Robins, 1980: 264-5).

Workhouse children and young people were classified and segregated according to age and gender into five different categories:

- Males above 15 years of age
- Boys between 2 and 15 years
- Females above 15 years
- Girls between 2 and 15 years
- Children under 2 years.

The system prescribed that any children over 2 years were to be separated from their parents. They wore uniforms to emphasis their poor law status as paupers. Life in the workhouse was highly regimented. While, officially, the three R's were taught, in practice there was very little emphasis on education or training. Barnes (1989: 11) observes that 'no special provision was made for children in the workhouse; neither were orphaned children eligible for outdoor relief. During the 1840s and 1850s the workhouses were the only refuge for most of the destitute and orphaned children in Ireland.' According to the First Annual Report of the Irish Local Government Board (1873: 43) there were 91,589 children under 15 years of age in the workhouses in 1851. As the Great Famine subsided, the number of children in workhouses fell to 77,000 or 6.5% of the age cohort under 15 years, as recorded in the Ryan Report (CICA, 2009: 1: 2.02). By 1872, partly due to the introduction of industrial schools, the number of children in Irish workhouses had fallen to 12,421. Emigration and population decline are also likely to have played their part in this dramatic fall in the youth population within Irish workhouses. Furthermore, the activities of voluntary organisations, which funded private orphanages, day schools and boarding-out societies, were also likely to have played their part in reducing the youth population in Irish workhouses.

Forced migrants, colonisation and child abuse

Those young people who survived the workhouse regime faced a grim future. Little opportunity was available in post-famine Ireland. The government decided that a system of orphan emigration for workhouse girls to the Australian colonies would simultaneously enhance the population and provide a future for destitute Irish female youth. It was a failure as a social experiment. Some 4,175 Irish orphan girls were sent to Australia during 1854 and 1856. Many ended up homeless and in prostitution (Robins, 1980: 197-221). This experiment in 'positive' eugenics underscores the state's response to poverty – social genetics rather than social welfare.

Transportation to Australia from the 1780s had been a common punishment for felons but also for victims of poverty, generally referred to as 'vagrants', which included the unemployed and 'lewd and idle women' – a less than subtle reference to prostitution (Powell, 1992). It is romanticised in the popular ballad 'The Black Velvet Band', in which a young man sentenced to transportation to Van Diemen's Land (Tasmania) laments his deception by a young woman into receiving stolen goods:

> One day, being out on a ramble, alone by myself I did stray,
>   I met with a young gay deceiver, while cruising in Ratcliffe Highway;
>   Her eyes were as black as a raven, I thought her the pride of the land,
>   Her hair, that did hang o'er her shoulders, was tied with a black velvet band
>
> (Wikipedia entry, 2014)

This ballad dates from the first half of the 19th century, probably between 1837 and 1853. Four waves of transportation between 1787 and 1868 had resulted in the transportation of many Irish people, most of whom regarded themselves as political and social martyrs (Hughes, 1988: 161-2).

Their fate in Australia is captured in a convict ballad dating from 1825–30 that expresses the stark reality of convict life:

> The very day we landed upon that fateful shore,
>   The planters came round us, full twenty score or more;
>   They ranked us off like horses and sold us out of hand,
>   They chained us up to pull the plough, upon Van
> Diemen's Land.
>
> (Hughes, 1988)

Life for children in this raw society was similarly harsh. Mendleshon (1979: 173) observes:

> Problems relating to children go right back to the beginnings of Australian settlement, and took an acute form because of the rawness of colonial conditions. As the oldest colony and the receptacle of a high proportion of convict migrants, New South Wales was initially presented with particular difficulties. In the early 1800s there were reports of unsupervised children roaming the streets, lacking in education and picking up a living where they could. Other reports spoke of the bad influences of parents and older companions of criminal origin. As the century wore on the rapid growth of urban population brought further strains, such as the prevalence of illegitimacy, which could not be cushioned or absorbed because of the absence in the new colony of a traditional pattern of social welfare or the necessary fixed capital assets such as orphanages, almshouses and hospitals.

Governor King, who established the first orphanage in Australia, noted 'finding that the greater part of the children in this colony are so much abandoned to every kind of wretchedness and vice, I perceived the absolute necessity of something being attempted to withdraw them from the vicious examples of their abandoned parents' (Mendlesohn, 1979: 173). The Governor also sought to address the large volume of 'convict' boys arriving in Australia by apprenticing them as carpenters to boat-makers, introducing to Australia a duel system of institutional care and boarding-out (Mendlesohn, 1979: 173). However, it wasn't until

1923 that Australian child welfare legislation was passed that established independent child welfare departments (Mendleshon, 1979: 181).

Attempts were made to re-establish a child migration scheme between Ireland and Australia during the 1930s. Raftery and O'Sullivan (1999: 265) note that following the establishment of the Irish Free State in 1922 an approach was made by the Christian Brothers to introduce child migration from Ireland to Australia:

> It is interesting to note that no child migration scheme ever developed directly from Ireland, despite the attempts of the Christian Brothers to persuade the Irish Government to send children to their institutions in Australia. In 1938, Brother Louis Conlon, manager of the Tardun orphanage in Western Australia, wrote to the Taoiseach, Eamon de Valera, inviting the Irish Government to participate in and provide financial assistance for a child migration scheme to Australia. Conlon visited Ireland to promote his cause and received some media attention. However, on the 17 August 1938, Conlon was told by the Cabinet Secretary that the Government would not sanction such a scheme. It was thought that de Valera did not approve of such forced migration as the solution to Ireland's problems. Irish children in industrial schools were thus spared having transportation to Australia added to their other miseries of hunger and abuse.

Evidence subsequently emerged during the 1980s and early 1990s of child abuse in Christian Brothers' institutions in Australia. This was known about in Dublin during the 1930s and 1940s. Whether the Irish government was aware of or influenced by this knowledge isn't established (Raftery and O'Sullivan, 1999: 262). On the other hand, British children were subject to forced migration to the colonies during the 20th century. A House of Commons Committee investigated the welfare of British child migrants and estimated that about 150,000 children were forced or deceived into migration to the colonies (Third Report of Select Committee on Health, 1998: para 11). The destinations included Canada, Australia, New Zealand and Zimbabwe. The motives, according to the 1998 select committee, were 'mixed': (1) philanthropic, (2) economic exploitation and (3) racist – the importation of 'good white stock'. Many of these former child migrants believe they are the victim of 'stolen' lives (Third Report of Select Committee on Health, 1998, para 41).

Poverty, class and institutionalisation

The question as to whether children were institutionalised on the basis of poverty and social class is fundamental to understanding the history of the reformatory and industrial school system in Ireland. Bruce Arnold (2009) has called this system 'the Irish Gulag'. But where did the children that populated a system that had all the characteristics of a Kafka or Solzhenitsyn novel come from? They were overwhelmingly from unskilled working-class backgrounds, as the Ryan Report reveals (CICA, 2009: 3: 3.08): 67% unskilled working class; 9% semi-skilled working class; 6% skilled working class; 4% non-manual; 1% managerial and technical; 1% professional worker and 12% unknown.

Out of 791 witnesses who gave evidence to the Confidential Committee of the *Commission to Inquire into Child Abuse*, chaired by Judge Sean Ryan, 530 (67%) stated that they were from unskilled working-class backgrounds. A further 97 witnesses reported that they didn't know their parents' skill levels.

In an analysis of the identities and status of the abused children in industrial and reformatory schools, Carol Holohan (2011: 108) has argued that the whole system was based on class, with the vast majority coming from working-class backgrounds and being cared for by lower order clerics with minimalist training. It produced an economic system based on slave labour, exploiting some of the neediest children in Ireland (Holohan, 2011: 112).

Paradoxically, the influence of poverty and the class origins of the children confined within the industrial and reformatory school system in Ireland has become the subject of heated debate. Essentially, the issue at stake is whether poverty or family failure was the cause of children's admissions. The evidence would appear to support the former point of view but it is complicated by the moral judgementalism that informed social attitudes at the time.

The Ryan Report (CICA, 2009: 1: 3.03), on the basis of an analysis of court archival records, concluded:

> Although the balance varied from decade to decade, the great majority of children were committed because they were 'needy'. The next most frequent grounds of entry were involvement in a criminal offence or school non-attendance. Each of these grounds involved committal by the District Court. The remaining two grounds, which over the entire period from 1936 to 1970 were less frequently

used, were being sent by a Health Authority and voluntary entry.

This conclusion that social need was the key factor leading to institutionalisation is important. It broadly supports Raftery and O'Sullivan's (1999: 22) contention that poverty was the root cause of institutionalisation:

> Approximately eighty per cent of all children committed, and over ninety per cent of girls, came under the category 'lack of proper guardianship'. In practice, this was a catch-all heading, which included children of unmarried mothers not eligible for adoption, children who had lost one or both parents, those whose parents were incapacitated through illness, or whose families were unable to look after them due to poverty. Homeless children came within this category, as did those whose families had been broken up because of desertion or the imprisonment of one parent. However, in all these cases, the language and procedure of the courts was to place the onus of guilt on the child. And the State, rather than attempting to address the poverty that existed in these families, chose instead to fund religious orders to effectively incarcerate these children.

Other scholars have questioned Raftery and O'Sullivan's (1999) 'poverty thesis' as being biased and over-simplistic. Keogh (2005) accuses Raftery and O'Sullivan of being 'polemical', while acknowledging 'the book is an important contribution to our understanding of the culture, ethos and history of the Irish industrial school system' (Keogh, 2005: 434). Maguire (2009: 10) also describes their book as 'a polemic and sensationalist piece of journalism'. Ferguson (2007) criticises Raftery and O'Sullivan on the basis that 'they fail to even mention cruelty and neglect' (Ferguson, 2007: 127). In her study, Maguire (2009: 37–43) raises the issue of 'defaulting parents' and links child poverty to family dysfunction as a significant factor in institutionalisation. The force of these criticisms underlines the sharp values and cultural divide that has informed the debate about industrial and reformatory schools. Historians (such as Keogh and Maguire) have come late to the debate, which has been led by social scientists and media exposure. The 'presentism' that Keogh (2005: 435) accuses Raftery and O'Sullivan of promoting reflects the debate in the public sphere as well as epistemological and methodological divisions between historical and social scientists about a report (the Ryan Report) largely produced by lawyers. However, in recent historical research, Sarah Anne Buckley (2013), in a study focused on the NSPCC, has come down strongly on the side of Raftery and O'Sullivan's 'poverty thesis' and the linkage of charity to power and social control.

The accuracy of these conflicting interpretations revolves around sources. There were three primary sources employed by the Ryan Report (2009): (1) court records; (2) files from the National Society for the Prevention of Cruelty to Children (NSPCC) and, post 1956, the Irish Society for the Prevention of Cruelty to Children (ISPCC);[2] and (3) witness evidence from survivors. Ferguson (2007: 124) used NSPCC records. Maguire (2009) drew upon 'a wide array of sources, including legislation, parliamentary debates, commission reports and annual reports from government departments' (p 13). She also had access to ISPCC files for three counties (Wexford, Wicklow and Mayo) from the late 1930s to the mid-1950s (Maguire, 2009: 14).

The Ryan Report (CICA, 2009: 5: 2) notes that NSPCC/ISPCC records are limited and provides two explanations for this: (1) they were mislaid in the changeover from NSPCC to ISPCC in 1956 (or more likely they were at least partly transferred to London), and (2) a fire in the Dublin headquarters in 1961. On the basis of a random survey of pre-1970 files, the Ryan Report (CICA, 2009: 5: 9) concluded 'that the main reason for children being committed to residential care was the poverty of their families'. However, the Ryan Report does acknowledge (on the basis of witness evidence) considerable complexity in 'social circumstances, including combinations of poverty, illness, neglect, parental death, non-marital birth and unemployment' stating that these ' were reported as significant factors in the admission of all 791 witnesses to the school system' (CICA, 2009: 3: 4.16). Given the broad evidential base of the Ryan Report, informed by nearly a decade of research and hearings, it is difficult not to accept its view as definitive, namely that the underlying cause of institutionalisation, as Raftery and O'Sullivan (1999) have argued, was structural poverty. However, both Ferguson (2007) and Maguire (2009), in taking issue with Raftery and O'Sullivan's (1999) 'poverty thesis', are also correct to the extent that the interaction between poverty and family circumstances often

2   The first Irish branch of the NSPCC was founded in Dublin in May 1889, with branches founded in Cork and Belfast in 1891. In 1956, the Irish Society for the Prevention of Cruelty to Children was founded as a successor to the National Society for the Prevention of Cruelty to Children, which had operated in Ireland from 1889 to 1956.

became the trigger for institutionalisation. In reality, removal from parental care meant placement in an industrial school.

Cullen (2012: 151) has offered an important insight into the complex relationship between poverty, family and institutionalisation:

> I believe that an important consideration in determining the reasons why the children were committed is the construction of poverty that operated within Irish society. The concept of the 'deserving poor' versus the 'undeserving poor' was connected with the 'moral' status of children. Children who were neglected or abused or were being reared in circumstances that were considered to be morally dubious were constructed as 'damaged' and contaminated by their experience. It was this combination of circumstances that gave rise to the stigmatisation of the children.
>
> While the majority of people were poor in Ireland at this time, being a lone parent, extreme poverty, and family breakdown were seen as incompatible with the Ideal Irish Identity and as a shameful indictment of the particular family and child. Families that did not fit with the strict rules of the conservative Catholic society of the time were subjected to marginalisation.

Maguire asserts in similar vein:

> … the industrial school system would not have existed in the first place if it did not serve some purpose to the state, and if it was not upheld and supported, every day, by an army of ISPCC inspectors and district court justices who sat in judgement on poor Irish families, and consigned to industrial schools children whose parents did not fit the mould of appropriate and respectable Irish parenthood. (Maguire, 2009: 10)

Both Cullen's and Maguire's argument is that families that did not conform to middle class standards of morality were dismembered by the state. But the families that were dismembered were working-class families living in poverty. Holohan (2011: 136) concludes: 'children who were poor, illegitimate, and abused were not considered part of the imagined nation and often paid a heavy price as they were defined as the other of Irish society.' The process of 'othering' poor children interacted with other social characteristics relating to legitimacy and ethnicity. Social genetics played a key role in the narrative of institutionalisation.

Social genetics and institutionalisation

Jane Barnes' (1989) study, entitled *Irish Industrial Schools 1868–1908*, examines the origins and development of the system as a form of social genetics. She notes that 'in order to carry out the central work of character formation and moral training, remaining links between the child and the home were ruthlessly cut ... conversion to a new set of values was to be the objective; purging the children of their parents' views and habits the method. The whole process amounted to social genetics' (Barnes, 1989: 88). Ferguson (2007) constructs institutionalisation as a strategy of 'ethnic cleansing'. The idea of social genetics is also taken up by Raftery and O'Sullivan (1999: 312): 'there was one constant theme that continuously informed the way in which industrial school children were treated. That was the clear perception from the religious that they were in some way less valuable and less worthy than other children.' While some of these children were illegitimate, they were almost certainly in the minority. A smaller group of the children were from ethnic minority backgrounds (eg, African-Irish, Travellers and so on) (Raftery and O'Sullivan, 1999: 312-13). All of the children in the Irish industrial schools were stigmatised by their social backgrounds and institutionalisation. They were treated as social outcasts. Irish civil society colluded in this policy of social genetics, which has some parallels with other European countries influenced by Social Darwinism (ie, survival of the fittest). In reference to the collusion of civil society, Raftery and O'Sullivan make a direct comparison with Nazi Germany (1999: 317-18).

Maguire (2009: 48) notes 'a remarkable degree of ambivalence towards illegitimate children amongst Irish clerics, lawmakers and judges'. This ambivalence reflected the view of civil society. In Ireland, illegitimacy was viewed as a threat to the blood lines or genes within families upon which property inheritance was based in a land-owning economy. The issues of blood and property arose during the adoption debate that took place between 1948 and 1952. In the wake of the First World War (1914–18), adoption had been introduced to England (1926), Northern Ireland (1929) and Scotland (1930). Following the Second World War (1939–45), the Adoption Society (founded in 1948) made a belated campaign to introduce similar legislation to Ireland; this met with powerful resistance. One officer of the Adoption Society recalled a rural TD (politician) telling him that to interfere with the line of succession to property was 'like interfering with a stud-book' (Whyte, 1980: 187). Manifestly, genes and property were fundamentally linked in Irish society. Illegitimacy (real or imagined) or membership of a minority ethnic group was viewed as a threat to the gene pool. Like the foundling children of the 18th century, who were viewed as carriers of syphilis, youths in industrial schools were regarded as the carriers of bad genes. Public anxiety about bad genes continued to be associated with the problem of syphilis, which was very often the product of sexual exploitation. Young girls were frequently targeted in cities by paedophiles offering sweets or money (Ferriter, 2009: 52). They were, instead of receiving care and protection, subjected to social exclusion in the form of a confinement and isolation from Irish society as a population of social outcasts. The Catholic Church made their remoralisation the centre of its agenda in an effort to 'cleanse' them of any links with their biological origins in a patriarchal society where the female victim in many cases was held responsible for the crime.

In order to facilitate remoralisation, young people were usually detained in industrial schools until they reached the age of 16 years, regardless of legality. Family ties were viewed as polluting. Mail was censored. Family visits were discretionary and rare. Parents (especially single parents) were made to feel uncomfortable. They were treated with distain by the clerical managers, often involving physical exclusion from the buildings, however inclement the weather. This policy of discouraging contact between children and their natural parents was carried out despite monetary payments from the parents (Raftery and O'Sullivan, 1999: 314-15). In a traditionalist society that professed to value the family, this would appear to be a fundamentally contradictory policy. Yet, as Raftery and O'Sullivan assert, both church and state cooperated in this policy:

> It is clear that families of a particular class of people, those who lived in poverty, were of less value and less importance in this context … While the bulk of this hostile attitude to family came from the religious orders, there is no doubt that the state colluded in it. Many children were deliberately committed by the courts to industrial schools hundreds of miles from their homes. This was a highly effective means of cutting off all contact with their families as the expense of traveling to visit was an effective barrier for very many of their parents … It was one of an arsenal of tactics used – particularly by nuns – to break the children's spirit and to

shape them for life – mainly as docile servants …' (Raftery
and O'Sullivan, 1999: 315-16)

Barnes (1989: 89) concludes that 'moral regeneration – which implied
incisive divorce from home and family – was the goal'. Raftery and
O'Sullivan assert that there is a contradiction in our perception of Irish
social policy, which has been widely viewed as non-interventionist and
pro-family. In reality it was highly directive towards these children's
incarceration in church-run industrial schools: 'this standard view
may now need to be re-examined in the context of the sheer scale
of the state's direct intervention in the lives of such vast numbers of
families, through committal of their children to industrial schools'
(Raftery and O'Sullivan, 1999: 338). However, this robust policy
of state interventionism did not extend to protecting children from
punishment and abuse once they were incarcerated in industrial schools.
The children were undergoing a process of remoralisation, intended
to change their attitudes and identity. This was the project of the
industrial school system. Remoralisation had replaced the foundling
hospitals policy of liquidation.

Vaccine trials on children in care: an unresolved issue

The *Irish Independent* raised the issue of vaccine trials on children in
care (McDonagh, 2010). This issue had been addressed by Justice Mary
Laffoy, the first Chair of the Commission to Inquire into Child Abuse,
without success. It is not covered in the Commission's final report (the
Ryan Report [CICA, 2009]) and remains an unresolved issue. The
inference behind the *Irish Independent* report is that there has been a
political cover-up. In fact, the investigation was not completed due to
legal proceedings, which ruled the issue was *ultra vires* (ie, beyond the
legal power of the Commission).

At the beginning of the 1990s, former residents of children's
institutions began to publicly report that they had been subjected to
clinical vaccination trials while in care. The then Minister of Health and
Children, Mr Michael Martin, in response to questions in Dáil Éireann
(the Irish Parliament) reported that an investigation was carried out by
the Chief Medical Officer (CMO) on clinical trials involving babies
and children in institutional settings over the periods 1960/61, 1970
and 1973. The main findings in the CMO's report were summarised
in the *Third Interim Report of the Commission to Inquire into Child Abuse*
(2003: 414) as follows:

Trial 1: This was a trial in which 58 infants, resident in five children's homes in the state, took part. It sought to compare the poliomyelitis antibody response after vaccination with a quadruple vaccine (diphtheria, pertussis − also known as whooping cough, tetanus (DTP) and polio combined) with standard vaccines in use at the time, which consisted of DTP and polio administered separately and at different sites. This trial was conducted between December 1960 and November 1961. The results of the trial were published in the *British Medical Journal* in 1962.

Trial 2: In one strand of this trial, 69 children resident in an orphanage in Dublin had blood taken. Twelve were subsequently administered intranasal rubella − that is German measles − vaccine. In another strand of this trial, 23 children living at home in a rural area in the Midlands were administered the same vaccine. The purpose of the trial was to investigate whether there was a propensity for intranasally administered vaccines to spread to susceptible contacts, for example pregnant women, and to estimate antibody levels and acceptability of the intranasal technique of vaccination. The trial was conducted during 1970. The results of the trial were published in the *Cambridge Journal of Hygiene* in 1971.

Trial 3: In this trial, 53 children in 'Mother and Baby' homes and children's homes in Dublin and 65 children living at home in Dublin were administered vaccine to compare the reactogenicity of the commercially available batches of Trivax vaccine (that is the proprietary name for Diptheria, Tetanus and Pertussis vaccine) and Trivax AD vaccine with a vaccine of equivalent efficacy but, in relation to the pertussis or whooping cough component, of lesser potency. This trial was apparently conducted in 1973. The outcome of this trial was not published.

In an ensuing Dáil debate (Dáil Éireann, 2000) the Minister for Health and Children stated:

The chief medical officer's report is a good one but it is incomplete. It raises as many questions as it answers and some of those questions go to the heart of our attitudes to children and their rights. The report is incomplete because in some areas the most rigorous interrogation of the system failed to produce documentary records of the trials. In some cases the consultant who conducted the trials believed they took place in particular homes, but the homes do not have files that substantiate this.

While we must remember that the trials were not recent, this lack of documentation is, at best, puzzling. It is certainly unsatisfactory. It is my hope that publication of this report, with the action I will propose to the House, will perhaps help us fill in the missing bits of the jigsaw by stimulating memories or helping to locate lost files. I have read and re-read this report and I have discussed it with the chief medical officer in detail. In spite of the information gaps and the indications that no child was medically harmed, each reading made me more sure that his work must be regarded as the beginning, not the end, of the matter. When a child comes into the care of the State, the State must fight fiercely for all that child's rights, including bodily integrity. The State does not have the right to view children in care as lesser citizens. Their bodily integrity is a basic human right which can never be watered down or infringed.

Clearly, when we look at vaccination trials, the issue of informed consent is immediately involved. I am not satisfied that the chief medical officer has been able to find solid, informed consent, on the record, given by the people who were entitled to give it. Let me put this in context. The history of drug trials includes some ghastly case studies where the rights of individuals were grievously ignored. There have been cases in other countries where prisoners and members of the armed forces were involved in the trials of substances without their knowledge or informed consent. There have even been cases – again, in other countries – where prisoners suffering a lethal illness were used as a 'control group'. In other words, they were not given a medicine which the authorities knew would save their lives. Instead, they were left untreated to suffer and die in the interests of providing a point of comparison.

The Chief Medical Officer's report had recorded that there were no statutory controls in force in Ireland regulating clinical trials. However, ethical standards were set by the Nuremberg Code (1947), the Helsinki

Declaration and the medical profession, as well as the Medical Research Council.

At the request of the Minister for Health and Children, the Commission to Inquire into Child Abuse, established in 1999 to investigate allegations of child abuse in institutional care was asked to investigate the vaccination trials issue. The Minister identified several core questions that needed to be answered:

- Why children in care received the experimental vaccines?
- Why were some of the recipients outside the normal age for the administration of the vaccines?
- Was the end result for commercial gain or public good?
- Why were the records of the trials so inadequate?

(*Third Interim Report of the Commission to Inquire into Child Abuse*, 2003: 212)

The Commission advertised in the media, both in Ireland and in the United Kingdom, seeking responses from survivors of the institutional care system who believed they had been involved in vaccine trials. The scope of the enquiry was enlarged to cover the period 1940–87. The Commission provided a questionnaire for survivors who wished to respond. It received a total of 877 replies from survivors who believed that they had been subjected to clinical vaccination trials while in institutional care.

The evidence from the 877 survivors of the Irish institutional care system that responded was as follows:

- one hundred and fifty-eight (158) correspondents positively alleged that they had been involved in a vaccine trial;
- two hundred and nineteen (219) correspondents suspected that they may have been involved in a trial;
- one hundred and forty-three (143) correspondents both alleged and suspected that they were participants in a vaccine trial;
- one hundred and thirty-six (136) correspondents indicated that they were not part of a vaccine trial;
- one hundred and eighty-four (184) correspondents indicated that they did not know whether they were involved in a vaccine trial or not;

- thirty-seven (37) correspondents failed to complete the relevant portion of the questionnaire.

(*Third Interim Report of the Commission to Inquire into Child Abuse*, 2003: 214-15).

The Commission to Inquire into Child Abuse, under its then Chair, Justice Mary Laffoy, set about establishing public hearings in relation to the vaccination trials. These hearings were called the Vaccination Trial Inquiry. It prepared a book of documents, held six days of public hearings in relation to procedural issues between March and July 2003, received applications for legal representation, appointed its own legal teams and established the vaccination trials as a division of the commission's investigation committee. However, following judicial review proceedings, the Vaccination Trials Inquiry was deemed *ultra vires* (beyond the power) of the Child Abuse Act 2000, which was the legal basis of the commission. On 25 November 2003, the Commission gave the High Court an undertaking that it would not proceed with the hearings until the matter was legally settled, which, given the *ultra vires* judgment, meant in effect that the Vaccination Trials Inquiry was terminated before its substantive hearings had started. The vaccination trials issues had been successfully prevented from coming into the public domain through an open inquiry.

The issue was, therefore, not due to a political cover-up but rather a judicial decision that prevented the Commission to Inquire into Child Abuse from pursuing its investigation. Clearly, there is an unresolved issue here that is to become the subject of a future investigation into Mother and Baby Homes established in 2015. The evidence that was revealed by the Commission's preliminary investigation gives serious cause for disquiet and manifestly needs to be fully investigated.

Philomena's story: forced adoptions and child deaths

The publication of a book called *The Lost Child of Philomena Lee* (Sixsmith, 2009) and a film called *Philomena* have raised major questions about mother and baby homes in Ireland during the 20th century. Philomena Lee's son was adopted by an American Catholic family during the 1950s. While she had signed a consent form, there is growing concern that many mothers of illegitimate children were coerced into 'forced adoptions' during this period. Because of the stigma of illegitimacy it wasn't possible for single mothers to keep their children. This led to tragic separations and in the case of Philomena (like many mothers who had been forced to give up their children for adoption) a subsequent search to be reunited with their child. In Philomena's case both mother and son searched for each other only to be foiled by his premature death. Her son had become legal counsel to two presidents of the United States. This dramatic story of Philomena provides an illustration of the Irish state's reluctance to support single mothers and the tragic consequences of that reluctance.

In Chapter 1, we have already noted the reports of child mortality in Tuam Mother and Baby Home during the 20th century. Connall O'Fatharta, in an article in the *Irish Examiner*, has suggested that child mortality rates in Bessborough Mother and Baby Home in Cork were as high as 68% in the 1940s.[3] These further revelations underline the importance of the Commission of Inquiry into Mother and Baby Homes, established by the Irish government during 2015. Its terms of reference will include 'forced adoption', child deaths in care and the vaccine trials.

Corporal punishment, 'black pedagogy' and social control

The concept of 'black pedagogy' is associated with the child development theorist Alice Miller (2007), who argued that the use of corporal punishment in the disciplining of children traumatised them for life. She contended that these abused children became damaged adults, suffering from depression and insecurity, which they passed on to their own children. Discipline in industrial schools was ruthlessly enforced. As Barnes puts it, 'although corporal punishment was cast in as favourable light as possible, strong evidence exists that some schools featured frequent and severe beatings'. She based this conclusion on an analysis of inspectors' reports, which 'while inspectors reported on the one hand a low incidence of corporal punishment, on the other they felt obliged to censure some managers for excessive use of the cane' (Barnes, 1989: 101). Once again we are confronted by contradictory behaviour by the state, raising fundamental issues about the social construction of the industrial school inmate's identity as victim, criminal and outcast. The Ryan Report (CICA, 2009: 1: 3.25) notes that 'children committed to these schools were seen as being criminals by staff and that a lot of the mistreatment experienced by the children emanated from this perception'.

The Ryan Report (CICA, 2009: 4: 6.14) concluded: 'Corporal punishment was the option of first resort for breaches of discipline.

---

[3]   *Irish Examiner* 25 August 2014 '68% of babies in Bessborough Home died'.

Extreme punishment was a feature of the boys' schools' including 'prolonged, excessive beatings'. The Ryan Report provides very detailed evidence of the shocking physical abuse of children in industrial and reformatory schools. In reference to Letterfrack Industrial School and Junior Reformatory, the Ryan Report (1: 8.214) concluded: 'public punishment increased the ordeal for the person being punished and had a frightening impact on the boys watching and listening. Such spectacles should have had no place in a facility dedicated to the care of children'. But they were part of the 'culture of fear' that pervaded the industrial and reformatory school system. The Ryan Report (3: 7.230) made reference to 59 witnesses from nine schools who reported their fear of the 'prospect of being stripped to be beaten or having to watch co-residents being beaten without their clothes'. One witness stated it was like watching *Mutiny on the Bounty*.[4] Other witnesses reported being raped, sometimes at gun point (CICA, 2009: 3: 7.231-7.233). Violence was endemic. Carol Holohan (2011: 7) concludes that children's experience in Irish industrial schools constituted systemic violence, not merely child abuse. The Ryan Report (3: 7.278) records that 308 witnesses reported that 'fear was their predominant response to the abuse that they both observed and experienced'. Emotional abuse was endemic. The Ryan Report (4: 6.39) concluded: 'a disturbing element of the evidence before the Commission was the level of emotional abuse that disadvantaged, neglected and abandoned children were subjected to generally by religious and lay staff in institutions'.

Orphans, bullying and racism

A witness told the Ryan Commission that 'we were terrified of those men in long trousers, we were just little fellas in short trousers' (CICA, 2009: 3: 7.278). Bullying was rampant within the industrial and reformatory school system and was linked to family origin and ethnicity. Orphans were particularly prone to being bullied, as witnesses reported in to the Ryan Report Commission:

> I wasn't a hard man. I came from a convent, I was an orphan. It was terrible for us, we got a terrible time, we got bullied by the kids as well. They would take your food off you, you wouldn't dare tell on them, they would batter you.

[4]   *Mutiny on the Bounty*: there have been several film versions of this story which is probably what is being referred to here.

It was a very, very cruel place, there was no sense in it or need for it, it was especially bad for the orphans, we were treated differently ... The Brothers promoted bullying especially of the orphans. (CICA, 2009: 3: 7.246)

The Ryan Report (3: 7.244) recorded '99 witness reports of bullying by co-residents from 16 schools'. The reason orphans were singled out for bullying was due to their assumed illegitimate status, placing them in the position of being 'moral dirt'. Children from mother and baby homes who were not placed for adoption were liable to be transferred to an industrial school. Their vulnerability was often exacerbated by their lack of any family connection. The Ryan Report (3: 7.236) commented 'the sons of lone mothers, "orphans" or "converters" were reported as particular targets for such abuse [denigration of family origin], being told that their mothers were "sinners", "slags" and "old whores"'. The Ryan Report (4: 3.36) records that 'there was a high number of orphans in Industrial Schools'. Racism was also a key factor in bullying. Seven witnesses' statements to the Ryan Report stated that they were 'verbally abused and ridiculed about their Traveller and mixed race backgrounds' (3: 7.236).

Br [X] called me a knacker [Traveller] and said my parents didn't want me, I felt worthless and degraded.
It was a very tough place for me, one nun locked me in a closet, beat the hell out of me with a leather strap. She didn't like blacks, she called me Baluba,[5] every time the Irish soldiers were attacked in the Congo she attacked me.

Unsurprisingly, the children institutionalised in these care facilities suffered from trauma. There are 18 reports of attempted suicide (CICA, 2009: 3: 7.282). There are also reports of the disappearance of children, following severe corporal punishment (3: 7.250-7.254).

Within the process of institutionalisation, a complex set of Foucauldian 'technologies of power' existed. Cullen (2012) has analysed a Kafkaesque world in which a number of psychological themes (shame, power, secrecy, isolation and fear) were employed within the Irish system of industrial and reformatory schools. She asserts that 'these themes are identified as objects/new realities that come together as "technologies of power"'. Because of these 'technologies of power,'

---

[5]   The Baluba was a Congolese tribe that killed several Irish soldiers who were on a peace-keeping mission during the 1960s.

Cullen (2012:17) argues, children in care became marginalised because they did not fit into the normative ideals of Irish family identity and the 'discourse of silence constructed the children as voiceless, and the discourse of othering perceived them as dehumanised'. This was the cultural tragedy that the Commission to Inquire into Child Abuse was required to interrogate and draw historical lessons from so that it could not be repeated in the future. But what was at the root of this cultural tragedy?

Sex, culture and child abuse

The issue of sexuality, which Diarmaid Ferriter has discussed in his major archival study of court records, *Occasions of Sin: Sex and Society in Modern Ireland* (2009), was at the core of many social problems in Ireland and particularly the practice of institutionalisation. Ferriter (2009: 172) asserts that control of sex and sexual relations was ambivalent; while the virtue of chastity was preached from the pulpits 'there was little discussion of one of the most prevalent sexual crimes – indecent assault against young children'. Arguably, there was an absence of a social vocabulary to define child abuse, which was variously described in the legal language of indecent assault, rape, incest and so on. Ferriter (2009: 23) also notes that 'a reluctance to replicate British legislation highlighted the tendency in Ireland to sometimes ignore or avoid issues to do with sexuality, pregnancy and illegitimacy'. The suppressed Carrigan Report (1934) reveals there was an awareness of sexuality in Ireland at this time but a reluctance to address its dark side (ie, child abuse). The Cussen Report (1936) similarly shut the lid on any public discussion of institutionalisation. The Children Act 1908 remained the principal statute in Ireland until it was eventually replaced by the Child Care Act 1991 and the Children Act 2001. Furthermore, the primacy of family rights in the Irish Constitution of 1937 up to 2012[6] has proven a major obstacle to child care reform, as has been highlighted by the Roscommon Child Care Report, 2010.

Within the world of poverty in which the slum defined everyday lived reality for a large section of the population, children were vulnerable to abuse. Ferriter (2009) notes that 'many of the legal cases of the early twentieth century reflect the extent to which living conditions contributed to sexual crime ... nor was it unusual, given the overcrowding, for parents to sleep in the same beds as their children'.

[6]   A referendum on inserting Children's Rights into the 1937 Constitution was carried in 2012 but the result was subsequently contested in the Supreme Court.

Incest inevitably became an issue. Ferriter (2009: 79) comments that 'many victims of what in 1908 legally became the crime of incest were subjected to rape over extended periods, an abuse sustainable because of the absence of a mother and the fear of being sent away'. Being 'sent away' meant incarceration in an industrial school where girls were disproportionately represented. Some (maybe particularly) female children were vulnerable to abuse in the dark alleyways and unlit corridors of tenement houses. Others sent away into service at a young age found themselves exploited by their employers (Ferriter, 2009).

Within the reformatory and industrial school system children were exposed to sexual abuse. The Ryan Report (CICA, 2009: 4: 6.18) concludes: 'Sexual abuse was endemic in boys' institutions. The situation in girls' institutions was different. Although girls were subjected to predatory sexual abuse by male employees or visitors or in outside placements, sexual abuse was not systemic in girls' schools.' The response of the religious authorities was to 'minimise the risk of disclosure' in cases involving clergy (4: 6.20). Even when extensive evidence subsequently emerged from police inquiries, criminal convictions and witness accounts of child sexual abuse in the past, religious congregations remained 'defensive and disbelieving' (4: 6.25).

Deinstitutionalisation and social change

Two Labour Party members of Dáil Éireann, Professor David Thornley and Dr John O'Connell, took up the issue of the implementation of the key recommendations of the Kennedy Report. During 1971, in a series of Dáil debates, they questioned ministers. In a response to a parliamentary question the Minister for Education, Mr Padraig Faulkner, pointed out that there was a long-term trend towards deinstitutionalisation and that "during the past 20 years the number of children in these schools has fallen from 6,000 to fewer that 2,000: also, there is a drop in the number of such schools from 52 to 28".[7]

In response to a series of parliamentary questions, the Minister for Justice, Mr Desmond O'Malley, provided a number of statistical reports on court committals (see Tables 8.1 and 8.2).

These statistics show large numbers of children being brought before the Dublin Metropolitan Court but very few committals. Even when orders were made they were often not enforced. What is clear is that the policy of institutionalisation was beginning to weaken. However, it seems to have been driven more by changing social values than

[7]   Dáil debates, Volume 252, 25 March 1971.

Table 8.1: Statistics regarding the number of cases involving children heard before the Dublin Metropolitan Court

Year	Cases
1961	14,413
1962	11,924
1963	11,818
1964	9,956
1965	8,882
1966	10,777
1967	9,832
1968	12,287
1960	13,654
1970	16,586

Source: Dail Debates: Volume 254, 17 June 1971 and Volume 255, 6 July 1971.

Table 8.2: Number of applications between 1961 and 1970 for committal to an industrial or reformatory school and actual committals

Year	Applications	Committals
1961	462	318
1962	535	292
1963	529	249
1964	388	164
1965	430	202
1966	384	155
1967	261	115
1968	229	73
1960	173	68
1970	193	61

Source: Dail Debates: Volume 255, 6 July 1971

any serious official attempt to provide alternatives in the community (O'Sullivan and O'Donnell, 2012). This lack of policy led to the establishment of the Task Force on Child Care in 1974, which reported in 1980. Its reform agenda finally bore fruit in the Child Care Act 1991. It ultimately led to the establishment of the Family and Child Care Agency in 2014.

Conclusion

In this chapter, we have examined the power dynamics of child abuse through the sociological lens of 'othering'. We set the analysis in its historical context, tracing developments up to the present day. Parental indifference historically emerges as a key issue, reflecting a wider societal indifference to abandoned children. Jonathan Swift in his satirical essay, *A Modest Proposal*, penned during the early 18th century, sought to confront society with its hypocrisy by advocating cannibalism. His use of the pamphlet as an instrument of media power was shocking. Swift intended it to be shocking. But he failed to break the silence. Media silence was the product of cultural collusion. There were 'known-knowns' but they were also unmentionables. Why? The answer lies in the cultural dynamics in which vulnerable groups are 'othered'. It resulted in devastating consequences for disadvantaged children. They were allowed to die with societal complicity during the 18th century. The 19th century witnessed their segregation in institutions, where children were brutalised and exploited, which offered no material change in their circumstances. This saga continued until the late 20th century. What is striking about this tragic narrative is its unrelenting bleakness. Genes and poverty underpinned the exclusionary process of 'othering'. The public silence that accompanied the abuse of children is a powerful testament to the darkness of child abuse, as a cultural signifier of the world that denied children rights. Recent research evidence indicates that society still has to break out of the power dynamic of 'othering' in relation to child abuse and develop a more socially inclusive response, particularly in relation to children from ethnic minorities. The hidden history of child abuse raises fundamental questions about child citizenship in Ireland.

NINE

The cultural politics of child abuse

> In those days of course you didn't have a voice, nobody thought you had a brain even. (Ryan Report [CICA, 2009: 3: 15.64])

This quotation, of words given as witness evidence to the Ryan Commission, testifies to the importance of the child's voice or, in this case, its enforced silence. The Ryan Report (CICA, 2009: 4: 7.14 and 7.15) recommended that 'children in care should be able to communicate without fear', adding 'childcare services depend on good communication'. The voice of the child is fundamental to good child protection practice. It is also a human rights concern that cannot be overstated. Child citizenship needs to be constitutionally acknowledged in a democratic society. Otherwise children become an oppressed minority, victimised by abuses of adult power.

In the light of proposals being made in the United Kingdom to privatise child protection services, allegedly with the support of some charities, the United Nations Convention on the Rights of the Child 1989 (UNCRC) becomes of urgent importance.[1] What we have learnt from the Ryan Report is that profit and charity in child protection results in the dehumanisation of children from socially disadvantaged backgrounds. Yet this Victorian legacy of child exploitation is once again visible in the shifting balance between 'state–civil society–market' that will determine welfare futures in the 21st century.

Children offer a vast market to be exploited for profit. In the article in *The Guardian* referred to earlier, Professor Eileen Munro, author of the influential UK Munro Report (2011), is reported to have stated that establishing a market in child protection would create perverse incentives for private companies to either take more children into care or leave too many languishing with dangerous families. The Ryan Report (CICA, 2009: 5: 4–9) clearly demonstrates that operating a child care system on a 'for profit' basis has a corrupting impact on both the state and civil society.

---

[1]   *The Guardian* 17 May 2014.

In this chapter we examine the cultural politics of child abuse. The chapter takes the narrative right up to the present day. We focus on two groups of children: (1) those from asylum-seeking backgrounds housed in direct provision accommodation and (2) the contemporary reality for children in care proceedings. What emerges from our analysis is that the issue of child abuse continues to be a disturbing reality in Irish civil society and the state remains reluctant to take responsibility for many child citizens who are born in Ireland. Their ethnicity clearly is an ongoing factor in abuse and social service failure.

Ethnic minorities, asylum-seekers and human rights

Inquiries such as the Ryan Report are usually classified as 'historical', suggesting these events and their accompanying truths can be consigned to the past. But that isn't so. The Australian journalist, John Pilger, in an article in *The Guardian* in 2013[2] entitled 'Australia's stop the boats policy is racist and lawless', points to a long tradition of abusing refugee and Aboriginal children. Pilger claims that between 2011 and 2012, 13,299 impoverished Aboriginal children were taken from their families. He concludes that another 'stolen generation' is being socially engineered in contemporary Australia. The link between impoverished children being 'boated' to Australia and contemporary migrant and Aboriginal children is direct. Their fates are likely to be similar in the sense that they are at risk of becoming both culturally and socially dispersed and open to economic exploitation. It underlines the reality that nation states can be abusers of children. Cultural attitudes towards poverty and ethnicity within any society are likely to shape the policy context in relation to children. Civicness and civility are vital cultural forces in building a tolerant and inclusive civil society.

In a series of investigative reports in *The Irish Times* about asylum seekers who have come to Ireland, Carl O'Brien reported that 'social services alerted [that there were] over 1,500 cases involving young asylum seekers', living in direct provision accommodation[3] funded by the state.[4] There are 4,360 people living in the direct provision system. They spend an average of three years and six months in direct provision accommodation. In some cases asylum seekers are incarcerated for over seven years (see Table 9.1). Most asylum seekers are from Africa

2   *The Guardian* 30 July 2013.
3   Direct provision accomodation refers to the institutional centres where asylum-seekers and refugees are housed.
4   *The Irish Times* 9 August 2014.

(3307), with 854 from Asia, 227 from Eastern Europe and 56 from elsewhere (see Table 9.2). There are 1,666 children living within the direct provision system (see Table 9.3).

Table: 9.1 How long have people been in the system?

Number of years	Number of people
1	823
2	550
3	414
4	450
5	511
6	603
7	479
Over 7 years	604

Source: Reception and Integration Agency

Table 9.2: Breakdown by continent of direct provision system residents (end December 2013)

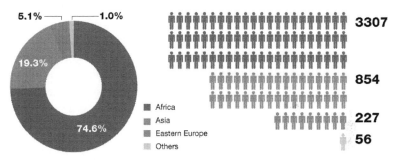

Source: Reception and Integration Agency

Table: 9.3 Breakdown by age and gender

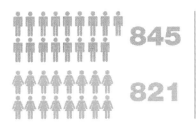

Age	Total Children	Boys	Girls
0-4	686	345	341
5-12	837	428	409
13-17	143	72	71

Source: Reception and Integration Agency

Asylum seekers receive board and lodgings, plus a weekly payment of €19.10 for an adult and €9.60 for a child. They live in 34 centres distributed around Ireland. These centres are converted hotels and hostels, convents and homes, and so on. Life for families within these facilities is difficult because of a lack of privacy and security. Adults are not allowed to work. Young people are denied the financial support to go to university. This discriminatory policy further marginalises asylum seekers forcing them into poverty. Each year there are nearly 1,000 applications for refugee status. There are only 150 positive decisions (O'Brien, 2014). The state-run reception and integration agency claims to ensure the welfare of asylum-seekers within the system. Since the system is privatised with the state paying more that €850 million to private contractors, it is difficult to know what standards are in operation within the centres (see O'Brien, 2014). However, over 1,500 child protection or welfare concerns involving young asylum seekers in direct accommodation have been reported to social services over the last five years. It suggests that there is a serious child protection problem within the direct provision system (see O'Brien, 2014). Human rights organisations take a critical view of the direct provision system in Ireland.

Samantha Arnold in an Irish study of 1,798 children in direct provision accommodation makes a link with the Ryan, Dublin and Cloyne reports, which she calls Ireland's 'dark past'. She argues 'Direct Provision is an example of government policy which has not only bred discrimination, social exclusion, enforced poverty and neglect, but has placed children at real risk … It is unlikely that an official inquiry into the treatment of asylum seekers children in Direct Provision accommodation would be instigated due to a simple lack of political will' (Arnold, 2012: 7). Arnold concludes 'Despite not having chosen to live in Ireland or seek asylum here, the children living in and growing up in Direct Provision are subjected to a cacophony of challenges disadvantaging them from the wider society of children growing up in Ireland to-day. These child victims have been largely invisible and certainly silent' (2012: 29).

Arnold's study demonstrates that there continues to be a major problem in Ireland regarding the 'othering' of children from ethnic minorities. It suggests that child poverty, social exclusion and cultural marginalisation define their lives. They live in inadequate accommodation where basic family life is very difficult to sustain. There have been complaints about hostels, and some of the hostels are now closed. The complaints and concerns often focus on provision for children (Arnold, 2012: 14-15). Like the children historically institutionalised, the children of asylum seekers and refugees lack support from civil society. That is what makes the violation of children's rights possible in 21st-century Ireland. It poses a major human rights issue.

Neglect, poverty and 'othering': the contemporary reality of children in care proceedings

In Ireland during 2011, 2,797 children were placed in voluntary care, compared with 3,358 as the result of court orders. Very little is known about children in voluntary care other than they are more likely to be in the care of relatives. What support and advice is available in these situations is uncertain (Coulter, 2013: 3). Due to the relaxation of the *in camera* rule in child care proceedings, it became possible to establish the Child Care Law Reporting Project, which has carried out research on 333 cases of child care proceedings in the courts. In November 2013, the Child Care Law Reporting Project published an interim report of its findings.

The Child Care Law Reporting Project concluded that 'in the majority of child care cases the primary reason children are taken into care is neglect, which can be, and often is, compounded by drug and alcohol abuse and mental illness' (Coulter, 2013: 5). It further noted that neglect was typically defined by the deprivation of food, warmth, hygiene, intellectual stimulation, supervision, and safety, attachment to or affection from adults and or medical care. Child neglect is intimately linked to poverty. The social reality reflected in Carol Coulter's (2013) interim report is of children growing up in households experiencing extreme poverty. It underlines the structural basis of child abuse in a political economy that divides society into rich and poor. *The Interim Report: Child Care Law Reporting Project* sets out the reasons for seeking a care order in an empirical study of court cases (see Table 9.4).

In Table 9.4, neglect emerges as the principal reason for the court application in over 20% of cases. The next highest category is 'multiple,' encompassing neglect, abuse, domestic violence, alcohol, drug abuse and mental illness. Abuse is reported as the third highest category in care proceedings, which can include sexual abuse or non-accidental injury to the child as well as physical abuse and emotional abuse. The fourth highest category was parental disability. Parental illness was also a significant reason for court proceedings, leading to children coming into care (Coulter, 2013: 18). In the light of media representations of child abuse, these findings are very significant. The findings underline the complexity of child abuse and its linkage with social deprivation.

In terms of the respondents' marital status, the Interim Report recorded that 41.2% were single parents. While in the majority of cases 57% both parents were cited as the respondents, in 33.9% of cases only the mother responded. Only 10.3% of respondents were married, with 11.4 % cohabiting. In an additional 12.9% of cases the parents were separated. In 5.1% of cases the parent was absent due to imprisonment, hospitalisation or death (Coulter, 2013: 19) (see Table 9.5).

Table 9.4: Reasons for seeking care orders

Reasons	Number	% of all applications
Neglect	72	21.6
Multiple	59	17.7
Abuse	44	13.2
Parental disability (intellectual, mental, physical)	40	12.0
Parental drug abuse	38	11.4
Parental alcohol abuse	24	7.2
Parent absent/deceased	20	6.0
Not recorded	11	3.3
Other	9	2.7
Domestic violence	6	1.8
Child's risk taking	6	1.8
Not applicable	4	1.2
Total	333	100.0

Source: C. Coulter, *Interim Report of Child Care Law Reform Project*, 2013: 38

Table 9.5: Respondent details in care proceedings

Respondents	Number	% of all respondents
Single	137	41.1
Not recorded	45	13.5
Divorced/Separated	43	12.9
Cohabiting	38	11.4
Married	34	10.2
Parent in hospital/prison	17	5.1
Other	10	3.0
Widowed	7	2.1
Not applicable	2	.6
Total	333	100.0

Source: C. Coulter, *Interim Report of Child Care Law Project*, 2013: 43

These findings indicate that a diversity of family forms characterises the background of cases coming before the courts in care proceedings. In over 40% of cases there is only a single parent, with one parent shouldering the responsibility in a larger proportion of cases. It is striking that in over 5% of cases coming before the courts in child care proceedings the parent was institutionalised. Another significant finding from the *Interim Report: Child Care Law Reporting Project* was the 'totally disproportionate' number of African children coming before the courts. Children who were of African origin were 20 times more likely than white Irish children to be the subjects of court proceedings (Coulter, 2013: 19-20). The *Interim Report: Child Care Law Reporting Project* sought to identify the reasons for the high proportion of children of African origin (which account for an estimated 22,524 or 0.5% of the Irish population) being made subjects of care proceedings. The Interim Report concludes:

> No easy explanations for this figure emerge from the statistics, though there are a few indicators. When the reasons for an order being sought was cross-referenced with ethnic background, abuse, parental disability (which we have found generally to be mental illness or intellectual disability) and parental absence emerged as the main reasons for African children coming into care. In the cases we reported on the website the abuse was usually physical abuse, linked to excessive parental discipline of the children. This raises issues of cultural difference that need to be addressed more broadly, rather than through the child care courts.
>
> In some of the cases we reported on the website African mothers were referred directly from direct provision hostels to psychiatric hospitals. It is not possible to state where the origin of their mental illness lay, but it is not unreasonable to speculate that the experiences which led them to seek asylum, combined with the experience of lengthy direct provision which has been analysed by FLAC,[5] were major contributory factors. The number of African children whose parents were absent relates to children who were either trafficked into Ireland or were abandoned by those

[5] Free Legal Aid Centres (FLAC) produced a report on the direct provision and dispersal system in 2009: 'One Size Doesn't Fit All'. See reference section for full details.

claiming to be their parents after arriving here. (Coulter, 2013: 20)

This identification of the treatment of asylum seekers and child trafficking raises challenging societal issues. It would appear that children of African origin in Ireland are highly vulnerable. The Child Care Law Reporting Project contrasted the disproportionately high levels of children of African origin appearing in court proceedings with the under-representation of children of Eastern European origin (ie, Poland, Latvia and Lithuania), which amount to 200,000 people or 4.4% of the population, yet this ethnic group accounted for only 3.3 % of respondents (see Table 9.6).

Table 9.6: Respondent ethnicity

Respondent Ethnicity	Number	% of all respondents
Irish	224	67.3
African	38	11.4
Mixed	28	8.4
Irish Traveller	12	3.6
European	11	3.3
U.K.	7	2.1
Not recorded	7	2.1
Middle Eastern	2	.6
Other	2	.6
Roma	1	.3
Not applicable	1	.3
Total	333	100

Source: C. Coulter, *Interim Report of Child Care Law Reform Project*, 2013: 43

The *Interim Report: Child Care Law Reporting Project* argues that there are profound 'societal issues' at the root of children coming before the courts in care proceedings. It suggests that the parents are often needy themselves 'with emotional and personal problems with poverty and social isolation, all impacting negatively on children' (Coulter, 2013: 15).

It also argues that much greater attention needs to be given to the voice of the child in care proceedings if Ireland is to become compliant with international law. The Interim Report asserts 'at the moment there is no consistency in the courts about whether and how the voice of the child is heard, or at what age it is appropriate to seek the views of the child' (Coulter, 2013: 29). Given that neglect is the primary reason for children becoming involved in care proceedings in the courts and parental incompetence is a pervasive problem, it would seem to be essential that the child's voice is heard in court proceedings.

The *Interim Report: Child Care Law Reporting Project* concludes that the social costs of failure to tackle the underlying social causes of children coming into care as a result of court proceedings will be high:

> Failure to tackle these problems will not come without a social cost. One of the themes that emerges from these reports is the impact of neglect, domestic violence, abuse or disrupted care in early life on the children themselves. They are much more likely to suffer from learning disabilities and conditions like ADHD which make it difficult for them to settle into school. Some of them also exhibit behavioural problems, which make it more likely they will be excluded from school and condemned to a lifetime of unemployment, marginalisation and poverty – and likely to require some level of State support for most of their lives. In the most severe of these cases the behavioural problems are such that the children are clearly on a trajectory that will lead them into criminality and indeed some of them have already embarked on crime well before they reach their teens. In other cases the behavioural problems will develop into psychiatric illness. In both these circumstances the costs to the State will be high. (Coulter, 2013: 16)

The choices facing society in terms of addressing child abuse are rooted in poverty, social division and the 'othering' of population groups on the basis of difference. There are answers to child abuse, but they are complex and costly. Watson et al (2012: vi) have calculated that in 2009, 24% of children were living in households experiencing social deprivation and 13% lived in households experiencing child specific deprivation' (ie, inadequate food, clothing, toys and play equipment, social participation opportunities and educational supports).

Public inquiries and child-centred services: the need for civicness and civility

The Ryan Report (CICA, 2009: 4: 7.06) recommended that 'childcare policy should be child-centred. The needs of the child should be paramount'. It advocated regular reviews, the enforcement of rules and regulations within a 'culture of respect' and the accountability of management at all levels (4: 7.07–7.13). It also declared that 'children who have been in child care facilities are in a good position to identity failings and deficiencies in the system, and should be consulted' (4: 7.18). In terms of ensuring that children's experiences are open and transparent, the Ryan Report recommended 'the full records of children in care must be maintained' (4: 7.20). Finally, the Ryan Report recommended uniform standards of practice across the country (4: 7.21).

The UK Munro Report (2011) highlighted the shortcomings of an over-bureaucratised child protection service that limits professional judgement by a too close adherence to rules. The concomitant loss is that we have a less child-centred service and an absence of relationship-building and trust:

> The demands of bureaucracy have reduced their capacity to work directly with children, young people and families. Services have become so standardised that they do not provide the required range of responses to the variety of need that is presented. (Munro, 2011: 6–7)

Munro poses a challenge to social workers and managers to reclaim their professional expertise and not to shy away from the exercise of professional judgement:

> This review recommends a radical reduction in the amount of central prescription to help professionals move from a compliance culture to a learning culture, where they have more freedom to use their expertise in assessing need and providing the right help. (Munro, 2011: 6–7)

While the development of practice procedures and protocols were originally intended to improve the quality and consistency of practice delivery, Munro's research reveals that these strategies have resulted in an over-regulation of social work and the promotion of more procedural-led practice. She claims that the centrality of relationship-building with families and children has been undervalued in a system that has become overshadowed by bureaucratic rules and protocols:

> Complying with prescription and keeping records to demonstrate compliance has become too dominant. The centrality of forming relationships with children and

families to understand and help them has become obscured. The review is making recommendations to enable social workers to exercise more professional judgement but is also concerned to improve their expertise. (Munro, 2011: 7-8)

Munro further acknowledges the practice challenges that a movement away from a prevailing culture of compliance will pose for practitioners and social work managers. However, she emphasises the necessity for social workers to embrace the uncertainty contained in the work and the responsibility of organisations to support practitioners to exercise greater professional judgement in practice situations where uncertainty and risk prevail:

A move from a compliance to a learning culture will require those working in child protection to be given more scope to exercise professional judgement in deciding how best to help children and their families. It will require more determined and robust management at the front line to support the development of professional confidence. (Munro, 2011: 5)

At the core of Munro's strategy is a rupture with the compliance culture and its replacement by a learning culture. While Munro's research was situated in the UK, the challenges posed for social workers and managers in child protection services have resonance internationally. In addition, an earlier UK report by Laming (2009), which was commissioned in the wake of the death of 'Baby P', highlighted the many challenges faced by child protection workers in the exercise of their roles and responsibilities. Moreover, in Ireland, the Roscommon Child Care Report (2010) made the case for a full review and revisions of child protection services. The intensification of media interest in all matters related to child protection and welfare has resulted in a proliferation of public inquiries that involve the interrogation of professionals and their work practices. Undoubtedly, social workers feel under threat when situated within a prevailing public climate of distrust, working in organisational contexts where systems of accountability have been developed in response to growing public concern.

Conclusion

In this chapter we have explored the contemporary challenges that confront child protection in Ireland. The chapter seeks to highlight the growing ethnic context of child deprivation. We started by analysing the circumstances of children in direct accommodation for asylum seekers. A disturbing picture emerges of children living in social conditions that are not conducive to high standards of child welfare or the vindication of their human rights. The chapter then moved on to analyse statistics from court referrals. Once again there are worrying signs. Neglect is a dominant feature in these court cases, suggesting poverty continues to shape the discourse of child protection. Finally, we looked at the role of the social worker and the need for greater professional autonomy in decision-making about the welfare of the child and, above all, the need to hear the voice of the child.

TEN

Conclusion

The only thing necessary for the triumph of evil is for good
[people] to do nothing. (Edmund Burke)

Child abuse is not a recent phenomenon. The mistreatment of children
– including infanticide, abandonment, severe physical punishment,
prostitution and hard labour – has been recorded throughout history.
While there is evidence to suggest that there has always been some
degree of public and state concern over cruelty to children (Corby
et al, 2012), this issue really only began to be recognised as a major
social problem during the late 19th century. Philanthropic organisations
in Britain and Ireland, most notably the National Society for the
Prevention of Cruelty to Children (NSPCC), were set up to meet
the needs of poorer children and campaign for legislation outlawing
child cruelty . By 1908, the main components of child protection
law that exist today were in place (Corby et al, 2012). Indeed, in
Ireland, the Children Act 1908 provided the main legal framework
for child care for over 80 years. The physical abuse of children was
'rediscovered' during the 1960s when Henry Kempe and his colleagues
published groundbreaking work on 'the battered child syndrome' – a
clinical condition in young children who had received serious physical
abuse, generally from a parent (Kempe et al, 1962). Their work had a
significant impact on the development of child protection policy and
practice in the United States, Britain and Ireland. However, *public*
awareness of the issue remained minimal until a series of high profile
cases – such as the Maria Cowell case in the UK – catapulted this issue
to the top of the political agenda. Professional and public concern over
the problem of child sexual abuse developed more slowly, emerging as a
serious problem in the 1970s (in the USA), 1980s (in Britain) and 1990s
(in Ireland). During the 1990s there was also a shift in emphasis from
intra- to extrafamilial abuse, particularly within institutional settings,
including residential homes and schools. In Britain, a number of high
profile child murder cases (notably that of Sarah Payne in 2000) also
received huge media coverage, fuelling public concerns over 'stranger
danger'.

The transformation of child welfare and protection from a marginal to a central issue of public concern and policy-making is nowhere more evident than in Ireland. Buckley and O'Nolan (2013) note that when the report of the Kilkenny Incest Investigation was published in 1993, child protection played a very minor role in the business of central government and the health and social services. Twenty years later, the sector is governed by a Department of Children and Youth Affairs, with a full Cabinet-level Minister and a standalone statutory Child and Family Agency. Over 30 pieces of child-related legislation have been enacted in the interim, and a referendum on inserting Children's Rights into the Irish Constitution was carried in 2012 (though the result was subsequently contested). Within this legislative framework, the Child and Family Agency bases its day-to-day operations 'on legislation, regulation and statutory guidance, as well as 185 separate policies, none of which were in existence in 1993' (Buckley and O'Nolan, 2013: 8).

As we have seen in the course of this book, child abuse inquiries have played an important part in raising public awareness of abuse and highlighting the experiences of some of the most stigmatised and excluded groups in society. The Climbié Inquiry (2003), for instance, paints a picture of the housing and financial difficulties experienced by families from abroad living in London (Stanley, 1999) while the brutality and deprivation of life within Ireland's industrial and reformatory schools are exposed in the Ryan Report (2009). Child abuse inquiries have also informed the development of policy and practice. In Britain, the Maria Colwell case is considered to have transformed child protection, while in Ireland, the Kilkenny Incest Inquiry helped secure additional resources for child protection services, expedited the full implementation of the Child Care Act 1991 and for the first time made child care a political issue. Inquiries have also been credited with introducing greater accountability and transparency (Buckley and O'Nolan, 2013).

Despite certain benefits, there have also been drawbacks to the proliferation of inquiries over the last few decades. According to Reder et al (1993), the critical atmosphere of public inquiries and accompanying media reporting has generated wholly unrealistic expectations that such deaths 'should never happen again' and beliefs that front-line professionals are incompetent. In the UK, child protection inquiries have also been associated with a culture of managerialism and defensive practice. One of the main conclusions of the Munro Review (2011) was that the child protection system had become over-bureaucratised and concerned with compliance at the expense of flexibility and the exercise of professional judgement. This situation was, in part, due to the publication of a series of high-profile inquiry reports, which focused 'too readily' on human error and added further bureaucratic procedures to an already over-burdened system: 'Each inquiry adds a few more rules to the book, increases the pressure on staff to comply with procedures, and strengthens the mechanisms for monitoring and inspecting practice so that non-compliance can be detected' (Munro, 2011: 19). While each addition makes sense when viewed in isolation 'the cumulative effect is to create a work environment full of obstacles to keeping a clear focus on meeting the needs of children' (Munro, 2011). Child abuse inquiries have also been criticised for their over-reliance on hindsight, considerable financial cost, undue influence on the development of policy, and repetitive findings and recommendations (Reder et al, 1993; Stanley, 1999; Corby, 2004).

Media interest in child abuse has played a vital role in promoting public awareness of this problem. From being a largely unacknowledged issue (prior to the 1960s), child abuse is now a major source of news reporting as well as featuring in television drama, films, call-in shows, soap operas and other genres, thereby reaching a diverse range of audiences. As we have seen, extensive news coverage helped to transform tragedies, such as the death of Maria Colwell and Victoria Climbié, into public scandals. Moreover, the media has been instrumental in calling powerful institutions to account for their handling of child abuse allegations. In Ireland, some of the most shocking and influential media coverage concerned clerical child abuse and its 'cover-up' by church and state authorities. The broadcast of a number of documentaries during the late 1990s and early 2000s, detailing the abuse of children in institutional and community settings, led to the setting up of three major inquiries into the church's handling of allegations of abuse (Ferns Report, 2006; Dublin Report, 2009; Ryan Report, 2009). Moreover, media coverage of child abuse prompted survivors to come forward and give testimony to these inquiries and provided opportunities for survivor groups to raise public awareness and campaign for change. Notwithstanding the many positive aspects of the media's interest in child abuse, there have also been a number of drawbacks. The media has been accused of sensational, simplistic and sometimes inaccurate coverage (Franklin and Parton, 1991); of creating 'moral panics' around child abuse (Silverman and Wilson, 2002) and of scapegoating the professionals, usually social workers, connected with child abuse cases (Franklin and Parton, 1991). The British tabloid press, in particular, have launched a series of personal attacks on those practitioners implicated in major child abuse inquiries (Fitzgibbon, 2008) leading to a crisis of confidence within the sector and increasingly defensive practice.

Why has child abuse become so prominent in the media? Probably because the media in contemporary society have become the interpreters and signifiers of an ethical civil society as organised religion is increasingly marginalised. In this transformed social landscape, civil society has become 'intertwined with communicative institutions, such as polls and mass media, and regulatory institutions, such as voting and offices with political power' (Dekker, 2010: 37). John Keane (2008) calls this cultural shift 'monitory democracy'. It means new democratic forms are emerging in a 'post-welfare state' world, where digitalisation is changing the social reality of human communication and policy. But it also means that in media-framing child abuse is represented as scandal. Janet Newman (2010: 273) argues that the nature of social services in an age of media-driven public scandals is being transformed by a paradox: 'how to cope with their declining public role, at a time that they have to take on new roles of engaging, disciplining and responsibilising the public'. Child abuse is at the core of this transformed social and political landscape, in which public scandals and inquiries increasingly define social values and highlight the importance of children's rights in an ethical civil society.

What is to be done about child abuse? The United Nations Convention on the Rights of the Child (UNCRC) 1989 suggests a strategy in its 3 Ps – provision, protection and participation. What should the implementation of these principles mean in policy terms? What will their impact be, in human rights terms, on the lives of children? Ultimately, the success or failure of a strategy for combating child abuse will depend on moving beyond rhetoric to address the reality of plural childhoods and the influence of social class on children's vulnerability. Poverty and vulnerability are closely interconnected in child abuse as this book has demonstrated. Let's look at the 3 Ps sequentially.

First, provision means tackling child poverty. As already noted in Chapter 9, approximately a quarter of all Irish children live in households that are experiencing basic social deprivation and 13% experience child specific deprivation (Watson, et. al, 2012). Child poverty needs to be tackled as the nation's number one social priority. Furthermore, there needs to be targeted supports within the community for families experiencing social deprivation, such as free childcare facilities. Aftercare services are vital for supporting vulnerable children leaving care and moving into the community, including support with accommodation, training and education, and income support. Youth work services need a great deal more investment and a philosophy based upon social education and personal development, which mainstream youth organisations currently practice. Outreach youth work is a vital part of connecting with vulnerable youth in the community (Powell et al, 2012). Youth clubs, youth cafes and youth projects need to be well-funded and open seven days a week – throughout the entire year.

Second, child protection services also need a great deal more investment. The establishment of the Child and Family Agency (TUSLA) in 2014 has represented a major step forward in Irish child protection. But without large scale investment its capacity will be constrained. As the UK Munro Report (2011) has advised, social workers ought to be encouraged to use their own professional initiative. More emphasis in social work training on human rights would broaden professional horizons, as would a deeper knowledge of child development. The media has an important positive role to play in child protection by challenging the culture of disbelief and highlighting children's vulnerabilities and the need for a clear commitment to children's rights in public policy. Mandatory reporting ought to be introduced immediately. It can protect many children from abuse by tackling under-reporting.

Third, participation is the vital new ingredient in children's rights discourse. It means putting the 'child's voice' at the centre of social policy and professional practice. That means active listening to children in an age-appropriate manner. All children have opinions about their welfare. But, historically, they have been shut out of the decision-making process (eg, case conferences, court proceedings, schooling and so on). There ought to be a cultural shift in relation to children's participation. Drawing on the work of Roger Hart, we have outlined in Chapter 6 a ladder of participation, ranging from tokenism to genuine inclusiveness in decision-making. In imagining children's futures we need to address their powerlessness, which is at the root of child abuse. That means rethinking children's rights in ways that empower them as active citizens with the capacity to participate in the determination of their own lives and have a real say in society. Adult power needs to be tempered by children's participation within an ethical civil society that values all citizens equally and takes human rights seriously.

References

Note: The reference list has been divided into three sections: inquiry reports (Ireland); parliamentary papers and government publications (pre-20th century); and general references (books, journal articles, etc). Unattributed newspaper articles have been referenced in the footnotes to each chapter.

Inquiry reports (Ireland)

Brosnan, K. (2008) *Monageer Inquiry: Report presented to Ms Mary Harney TD, Minister for Health and Children, and Mr Dermot Ahern TD, Minister for Justice, Equality and Law Reform*. Dublin: Department of Health and Children.

Brosnan, K. Luny, L. and McHugh, J. (2009) *Report of the Monageer Inquiry*. Dublin: The Stationery Office.

Bruton, M. (1998) *West of Ireland Farmer Case: Report of review group, presented to North Western Health Board, July 1998* [also known as the McColgan Case], Manorhamilton: North Western Health Board.

CICA (Commission to Inquire into Child Abuse) (2009) *Report of the Commission to Inquire into Child Abuse, Volumes I–V* [also known as the Ryan Report], Dublin: Government Publications.

CIRISS (Commission of Inquiry into the Reformatory and Industrial School System) (1936) *Report of the Commission of Inquiry into the Reformatory and Industrial School System* [also known as the Cussen Report], Dublin: Stationery Office.

CIRISS (1970) *Report of the Commission of Inquiry into the Reformatory and Industrial School System* [also known as the Kennedy Report], Dublin: Government Publications Office.

Coulter, C. (2013) *Interim Report: Child Care Law Reporting Project*, Dublin: Child Care Law Reporting Project (CCLRP).

DCYA (Department of Children and Youth Affairs) (2014) *Report of the Inter-Departmental Group on Mother and Baby Homes*, Dublin: DCYA.

Department of Health (1996) *Report on the Inquiry into the operation of Madonna House*, Dublin: Government Publications.

DJELR (Department of Justice, Equality and Law Reform) (2009) *Report by the Commission of Investigation into the Catholic Archdiocese of Dublin*, Dublin: Government Publications.

DJELR (2011) *Report into the Catholic Diocese of Cloyne*, Dublin: Government Publications.

Gibbons, N. (2010) *Roscommon Child Care Case: Report of the Inquiry Team to the Health Service Executive, 27 October 2010.* Dublin: Health Service Executive.

Houses of the Oireachtas (1996) *Interim Report of the Joint Committee on the Family: Kelly – A child is dead: Report of a Committee of Inquiry,* Dublin: Government Publications.

McGuinness, C. (1993) *Kilkenny Incest Investigation: Report presented to Mr. Brendan Howlin TD, Minister for Health by South Eastern Health Board, May 1993.* Dublin: The Stationery Office.

Murphy, F.D., Buckley, H. and Joyce, L. (2005) *The Ferns Report: Presented to the Minister for Health and Children.* Dublin: Government Publications.

Murphy, R.H. (1998) *Report of the Independent Inquiry into Matters Relating to Child Sexual Abuse in Swimming. Submitted to the Minister for Tourism, Sport and Recreation and to the Minister for Education and Science, 27 May 1998,* Dublin: Government Publications.

Reilly, M. (2012) *Report on the Inspection of St Patrick's Institution.* Dublin: Office of the Inspector of Prisons.

Shannon, G. and Gibbons, N. (2012) *Report of the Independent Child Death Review Group,* Dublin: Government Publications (Department of Children and Youth Affairs).

Third Interim Report of Commission to Inquire into Child Abuse (2003), Dublin: Stationery Office.

Parliamentary papers and government publications (pre-20th century)

First Annual Report of the Irish Local Government Board (1873), Dublin.

Journal of the Irish House of Commons for the years: 1758, 1791, 1792, 1798.

Report of the Inter-departmental Committee on Child Care (1896)(Mundella Report), Local Government Board, London.

Report of the Reformatory and Industrial Schools Commissioners, HC 1884, c3876 XLV. 1.

Third Report of the Commissioners of Irish Education Enquiry, 1826-7.

Thirty-fourth Report of the Inspector of Reformatory and Industrial Schools of Ireland, 1896, c8204, XLV.

General references

Adorno, T. (1998) *Critical modes: Interventions and catchwords*, New York: Columbia University Press.

Alderson, P. (2013) *Young children's rights*, London: Jessica Kingsley.

Anheier, H., Kaldor, M. and Glasius, M. (2012) 'The Global Civil Society Year Book: Lessons and Insights 2001–2011', in M. Kaldor, H. Moor and S. Selchon (eds) *Global civil society 2012*, London: Palgrave Macmillan.

Archard, D. (1993) *Children: Rights and childhood*, London: Routledge.

Aries, P. (1973) *Centuries of childhood*, London: Penguin.

Arnold, B. (2009) *The Irish Gulag.* Dublin: Gill and MacMillan.

Arnold, S. (2012) *State sanctioned child poverty and exclusion.* Dublin: Irish Refugee Council.

Ayre, P. (2001) 'Child protection and the media: Lessons from the last three decades', *British Journal of Social Work,* 31: 887–901.

Barnes, J. (1989) *Irish industrial schools 1868–1908: Origins and development*, Dublin, Irish Academic Press.

Barrie, J.M. (1993) *Peter Pan*, Bristol: Parragon.

Baxter, C. (2011) 'Behind Murakami's Mirror', *New York Review of Books*, 8 December.

Beck, U. (1992) *Risk Society*, London: Sage.

The Black Velvet Band, wiki article, 18 September 2014. Online at: http://en.wikipedia.org/wiki/The_Black_Velvet_Band

Blanshard, P. (1954) *The Irish and Catholic power*, London: Verschoyle.

Bodó, B. (2003) *Tiszazung: A social history of a murder epidemic*, New York: Columbia University Press, Eastern European Publications.

Boswell, J. (1998) *The kindness of strangers.* Chicago: Chicago University Press.

Brandsen, T. Dekker, P. and Evers, A. (eds) (2010) *Civicness in the governance and delivery of social services,* Baden Baden: Nomos.

Brannan, C., Jones, J. and Murch, J. (1993) *Castle Hill Report*, Shrewsbury: Shropshire County Council.

Brooke, H. (1830) *The interests of Ireland,* Dublin.

Buckingham, D. (2000) *After the death of childhood: Growing up in the age of electronic media,* Cambridge: Polity Press.

Buckingham, D. (2011) *The material child*, Cambridge: Polity Press.

Buckley, H. and O'Nolan, C. (2013) *An examination of inquiries,* Dublin: Department of Children and Youth Affairs.

Buckley, S.A. (2013) *The cruelty man: Child welfare, the NSPCC and the State of Ireland*, Manchester: Manchester University Press.

Burns, K. and Lynch, D. (2012) 'Politics, democracy and protecting children', in A. Burns and D. Lynch (eds) *Children's rights and child protection: Critical times, critical issues in Ireland*, Manchester: Manchester University Press.

Butler, I. and Drakeford, M. (2003) *Scandal, social policy and social welfare*, Bristol: Policy Press.

Butler, I. and Drakeford, M. (2008) 'Booing or cheering? Ambiguity in the construction of victimhood in the case of Maria Colwell', *Crime, Media, Culture*, 4(3): 367-385.

Butler, I. and Drakeford, M. (2012) *Social work on trial: the Colwell Inquiry and the state of welfare*, Bristol: Policy Press.

Byron, T. (2008) *Safer children in a digital world* (the Byron Report), London: UK Department of Children, Schools and Families.

CARE (1972) *Children deprived: CARE memorandum on deprived children and deprived children's services in Ireland*, Dublin: CARE.

CARE (1974) *CARE Newsletter* 1(2), November.

Carrigan Report (1931) *Report of the Committee on the Criminal Law Amendment Acts (1880-1885) and Juvenile Prostitution*, Dublin: Government Publications Office.

Checkoway, B. (2011) 'What is youth participation?' in *Children and Youth Services Review*, 33: 340-45.

Cheit, R.E., Shavit, Y. and Reiss-Davis, Z. (2010) 'Magazine coverage of child sexual assault 1992-2004', *Journal of Child Sexual Abuse*, 19(1): 99-117.

Clyde, J. (1992) *The report of the inquiry into the removal of children from Orkney*, Edinburgh: Her Majesty's Stationery Office.

Cohen, A. (2007) 'Introduction: Childhood between past and present', in Cohen, A. and Rutler, J. *Constructions of childhood in Ancient Greece and Italy*, Athens, American Schools of Classical Studies.

Coldrey, B.M. (1996) 'The sexual abuse of children: the historical perspective', *An Irish Quarterly Review*, 85(340): 370-80.

Considene, M. and Dukelow, F. (2009) *Irish social policy: A critical introduction*, Dublin: Gill and Macmillan.

Corby, B. (2004) 'The costs and benefits of the North Wales Tribunal of Inquiry', in N. Stanley and J. Manthorpe (eds) *The age of inquiry: Learning and blaming in health and social care*, Abingdon: Routledge.

Corby, B., Doig, A. and Roberts, V. (1998) 'Inquiries into child abuse', *Journal of Social Welfare and Family Law*, 20(4): 377-95.

Corby, B., Doig, A. and Roberts, V. (2001) *Public inquiries into abuse of children in residential care*, London: Jessica Kingsley.

Corby, B., Shemmings, D. and Wilkins, D. (2012) *Child abuse: An evidence base for confident practice* (4th edn), Maidenhead: Open University Press.

Costin, L. Karger, H. and Stoesz (1997) *The politics of child abuse in America*, New York: Oxford University Press.

Coulter, C. (2010) 'Litany of questions over children left to child abuse', *The Irish Times* 16 February.

Crosson Tower, C. (1996) *Understanding child abuse and neglect*, Boston: Allyn and Bacon.

Cullen, C. (2012) *A discourse analysis of the Ryan Report: Construction of children in care in Irish social policy*, Doctoral thesis in social science, Cork: National University of Ireland.

Deetman, W. *Reports into child abuse in the Netherlands, 2011 and 2013.* Amsterdam.

De Francis, V. (1969) *Protecting the child victim of sex crimes committed by adults*, Denver: American Humane Association.

Dekker, P. (2010) 'Civicness: from civil society to civic services?', in T. Brandsen et al (eds) *Civicness in the governance and delivery of social services*, Baden Baden: Nomos.

deMause, L. (1974) 'The evolution of childhood', in L. deMause (ed) *The history of childhood,* New York: The Psychohistory Press.

deMause, L. (1976) *History of childhood*, London: Souvenir.

Department of Children and Youth Affairs (2013) *State of the nation's children: Ireland 2012*, DCYA, Dublin.

Dickson, G. (2010) *The children's crusade*, London: Palgrave Macmillan.

Doerner, K. (1981) *Madmen and the bourgeoisie*, Oxford: Blackwell.

Donnelly, S. and Inglis, T. (2010) 'The media and the Catholic Church in Ireland: Reporting clerical child sex abuse', *Journal of Contemporary Religion*, 25(1): 1-19.

Donzelot, J. (1980) *The policing of families*, London: Huchinson.

Elias, N. (1994) [1939] *The civilising process*, Oxford: Blackwell.

Farson, R. (1974) *Birthrights*, New York: Macmillian.

Ferguson, H. (1993) 'Surviving Irish childhood: child protection and the death of children in child abuse cases in Ireland since 1884', in H. Ferguson, R. Gilligan and R. Torode (eds) *Surviving childhood adversity: Issues for policy and practice,* Dublin: Social Studies Press, Trinity College.

Ferguson, H. (Winter 1993-94) 'Child abuse inquiries and the Report of the Kilkenny Incest Investigation: a critical analysis', *Administration*, 41(4): 385-410.

Ferguson, H. (1995a) 'Child welfare, child protection and the Child Care Act 1991: key issues for policy and practice', in H. Ferguson and P. Kenny (eds) *On Behalf of the Child: Child welfare, child protection and the Child Care Act 1991,* Dublin: A.A. Farmar.

Ferguson, H. (1995b) 'The paedophile priest: a deconstruction', *An Irish Quarterly Review*, 84 (335): 247-256.

Ferguson, H. (2007) 'Abused and looked after children as "moral dirt"', *Journal of Social Policy*, 36(1): 123–39.

Ferguson, H. (2011) *Child protection practice,* Basingstoke: Palgrave MacMillan.

Ferriter, D. (2004) *The transformation of Ireland, 1900–2000,* London: Profile Books.

Ferriter, D. (2009) *Occasions of sin: Sex and society in modern Ireland,* London: Profile Books.

Field-Fisher, T.G. (1974) *The Report* of the Committee of Inquiry into the *care and supervision provided in relation to Maria Colwell,* London: Her Majesty's Stationery Office.

Finkelhor, D. (1979) *Sexually victimized children,* New York: Free Press.

Fitzgibbon, W. (2012) *Probation and social work in trial,* London: Palgrave.

FLAC (Free Legal Aid Centres) (2009) *One size doesn't fit all: A legal analysis of the direct provision and dispersal system in Ireland, 10 Years On,* Dublin: FLAC.

Flannery, T. (2009) *Responding to the Ryan Report,* Dublin: Columba Press.

Fleischhauer, J. and Hollersen, W. (2010) 'The sexual revolution and children: How the left took things too far', *Spiegel Online*, 2 July 2010. Online at: http://www.spiegel.de/international/zeitgeist/the-sexual-revolution-and-children-how-the-left-took-things-too-far-a-702679-3.html

Foley, P., Parton, N., Roche, J. and Tucker, S. (2003) 'Contradictory and convergent trends in law and policy affecting children in England', in C. Hallett and A. Prout (eds) *Hearing the voices of children: Social policy for a new century,* London: Routledge Falmer.

Foucault, M. (1967) *Madness and civilization,* London: Tavistock.

Foucault, M. (1979) *History of sexuality (Volume 1),* Harmondsworth: Penguin.

Foucault, M. (1980) *Power/Knowledge,* Sussex: Harvester.

Foucault, M. (1991) *Discipline and punish,* London: Penguin.

Franklin, B. and Parton, N. (1991) 'Media reporting of social work: a framework for analysis', in B. Franklin and N. Parton (eds) *Social work, the media and public relations,* London: Routledge.

Furedi, F. (2013) *Moral crusades in an age of mistrust: The Jimmy Savile scandal,* Basingstoke: Palgrave Macmillan.

Garvin, T. (2004) *Preventing the future: Why was Ireland so poor for so long?* Dublin: Gill & Macmillan.

Giddens, A. (1998) *The third way,* Cambridge: Polity.

Gilligan, R. (1991) *Irish child care services: policy, practice and provisions,* Dublin: Institute of Public Administration.

Gilligan, R. (2009) 'The "public child" and the reluctant state?', *Eire-Ireland : A journal of Irish studies* 44 (1&2): 265-290.

Greenslade, R. (2012) Blog post, *Greenslade Blog,* weblog post, 23 July 2013, Online at: http://www.theguardian.com/media/greenslade

Griffin, C. (1993) *Representations of youth: The study of youth and adolescence in Britain and America,* Oxford: Polity Press.

Griffiths, D.L. and Moynihan, F.J. (1963) 'Multiple epiphysial injuries in babies ("Battered Baby" syndrome)', *British Medical Journal,* 2(5372) (December 21): 1558-61.

Hart, R. (1992) *Children's participation from tokenism to citizenship,* Florence: UNICEF Innocenti Research Centre.

Hatty, S.E. and Hatty, J. (2001) 'Australia', in B.M. Schwartz-Kenney, M. McCauley and M.A. Epstein (eds) *Child abuse: A global view,* Westport, Connecticut: Greenwood Press.

Higonnet, A. (1998) *Pictures of innocence,* New York: Thames and Hudson.

Higonnet, A. (2002) 'Picturing innocence: an interview with Anne Higonnet' ,*Childhood,* 9.

The Historical Institutional Abuse Inquiry (2014) *Terms of Reference.* Online at: http://www.hiainquiry.org/index/acknowledgement_forum/terms-of-reference.htm

Holland, K. (2014) 'Media matters', *The Irish Times* 25 April.

Holohan, C. (2011) *In plain sight: Responding to the Ferns, Regan, Murphy and Cloyne Reports,* Dublin: Amnesty International.

Holt, J. (1974) *Escape from childhood,* New York: E.P. Dutton.

Hooper, J. and Siddique, H. (2010) 'Catholic anger as Church puts female ordination on par with sex abuse', *Guardian,* 17 July.

House of Commons Health Committee (2003) *The Victoria Climbié Inquiry Report: Sixth Report of Session 2002-3,* London: HMSO.

Hughes, R. (1988) *The fatal shore,* New York: Vintage.

ICCL (Irish Council for Civil Liberties) (1977) *Children's rights under the constitution,* Dublin: ICCL.

Inglis, T. (1998) *Moral monopoly: The rise and fall of the Catholic Church in modern Ireland,* Dublin: University College Dublin Press.

Invernizzi, A. and Williams, J. (2008) *Children and citizenship*, London: Sage.

Irish Catholic Bishops' Advisory Committee on Child Sexual Abuse by Priests and Religious (1996) *Child Sexual Abuse: A Framework for a Church Response*, Dublin: Veritas.

James, A. and James, A.L. (2004) *Constructing childhood: Theory, policy and social practice*, Basingstoke: Palgrave Macmillan.

James, A. and James, A.L. (2008) *Key concepts in childhood*, London: Sage.

James, A., Jenks, C. and Prout, A. (1998) *Theorising childhood*, Cambridge: Polity.

James, A., Curtis, P. and Birch, J. (2008) 'Care and control in the construction of children's citizenship' in A. Invernizzi and J. Williams (eds) *Children and citizenship*, London: Sage.

Jenks, C. (2005) *Childhood*, London: Routledge.

Johnny, L. (2006) 'Reconstructing childhood', *International Education Journal*, 7(1): 17-25.

Kadushin, A. (1980) *Child welfare services* (3rd edn), New York: Macmillan.

Kampmark, B. (2012) *The sacred child*, New York: Nova Science.

Keane, J. (2008) *Children and civil society*, Seminar Paper, Sydney University.

Keenan, M. (2012) *Child sexual abuse and the Catholic Church: Gender, power and organizational culture*, Oxford: Oxford University Press.

Kearney, J.F. (1813) *Institution for administering aid to the sick*, Dublin.

Kempe, C., Silverman, P., Steele, B., Droegemueller, W. and Silver, H. (1962) 'The Battered-child syndrome', *Journal of the American Medical Association*, 181: 105-112.

Kempe, R. and Kempe, C. (1978) *Child abuse*, London: Fontana/Open Books.

Keogh, D. (2005) *Twentieth century Ireland*, Dublin: Gill and Macmillan.

Kertzer, D. and White, M. (1994) 'Cheating the angel-makers', *Continuity and Change*, 9 (03): 451-80.

Kilgallon, W. (1995) *Report of the Independent Review into Allegations of Abuse at Meadowdale Children's Home and related matters*, Morpeth: Northumberland County Council.

Kilkelly, U. (2012) 'Learning lessons from the past: legal issues arising from Ireland's child abuse inquiries', *Irish Journal of Applied Social Studies* (12)1: 8-24.

Kirby, P. (1995) 'The death of innocence: Whither now? Trauma in church and state', *Studies: An Irish Quarterly Review*, 84 (335): 257-65.

Kirkwood, A. (1993) *The Leicestershire Inquiry 1992,* Leicester: Leicestershire County Council.

Kitzinger, J. (2000) 'Media templates: Patterns of association and the (re)construction of meaning over time', *Media, Culture & Society,* 22(1): 61-84.

Kitzinger, J. (2004) *Framing abuse: Media influence and public understanding of sexual violence against children,* London: Pluto.

Kuijvenhoven, T. and Kortleven, W.J. (2010) 'Inquiries into fatal child abuse in the Netherlands: A source of improvement?', *British Journal of Social Work,* 40: 1152-73.

Lalor, K. (1998) 'Child sexual abuse in Ireland: An historical and anthropological note', *Irish Journal of Applied Social Studies,* 1(1): 38-53.

Lalor, K. (2001) 'Child sexual abuse in Ireland: A brief history', in K. Lalor (ed) *The end of innocence: Child sexual abuse in Ireland,* Cork: Oak Tree Press.

Laming, H. (2003) *The Victoria Climbié Inquiry Report: Report of an inquiry by Lord Laming,* Cmnd 5730, London: HMSO.

Laming, Lord (2009) *The protection of children in England: A progress report,* London: The Stationery Office.

Lavan, A. (1998) 'Social work in Ireland', in S. Shardlow and M. Payne (eds) *Contemporary issues in social work: Western Europe,* Aldershot, Hants: Arena.

Law Commission of Canada (2000) *Restoring Dignity Responding to Child Abuse in Canadian Institutions: Executive Summary.* Canada: Minister of Public Works and Government Services.

Levene, M. (2005) *Genocide in the age of the nation state: Volume 2: The rise of the West and the coming of genocide,* London: IB Taurus.

Liebel, M. (2008) 'Citizenship from below: children's rights and social movements' in A. Invernizzi and J. Williams (eds) *Children and citizenship,* London: Sage.

Liebel, M. (2012) *Children's rights from below,* London: Palgrave Macmillan.

Lipson, M. and Vallentyne, P. (1992) 'Child liberationism and legitimate inference', *Journal of Social Philosophy,* XXX(23): 5-15.

Lis, C. and Soly, H. (1979) *Poverty and capitalism in pre-Industrial Europe,* Harvester Press, London.

Luddy, M. and Smith, J. (2009) 'Editor's Introduction', *Éire-Ireland,* 44 (1 & 2) 5-8.

McCullagh, C. (2002) *Media power: A sociological introduction,* London: Palgrave.

McDonagh, P. (2010) 'More vaccine trials were kept secret by the state', *Irish Independent,* 27 August.

McDowell, R.B. (1979) *Ireland in the Age of Imperialism and Revolution*, Oxford: Clarendon.

McGuinness, C. (2012) 'It is a long way from Kilkenny to here: Reflections on legal and policy developments before and since the publication of the *Kilkenny Incest Investigation*', in K. Burns and D. Lynch (eds) *Children's rights and child protection: Critical times, critical issues in Ireland*, Manchester: Manchester University Press.

McKay, S. (1998) *Sophia's story*, London: Gill and Macmillan.

McLuhan, M. (1962) *The Guttenberg Galaxy*, Toronto: University of Toronto.

McLuhan, M. (1964) *Understanding media*, New York: McGraw Hill.

McLuhan, M. (1967) *The medium is the message*, New York: Random House.

Maguire, M. (2009) *Precarious childhood in post-independent Ireland*, Manchester: Manchester University Press.

Malinowski, B. (1948) *Magic, science and religion*, Glencoe: Free Press.

Malthus, T. (1878) *Essay on the principle of population*, London: (unknown)

Mann, M. (2005) *The dark side of democracy*, Cambridge: Cambridge University Press.

Mendleshon, R. (1979) *Social welfare in Australia 1900–1975*, Sydney: Allen and Unwin.

Meyrowitz, J. (1985) *No sense of place: The impact of the electronic media on social behavior*, New York: Oxford University Press.

Mian, M., Bala, N. and MacMillan, H. (2001) 'Canada', in B.M. Schwartz-Kenney, M. McCauley and M.A. Epstein (eds) *Child abuse: A global view*, Westport, Conneticut: Greenwood Press.

Miller, A. (2007) *The drama of the gifted child*, New York: Basic Books.

Mokyr, J. (1980) *Why Ireland starved*, London: Allen and Unwin.

Morton, R. (1972) *Venereal disease,* Harmondsworth: Penguin.

Mollan, C. (1979) *Children first*, Dublin: Arlen House.

Munro, E. (2004) 'The impact of child abuse inquiries since 1990', in N. Stanley and J. Manthorpe (eds) *The age of the inquiry*, London: Routledge.

Munro, E. (2011) *The Munro Review of Child Protection: Final Report – A child-centred system.* London: the Department of Education.

Murakami, H. (2011) *1Q84*, New York: Knopf.

Myers, J. (2011) 'A short history of child protection in America', in J. Myers (ed) *The APSAC handbook on child maltreatment,* Thousand Oaks: Sage.

Najemy, J. (2008) *A History of Florence 1200-1575*, Blackwell, Oxford.

Nelson, B. (1984) *Making an issue of child abuse: Political agenda setting for social problems*, Chicago and London: University of Chicago Press.

Newman, J. (2010) 'Civicness and the paradoxes of contemporary governance', in Blanden et al (eds) *Civicness in the governance and delivery of social services*. Baden Baden: Nomos.

O'Brien, C. (2010a) 'Child deaths while in care or contact with services', *The Irish Times,* 5 June.

O'Brien, C. (2010b) 'HSE accused of potential dereliction of duty over foster care'. *The Irish Times*, 13 July.

O'Brien, C. (2014) 'Lives in limbo', *The Irish Times.* 9 August.

OECD (1962) *Investment in Education: Report of survey team appointed by the Minister of Education,* October, Dublin: Stationery Office.

O'Gorman, C. (2009) *Beyond belief*, London, Hodder and Stougthon.

O'Reilly, E. (1992) *Masterminds of the right*, Dublin: Attic Press.

O'Sullivan, E. and O'Donnell, I (2012) *Coercive confinement in Ireland*, Manchester: Manchester University Press.

O'Toole, F. (2009a) 'Law of anarchy, cruelty in care', *The Irish Times*, 23 May.

O'Toole, F. (2009b) 'Ryan Report', *The Irish Times*, 28 December.

Panter-Brick, C. and Smith, M. (2000) *Abandoned children*, Cambridge: Cambridge University Press.

Parton, N. (1985) *The politics of child abuse*, London: MacMillan.

Parton, N. (1991) *Governing the family: Child care, child protection and the state,* London: MacMillan.

Parton, N. (2004) 'From Maria Colwell to Victoria Climbié: Reflections on public inquiries into child abuse a generation apart', *Child Abuse Review*, 13(2): 80-94.

Parton, N. (2006) *Safeguarding childhood: Early intervention and surveillance in late modern society*, Basingstoke: Palgrave MacMillan.

Phelan, D. (1835) *Statistical Enquiry into the present state of the medical charities of Ireland*, Dublin.

Pinkney, S. (2000) 'Children as welfare subjects in restructuring social policy', in G. Lewis, S. Gewirtz and J. Clarke (eds) *Rethinking social policy*, London: Open University/Sage.

Pollock, L. (1983) *Forgotten children: Parent-child relations from 1500 to 1900,* Cambridge: Cambridge University Press.

Postman, N. (1994) *The disappearance of childhood*, New York: Vintage Books.

Powell, F. (1992) *The politics of Irish social policy 1600-1900,* New York: Edward Mellen Press.

Powell, F. (2013) *The politics of civil society: Big society and small government*, Bristol: Policy Press.

Powell, F., Geoghegan, M., Scanlon, M. and Swirak, K. (2012a) 'The Irish charity myth, child abuse and human rights: Contextualising the Ryan Report into care institutions', *British Journal of Social Work*, January, pp 1–17.

Powell, F., Geoghegan, M., Scanlon, M. and Swirak, K. (2012b) *Youth policy, civil society and the modern Irish state*, Manchester: Manchester University Press.

Qvortrup, J., Corsaro, W. and Honig, M.S (eds) (2011) *The Palgrave handbook of childhood studies*, London: Palgrave Macmillan.

Raftery, M. (2009) 'Report a monument of a society's shame', *The Irish Times*, 21 May.

Raftery, M. and O'Sullivan, E. (1999) *Suffer the little children: The inside story of Ireland's industrial schools*, Dublin: New Island Books.

Reder, P., Duncan, S. and Gray, M. (1993) 'A new look at child abuse tragedies', *Child Abuse Review*, 2(2):89–100.

Richardson, V. (1999) 'Children and social policy', in S. Quinn, P. Kennedy, A. O'Donnell and G. Kiely (eds), *Contemporary Irish social policy*, Dublin: University College Dublin Press.

Rismyhr Engelund, S. (2012) 'Introductory essay: "The Other" and "othering"', *New Narratives: Multicultural Literature at the University of Oslo,* weblog post, no date but comments indicate 2012. Online at: http://newnarratives.wordpress.com/issue-2-the-other/other-and-othering-2/

Robins, J. (1980) *The lost children: A study of charity children in Ireland 1700–1900*, Dublin: Institute of Public Administration.

Rogers, J. (1734) *Essay on epidemic diseases*, Dublin.

Rose, J. (1984) *The case of Peter Pan: The impossibility of children's fiction*, London: Macmillan.

Royal Commission into Institutional Responses to Child Sexual Abuse (2013) 'Terms of reference'. Online at: http://www.childabuseroyalcommission.gov.au/about-us/terms-of-reference

Scull, A. (1979) *Museums of madness*, London: Palgrave Macmillan.

Shannon, G. (2013) *Sixth Report of the Special Rapporteur on Child Protection: A report submitted to the Oireachtas*. Online at: http://www.dcya.gov.ie/documents/Publications/SixthRapporrteurReport.pdf

Shorter, E. (1975) *The making of the modern family*, Huntington, NY: Fontanta.

Silverman, J. and Wilson, D. (2002) *Innocence betrayed: Paedophilia, the media and society,* Cambridge: Polity Press.

Sixsmith, M. (2009) *The lost child of Philomena Lee,* London: MacMillan.

Skehill, C. (1999) *The nature of social work in Ireland*, New York: Edwin Mellen Press.

Skehill, C. (2004) *History of the present of child protection and welfare social work in Ireland,* New York: Edwin Mellen Press.

Skidmore, P. (1995) 'Telling tales: Media power, ideology and the reporting of child sexual abuse in Britain', in D. Kidd-Hewitt and R. Osbourne (eds) *Crime and the media: The post modern spectacle,* London: Pluto Press.

Smart, C. (1999) 'A history of ambivalence and conflict in the discursive construction of the "child victim" of sexual abuse', *Social and Legal Issues,* 8(3): 391–409.

Soukup, P.A. (1997) 'Church, media and scandal', in J. Lull and S. Hinerman (eds) *Media scandals: Morality and desire in the popular culture marketplace,* Cambridge: Polity Press.

Staffordshire County Council (1991) *The Pindown experience and the protection of children: The Report of the Staffordshire Child Care Inquiry 1990,* Stafford: Staffordshire County Council.

Stanley, N. (1999) 'The institutional abuse of children: An overview of policy and practice', in N. Stanley, J. Manthorpe and B. Penhale (eds) *Institutional abuse: Perspectives across the life course,* London: Routledge.

Steinberg and Kincher (1997) *Kinderculture,* Bolder, CO: Westview Press.

Swift, J. (1965) 'A modest proposal', in P. Pinkus (ed) *Jonathan Swift: A Selection of his Works,* London: Macmillan.

Task Force on Child Care Services (1980) *Task Force on Child Care Services: Final Report,* Dublin: Stationery Office.

Tatar, M (2003) *The hard facts of the Grimms' Fairy Tales,* Princeton and Oxford: Princeton University Press.

Third Report of Select Committee on Health (1998), London, House of Commons.

Thompson, J.B. (1997) 'Scandal and social theory', in J. Lull and S. Hinerman (eds) *Media scandals: Morality and desire in the popular culture marketplace,* Cambridge: Polity Press.

Tuairim (1966) *Some of our children: A report on the residential care of deprived children in Ireland.* London: Tuairim.

Tyrell, P. (2006) *Founded on fear,* Dublin: Irish Academic Press.

United Nations Convention on the Rights of the Child (1990) Online at: http://www.unhchr.ch/htm//menu2/6/treaties/crc.htm

Utting, Sir William (1991) *Children in the public care: A review of residential child care,* London: HMSO.

Utting, Sir William (1997) *People like us: The report of the review of the safeguards for children living away from home,* London: HMSO.

Watson, D., Maitre, B. and Wheland, C. (2012) *Understanding childhood deprivation in Ireland,* Dublin: Department of Social Protection.

White, I. and Hart, K. (1995) *Report of the management of child care in the London Borough of Islington*, London: Borough of Islington.

Whyte, J.H. (1980) *Church and state in modern Ireland 1923-1979*, Dublin: Gill and Macmillan.

Wilczynski, A. and Sinclair, K. (1999) 'Moral tales: Representations of child abuse in the quality and tabloid media', *The Australian and New Zealand Journal of Criminology*, 32: 262-83.

Winter, G. A. (1990) *The Report of the Archdiocesan Commission of Enquiry into the Sexual Abuse of Children by Members of the Clergy*, Newfoundland: Archdiocese of St. John's.

Wodsworth, W.D. (1876) *A Brief History of the Ancient Foundling Hospital of Dublin, from the year 1702, with some account of similar institutions abroad*, Dublin: A. Thorn.

Wollheim, R. (1971) *Freud*, London: Fontana.

Wood, K. (1993) *The Kilkenny Incest Case*, Dublin: Poolbeg.

Young-Bruehl, E. (2012) *Childism: Confronting prejudice against children*, New Haven: Yale University Press.

Zelizer, V. (1994) *Pricing the priceless child: The changing social value of children*, Princeton: Princeton University Press.

Zipes, J. (2012) *Fairy tales and the art of subversion*, London: Routledge.

Index

L

M